The Home Shop Machinist
PROJECTS
Two

The Home Shop Machinist
PROJECTS
Two

Compiled and edited by
Joe D. Rice

THE HOME SHOP MACHINIST, INC.
Traverse City, Michigan

PHOTO CREDITS
Page 1: Charlie Dondro, May/June '85 cover
Page 53: Philip Duclos, July/August '84 cover
Page 103: Harold Mason, November/December '85
Page 115: Philip Duclos, March/April '85 cover
Page 133: R. S. Hedin, July/August '85 cover
Page 185: Guy Lautard, November/December '84 cover

The Home Shop Machinist
PROJECTS
Two

The Home Shop Machinist, Inc.
P.O. Box 1810
Traverse City, Michigan 49685-1810

International Standard Book Number 0-941653-01-3
Library of Congress Catalog Card Number 83-640315

Typeset and printed at Village Press, Traverse City, Michigan, USA

INTRODUCTION

PROJECTS TWO is the second book to come from *The Home Shop Machinist*. Like **Projects One**, it is an edited compilation of most (but not all) articles published in the magazine during the years 1984 and 1985. The magazine's back issues are long gone, due to the rapid increase in circulation that was experienced during those years. We are happy that you have the opportunity to enjoy those articles now, especially if this is the first time you've ever seen them.

If you have **Projects One**, you will undoubtedly become aware right away of the maturity of the material in this book compared to the first two years (1982-83). The first year, especially, was made up primarily of shop articles taken from *Live Steam* magazine files — not that doing that makes them less mature; they're simply a little more limited in scope because they are specific to the model engineering hobby. By 1984, our files for *The Home Shop Machinist* were beginning to bulge with fine articles for the machinist who might not be a model engineer at all.

Some articles high on the all-time popularity list appeared in the years 1984 and 85. Certainly Harry Bloom's "Reconditioning a Lathe" ranks at the top of all the "Techniques" articles we ever published. And also in these years, today's very familiar, and popular names began showing up with regularity, such as Rudy Kouhoupt, Philip Duclos, Guy Lautard, J. O. Barbour, Jr., William F. Green, and John Dean. Not only are these people consumate craftsmen, they are also prolific writers. They — and quite obviously all the others — derive considerable pleasure from sharing their skills and knowledge (shop wisdom) with everyone, and I consider that to be a most noble calling.

Again, as with our first book, I hope **Projects Two** gives you many hours of pleasure both in your easy chair and in your shop!

Joe Rice, Editor

CONTENTS

HOBBY PROJECTS

TECHNIQUES

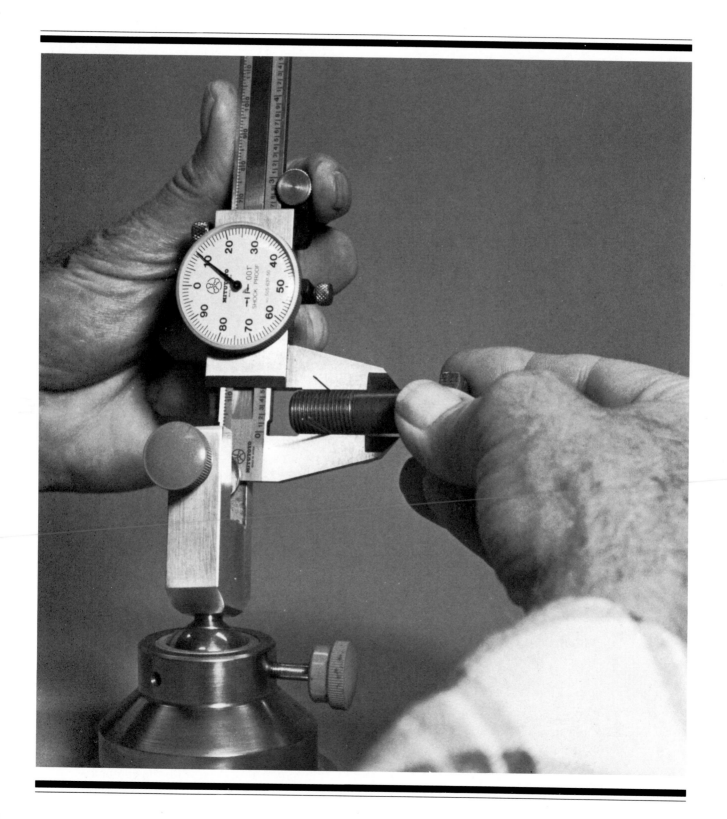

1 *Before*

2 *After*

Reconditioning a Lathe

by Harry Bloom

Photos by Author

FOREWORD

This article was originally conceived with the Atlas lathes in mind, and their "fine tuning." I was not able to obtain an Atlas lathe until I was 80% complete with the Sheldon lathe described. Basically, the article is focused on obtaining consistent, accurate work from a lathe, through the reconditioning process. Scraping is not a fast process. It is very time consuming and tedious. If you get frustrated or tired, just walk away from it. It took me about seven hours to scrape the cross slide and about 15 hours to scrape just the "V" and flat slides of the carriage the first time. Needless to say, I did not do it all in one day. So have patience; you will be more than pleased with the end result, if you are careful. The process described is based very closely upon the book, Machine Tool Reconditioning. *I modified and adjusted as conditions allowed. If this is your first crack at reconditioning, follow the book to the letter. What worked for me may not work for you.*

During the past few years, the economy has been closing and/or consolidating plants and occasionally selling off assets. Some of these assets are of interest to those of us with machine shops in our homes or elsewhere. Those assets that we are concerned with are the lathes, mills, grinders, and other equipment. For the majority of us, most of these machines are much too large; however, one occasionally comes along that is just right.

Don't be misled into thinking that the machines made available are going to be in excellent condition (unless there is a forced sale, where all assets are sold). For the most part, the businesses that are selling off assets are selling machines that are of least value to them. Generally, you can assume that these machines are ready for the scrap pile or close to it. With the above in mind, we are now ready to buy that "new" machine that we've wanted. I have needed a lathe larger than my 9" South Bend to enable more efficient manufacture of certain equipment that I sell to my customers in the fence business.

My search for a "new" lathe succeeded in January, 1983, when I bought a Model M 13" x 36" Sheldon. As you can tell from Photos 1, 3 and 4, the lathe is in need of a thorough cleaning and painting. This lathe had been sitting in an open-sided shed, exposed to the elements for some time. What is not readily apparent is that the lathe needs to be reconditioned. The first order of business was to run a preliminary check on the bed.

I mounted an indicator on the compound rest and indicated the inside inverted V-way

2

3

4

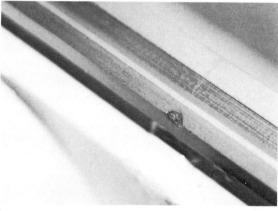

5

(hearafter referred to as V-way) of the bed from the headstock to the extreme right end of bed. This check showed a variance of about .010″. Keep in mind that this is not a reliable check, especially if the variance is much smaller. At the time of the check, the bed had not been leveled, which is a crucial factor. A machine tool must be leveled to conduct an accuracy check, or to turn out accurate work. However, given the bed length and the degree of variance, the test told me that the bed needed work. If the bed needs reconditioning, so does the rest of the machine, as far as I'm concerned.

My next problem was getting the machine into my basement. Considering the 1550 lb. weight of the machine, this necessitated a complete disassembly and then moving the machine (Photos 1, 3 and 4 were taken at my place of employment). Upon removing the headstock, a bunch of shims of assorted sizes fell off. You can imagine my chagrin; the fun and games had started. Anytime the headstock is shimmed, you have problems of major, if not catastrophic, proportions. A headstock should never be shimmed. (I'm saying this but chances are I will shim the headstock to avoid scraping its slides.) A little cleaning in the area of a big nick on the rear inside of the V-way of the bed revealed a crack. (Photo 5)

The shims are explained; but what do I do now? The crack, as you can see (Photo 6), extends across both rear ways and about 3″ down into the vertical part of the bed. I consulted a machinist friend, who told me the lathe was worth saving.

Several phone calls to machine shops in town all led me to one shop that specialized in machinery rebuilding. I took the bed to the shop

6

for a price quote. The shop manager was leery of repairing the crack, but asked that I leave the bed with him for a while. Three weeks later, I called. He had consulted with his welder, and their recommendation was to drill a hole at the bottom of the crack and grind vees on both sides up to the bottom of ways and braze the crack, then plane the bed. The price quoted was $350.00. I agreed to the procedure and, three weeks later, I picked up the bed. In the meantime, I stripped the cabinet of its old paint and repainted it, sent the motor out for overhaul ($50.00) and ordered six new belts for the power transmission system, which cost about $45.00.

It may seem crass to some, but I am going to discuss prices and costs associated with the lathe and its reconditioning. Cost is a very important factor that can't be overlooked. You must ask yourself if the machine is worth it. Not just this 13″ Sheldon; I obviously feel it's worth it, or I wouldn't be doing it, but your lathe or whatever. Will you get a fair value received? What does a new machine of comparable size cost? How much time is involved for value received? Only after you have answered these questions and many more, can you make an intelligent decision. But consider this, after you have reconditioned your machine, you will have a machine that is equal to or better than the same machine when it left the factory for the first time. The Sheldon cost me $900.00 and, by the time I'm finished with the machine and tool it, I will have spent about $2,500.00. I might point out that this is about $2,000.00 to $3,000.00 less than a comparable machine. (A 13″ geared head lathe made in Taiwan, tooled, would cost about $5,700.00).

By now, you are probably wondering what the reconditioning process entails. The goal of reconditioning is to return the machine to the original factory specifications or better. In the case of a lathe, I want it to turn, face, bore, thread, and whatever else accurately. I don't want it to turn tapers, unless intentionally set. I want to be able to turn a bar and get the same results over the entire length. I will rework the flat bearing by the process of scraping. I will make use of a surface plate, parallels, straight edges, a dial test indicator, a master precision level, precision squares, scrapers, and assorted other tools.

In the end, I want the lathe to meet the following accuracy checks. These are the tests (see test sheet) that the lathe must or should pass. If you do good work and perform accuracy checks as you progress, these accuracies are easy to obtain; in fact, don't be surprised if, after you have assembled the lathe, that all tests affected by scraping succeed. Certain tests are affected by other factors. These tests are the spindle tests for the head and tail stocks. I had a problem with the headstock spindle center runout until I tightened the bearing preload. The actual values given are eyeball estimates. My dial indicator is calibrated to .0005″; anything closer has to be estimated. Of course, I could buy an indicator calibrated in .0001″. Some tests I have not conducted at time of writing, and I left these blank, due to a more urgent project.

I will briefly discuss the major tools, but I strongly urge you to obtain the book, *Machine Tool Reconditioning* by Edward F. Connelly, published by Machine Tool Publications. I have the 11th printing (1978). I bought the book in 1979 when I redid my 9″ South Bend, and have never regretted the purchase. (The book is advertised in *Live Steam* and *The Home Shop Machinist*.)

The Surface Plate

The most common type surface plates, from what I have been able to discover, are the granite variety. Granite surface plates are available in three grades: AA, A and B. AA is the most expensive; A is next, and B is the cheapest. I have a B grade 18″ x 24″ surface plate ($220.00). Each surface plate is furnished with a certificate of accuracy. The surface plate will be your reference surface for flatness, against which you check most of your work. A plate 12″ x 12″ ($100.00) will suffice in most cases, although a 12″ x 18″ ($125.00) is not much more expensive. If you are reconditioning a 9″ South Bend, a

TEST SHEET — SHELDON MACHINE CO. Inc.

Each Sheldon Lathe must pass this Rigid Test

Each Lathe must pass the 19 accuracy checks on this Test Sheet before leaving the factory. This individual Test Sheet is delivered with the lathe as a Guarantee that it is a true precision machine tool.

7

8

9

12″ x 18″ will be easier to use than a 12″ x 12″, especially when you get to the carriage. When you are checking height on the V-slides, it is better to slide the surface gauge on the plate rather than lifting it off and putting it back down. The vibration when returning the surface gauge to the plate is enough to upset the dial test indicator.

Parallels

You can buy them or make them. If you make them, be careful; the steel you have is not necessarily flat or parallel. I regularly use a *matched* pair of ¾″ toolbits as parallels (Photo 7).

Straight Edges:

Make these tools. They are extremely expensive if bought; a granite edge 36″ long costs about $300.00, and is heavy. Except in certain instances, they are not very useful for our size of work. For the small sizes we are concerned with, we are better off making our own. Straight edges must be made to surface plate accuracy. You can get by with an angle straight edge, but having a regular straight edge is also advantageous. I have four straight edges—two regular and two angle (Photo 8).

The larger ones are made for Meehanite. I scraped the two smaller ones (the rectangular is ⅜″ x 1″ x 18″; the angle is ½″ x 1″ x 12″). I caution you again—flat ground stock you purchase is not necessarily flat or straight; check it out on your surface plate. If you have never scraped before, this is where you should start. With care, you should be able to make edges a little longer than the diagonal of your surface plate. The larger straight edges were surface ground by a local shop on an automatic

surface grinder less than a year old. It cost $50.00 to get the edges ground, and was worth it. The rectangle is 1½″ x 2¼″ x 24″, the angle 1″ x 1½″ x 18″, milled and then ground at a 45° angle.

Scrapers

Can be made or purchased. The commercial variety costs between $40 and $50 (Photo 9). I prefer to make my own from worn out files. *MTR (Machine Tool Reconditioning)* gives detailed instructions on making your own from files. My procedure is as follows: Grind teeth off on both sides for about an 1½″ to 2″, and dull the rest of the teeth. I then grind a radius on the end and hone the blade to a very sharp edge (Figure 10).

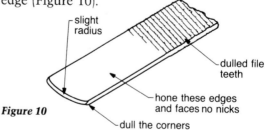

slight radius

dulled file teeth

hone these edges and faces no nicks

dull the corners

Figure 10

I have several scrapers of various widths and configurations. You will need at least one scraper for dovetails (Figure 11). I do not anneal, forge, and reharden these old files; I simply touch them to the sharpening stone more frequently. I have toyed with various ideas for scrapers, namely, adapting a cutoff blade for scrapers and having a carbide tip soldered on a piece of steel; however, so far, I have not acted on those ideas.

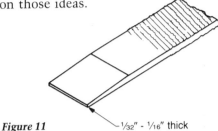

Figure 11   1/32″ - 1/16″ thick

For those of you who are interested, power scrapers are available. I have literature for the *BIAX* brand distributed by DA-PRA Inc. There are variable speed and variable stroke models available. The prices range from $1,100.00 to $1,200.00 for the basic scraper. They are undoubtedly great labor and time savers; however, I don't think they are cost effective for our purposes. (That still does not change the fact that I still want one. It's nice to dream every so often.)

Precision Level

The only good a carpenter's level will do is to rough in the bed; other than that, don't waste your money unless you already have one. You will need a level that shows a distinct bubble movement when a .003″ shim is placed under one end. A 12″ #98 Starrett with graduated vial (Photo 12) will do nicely. They cost about $50.00. However, they are graduated in .005″. As you will see in the article, I needed a more sensitive level. A Master Precision Level with a sensitivity of .0005″ per foot and graduated in the same increments was purchased. I selected a Scherr-Tumico (Photo 13) level costing $240.00.

Starrett's #199 costs about $254.00 and Brown and Sharpe's costs $588.00. There are imported levels that cost between $110.00 and $140.00. Several factors influenced my purchase. Scherr-Tumico has a flat base; the imports have a vee groove, which is not suitable for my purposes. Also, the S-T is 1½″ wide, Starrett is 1⅝″, imports are 1⅞″ to 2″. All the levels mentioned above have vial adjusting screws, another important consideration. The first test done with the level is to check it. Place it on a level surface and then turn it 180°. If you get the same reading, you're okay. If not, work the adjusting screw, and repeat the test.

Precision Squares

Precision squares are used in alignment checks. Squareness is specified in squareness per foot. The cost is about $50.00.

Dial Test Indicators

An indicator calibrated in .0005″ is minimum acceptable. The cost is about $55.00.

Surface Gauge

If you don't have one, get one, or make one. It is very useful (almost indispensable) in performing checks. The cost is about $30.00.

Marking Medium

I use *Canode Blue*, a commercial compound. There are other brands available, so check with your local supplier.

12

Sharpening Stones

The use is obvious, but I keep three sharpening stones for use in scraping only. After each use of the scraper, I stone the burrs off. You will need the regular style plus triangular shape or some other shape to stone dovetails.

I have tried to mention the major tools and equipment that you will need. I'm quite sure I've missed some, so here is my apology in advance. I again strongly suggest that you get a copy of *Machine Tool Reconditioning*. The book tells you in more detail what you need, how to make it and how to proceed on

13

reconditioning. Besides, I am not going into the detail that Connelly goes into.

Before I get to the reconditioning process, a word about "flat." Flat is the working surface of the surface plate. The certificate of accuracy guarantees the following: If you have two parallel planes, they will be separated by a distance no greater than the certificate shows. If I'm reading the certificate on my plate correctly, the planes are no further than .00015"apart. A straight edge is a long narrow surface plate, and parallels are, by definition, two parallel straight edges.

Scraping is the process of removing a small particle of metal. It is not an indiscriminate process; you control where and how much metal is removed. In the beginning, you remove large amounts of metal with heavy long strokes, gradually refining the removal to minute flecks. At the same time, you are endeavoring to scrape straight down (parallel to original factory plane) (see 35 *MTR*).

There is a scraping cycle to be followed which entails seven steps.

(1) Removal of burrs
(2) Spreading marking medium
(3) Application of spotting tool
(4) Analysis of markings
(5) Scraping of indicated high spots
(6) Cleaning of surface
(7) Removal of burrs, etc., as cycle is repeated

After many repetitions of the scraping cycle, you will have a flat surface with necessary bearing quality. Often in the process, alignment checks will be performed, because the piece being scraped must align properly with another member. The carriage must align properly with the bed, etc.

Reference has been made to spotting tools. These are the surface plate, straight edges and templates. The templates are the various machine components that have been scraped. For example, the cross slides will be used as a template for scraping the cross slide ways of the carriage, in conjunction with straight edges. For this reason, we will follow logical, definite order on the sequence of scraping the members. *MTR* gives two scraping orders for the engine lathe. The one I recommend you follow is the first one, which is:

1. Cross slide
2. Compound rest top
3. Compound rest bottom
4. Carriage

5. Outer ways of bed
6. Tailstock base
7. Inner ways of bed
8. Headstock

This is the sequence I use when I scrape a lathe with the bed configuration in Figure 14.

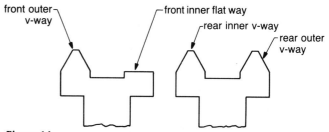

Figure 14

The Sheldon lathe has a bed configuration as shown in Figure 15. Because of the bed configuration and other reasons, I changed the sequence (some might say drastically) when I scraped the bed. My scraping sequence went as follows:

1. Same as MTR
2. Same as MTR
3. Same as MTR
4. Flat ways of bed
5. Carriage
6. V-ways of bed
7. Tailstock
8. Headstock (did not scrape)
9. Carriage
10. Tailstock

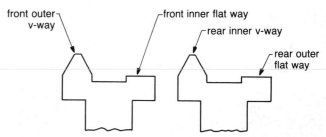

Figure 15

My reasoning to change the sequence is as follows: If you recall, I had a crack repaired and the bed planed. The planing removed .032" straight down. I originally intended to stone the bed and not scrape it. With the amount removed from the bed plus the amount removed from scraping the carriage, I was going to have tremendous problems realigning the lead screw. Therefore, I elected at the outset to attach (glue) way strip bearing material to the carriage slides to build the height back up. Unfortunately, the planing job was not quite perfect.

It was at this point that I decided to scrape the bed. More about this later. Before you scrape a piece, check it to determine how much has to

7

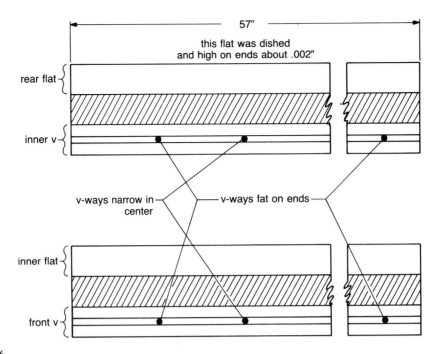

57"

this flat was dished
and high on ends about .002"

rear flat

inner v

v-ways narrow in center   v-ways fat on ends

inner flat

front v

Figure 16

17

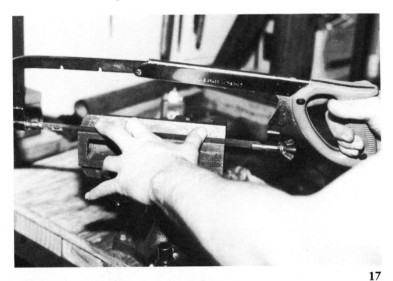

18

be removed. If a rather large amount must be removed, it is better if you can mill, shape or otherwise machine it off rather than scrape. I try to leave about 1 to 3 thousandths to scrape after machining. I only machine if I have a reference surface to work from. If you do not have the equipment to machine, you can try using a hand grinder, files, or indiscriminate scraping. *Check your progress often.* Do not remove so much metal that you make things worse.

One other procedure that is necessary is cutting relief grooves. I cut these grooves with a hacksaw (Photo 17) wherever I have an inside corner.

These grooves are necessary for the spotting tool, usually the angle straight edge, to properly do its job (Photo 18).

The cross slide (Photos 19 and 20) (p. 258-261, *Machine Tool Reconditioning* is composed of five surfaces which get scraped: the swivel way, the two flat slides, the guided slide and the gibbed surface.

The swivel way (Photo 19) is the first surface to be scraped. I referenced this surface to the machine surface between the guided slide and the gibbed surface. Most of the factory scraping marks were still visible and it was relatively easy scraping, with a total of about .002" being removed. The surface was low around the periphery (see photo). After scraping, the swivel ways are parallel within .0005" of the reference surface.

8

19

20

21

The flat slides were inspected on the surface plate using surface gauge and dial test indicator (DTI) (Photo 21). I make sketches like Figure 22 whenever possible as a guide to help me direct attention in scraping high sections.

All spotting for this member was performed on the surface plate. Spotting is performed in the following manner:

Marking medium (bluing) is applied to the spotting tool in an even coat, the heaviness determined by estimated amount of scraping. The surface to be spotted is moved across the spotting surface. Use two to five short strokes resulting in the transfer of marking medium.

As a result, the high spots are indicated and scraped. When spotting the surface, use discretion in the amount of pressure applied. False markings are an ever present hazard. Rework the bluing on the spotting tool into an even coat. (Read *MTR*, Chapters 10 and 11.)

When you are starting a new scraping cycle, change the direction from which you scrape. The scraping is easier and you get rid of chatter marks.

The guided slide is the next surface to be scraped. I used the angle straight edge and, to some extent, the guiding way of the carriage to spot this surface. The guiding way is used to indicate that the correct angle is being scraped. I did not scrape any marking spotted by the guiding way. I used it as a crude reference.

I chose not to scrape the gibbed surface at this time. The reasoning is that this machine has tapered angular gibs on the cross slide and compound rest. I wanted to scrape the gibbed way first, before mating the gibbed surfaces. I was trying to avoid making new gibs. If your machine has flat gibs, go ahead and scrape this

+2	0
Figure 22	
+3	+2

NUMBERS ARE THOUSANDTHS OF AN INCH

9

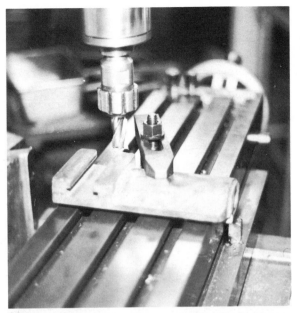

23

25

24

surface. Parallelism is to be obtained with the guiding slide.

The Compound Rest Top (Photo 23) (pp. 262-264, *MTR*) is composed of five surfaces to be scraped: the tool post ring support, the two flat slides, the guided slide, and the gibbed surface.

The feed screw is a new factor to be considered. Endeavor to maintain parallelism vertically and horizontally with the screw. We are trying to minimize the amount of binding that will occur with the screw.

I scraped this member in the order listed above. I did not scrape the gibbed surface for reasons already stated. Again, I used the surface plate and angle straight edge.

The Compound Rest Bottom (Photo 24) (p. 264-268, *MTR*) is also composed of five surfaces to be scraped: the swivel slide, the two flat ways, the guiding way, and the gibbed way.

The scraping order is the same as listed. Depending on the construction of your lathe, you may have to use parallels to scrape this member. On some lathes, there is a boss in the center of the swivel slide. If this is the case, then the swivel way, which has already been scraped finished, is the only spotting tool available. To scrape the flat ways, parallels must be used.

In the case of my Sheldon, there is no boss, but a pivot pin that is removable. Because of this, I used the surface plate to spot. (By now, you have probably noticed a confusion of terms — swivel way, swivel slide, flat ways, flat slides, etc. The flat slides slide over/on the flat ways. The sliding surfaces are movable, the ways are not.)

The guiding way is scraped using the angle straight edge and the guided slide of the compound rest top. Because the guided slide is scraped finished, it is now suitable for use as a template, and I scraped the markings produced by this member. I also used the guided slide and angle straight edge to spot the gibbed way. Parallelism was checked often using dowel pins, micrometer, vernier caliper or DTI, whichever lent itself to the easiest check (see Photo 25).

The tapered angular gib can now be fitted to the compound rest top and bottom members. In the case of the Sheldon, enough metal had been removed that the gib could now properly be fitted. I had a choice — make a new one or attach a shim strip (Photo 26). I used a cyanoacrylate-based adhesive to attach a .060"

26

27

30

31

28

32

cross slide dovetail

*   front v-slide

rear flat slide

*original machined on same plane   *Figure 29*

11

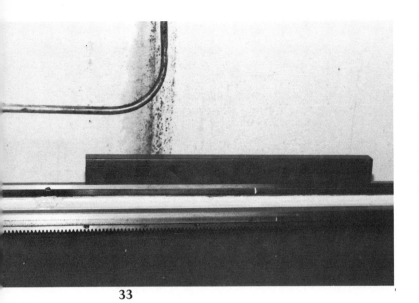

33

34

brass strip to the gib face that did not have a sliding member in contact.

The gib is fitted in the following manner: Marking medium is applied to the gib way and gibbed surface. The gib is inserted and lightly tapped to seat. It is then lightly tapped from the small end to remove it. The markings were analyzed and then scraped. This procedure has to be repeated many times until proper fit is obtained. Once obtained, the adjusting screw is placed and sliding fit is checked, as well as parallelism, and adjustments made if necessary. The same procedure is used later on to fit the gib for the cross slide to the carriage gib way. The three members just scraped are assembled and an alignment check is performed (Photo 27) (p. 268, *MTR*). The tolerance for this alignment is .0035" per foot. My check showed about .0015" per foot. You may ask "Why so tight on these members?" If you are turning a taper or in feeding for threading, the tool bit must be on the lathe center line. Strive to hold this tolerance or tighter. Besides, the tolerances are going to get a lot closer.

The Carriage and Bed (Photo 28) (p. 268-276 and 278-291, *MTR*) is composed of seven to nine surfaces to be scraped, depending on style of bed: the two flat ways, guiding way, gib way, one or two pair V-slides (if one pair, then one flat way), and the gibbed surface. If you are reworking a lathe and the bed has V-ways front and rear, follow *MTR*. In the case of the Sheldon with an outer V-way and outer flat way, plus a design of the carriage, I added a surface to scrape for a reference point from which to scrape the flat way. See Figure 29 and the reasoning becomes apparent. With the carriage set on parallels on the surface plate, I scraped the surfaces parallel so that I could safely use these surfaces for a

reference from which to scrape the flat ways. Once this was accomplished, I then checked the flat ways for parallelism. The check revealed that it would be advantageous to machine the flat ways and then scrape (see Photo 30 for milling setup.)

By this method, I could reduce the use of the cross slide as a template and rely more on the surface plate and straight edge for scraping. In addition, it is easier to check vertical alignment of the cross feed screw (Photos 31 and 32). Excepting this change, I scraped the guiding way and gibbed way per *MTR*. I did not scrape the Vee or flat slides next. More on why later.

As you will recall, I intended to stone only the bed; however, I discovered that this was not possible (Figure 16). I decided to scrape the flat ways of the bed; the problem was assuring accuracy, and doing it in the least time-consuming manner. After much discussion and brainstorming, I hit upon the following procedure. I would use the 24" straight edge (Photo 33) and a master precision level (I finally had to buy one) and scrape the rear outside flat way of the bed.

I would start at the tailstock end and work left. The spotting and scraping procedure would be as follows: Divide the bed into sections; the first is 24" long, and the rest are 12". Finish section 1, then advance to section 2. Finish section 2, then advance to section 3. After the first section is scraped, I have a reference surface for the next section, which is half the length of the straight edge. The master precision level is used extensively to check progress and to find isolated high spots. Remember that this level is sensitive to .0005" per foot and you can easily estimate a ¼ to ⅓

35

36

37

division. After the rear flat way had been scraped, I would scrape the front inner flat way in the same manner. I would also have to reference this flat way to the finished rear flat way, and for parallelism, I would use matched parallels and suitable shim stock. Once the shim stock is picked I cannot change it. The flat ways do not have to be in the same plane, just parallel (Photo 34).

Once I settled on the procedure for scraping the flat way, I had to level the bed (p. 279-282, MTR). Since I had the final location for the lathe picked out, I bolted the cabinet to the floor (concrete) and leveled the bed. I cannot overemphasize the importance of leveling – **if the lathe is not leveled, you will not do accurate work.**

It took me ten hours, with a lot of coffee breaks, to scrape the flat ways of the bed. I was then ready to scrape the carriage slides. I placed the carriage on the bed and checked levelness (Photo 35). The rear flat slide is so high, that I decided to machine about .015″ off and then scrape (Photo 36).

I applied bluing to the bed and scraped the slides, checking alignments and levelness frequently (Photo 37) (p. 275, MTR). I also spotted with a straight edge. It took me about 15 hours to scrape the carriage slides. I finished the slides and ran an alignment check on the inside "V" way (Photo 38).

The "V" ways went every which way but straight. The average error was about .0025″. I literally went through the roof when I discovered the error. After I cooled off, I realized that perhaps I was expecting too much from the planing job. Preparatory to planing

38

the bed "V" ways, the bottom surface, where the feet attach, was ground (Figure 39).

The bed had to be turned upside down and jacks used to level the bed on the grinder. The center surface that was ground was, in all probability, low. As a result, when the bed was set up on the planer, that center surface bowed

13

the bed ever so slightly. The "V" ways were wider on the ends than in the middle. Nevertheless, the planing job was worth every penny of the cost, considering the bed's original condition.

I decided to scrape the front side of the front "V" way, and then the rear side, using basically the same procedure I used for scraping the flat ways. I frequently checked levelness. I then scraped the rear inside way using the straight edge and checking with a DTI mounted on carriage. Another problem to be aware of is "wind" (p. 283-284, *MTR*). You must frequently check for "wind" and take precautions or corrective measures. (Refer back to Photo 35 for checking procedure.)

It took me about 20 hours to scrape the "V" ways. The bed has been checked for levelness in all directions; the "V" ways are parallel. The bed is aligned within .00075" over the 57" length. The "V" ways are parallel within .00025". With no problems from the crack, I expect this lathe to last for many years.

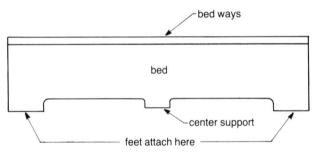

bed ways

bed

center support

feet attach here

Figure 39

AUTHOR'S NOTE

I recently discovered a slightly warped straight edge when I was checking the accuracy of my surface grinder. I urge you to be aware of this ever-present problem; straight edges can, for a variety of reasons, warp. Frequently check them against your surface plates. The only sure-fire remedy for a warped edge is to re-scrape or re-grind it.   H.B.

I am now ready for the home stretch. I mounted the headstock and ran all the checks listed in *MTR*, p. 298-302. I did not expect any problems and found none. The only area that may be questionable is the spindle taper run-out test. I borrowed a no. 5 Morse taper shank drill bit (See Photo 40) and ran my checks on vertical and horizontal alignments.

I first checked for sag – which was negligible – then ran the tests. The drill bit has a slight taper which must be considered. The alignments are well within tolerance. The drill bit does not lend itself very effectively for spindle

40

taper run-out test. From what I could determine, the taper run-out was out about .0015" at the end of this bit, which is about 17" from the spindle. Some of the error can be attributed to dirt and manufacturing error. Spindle bearing clearance will also effect this test, as well as the other tests.

The Tailstock: (p. 291-298, *MTR*) The tailstock is composed of two members to be scraped, the tailstock top and the tailstock base. The bottom surface of the top, the "V" slides, flat slide, and top surface of the base are scraped. The surfaces are scraped in the order listed.

The bottom surface of the top should need but a minimum of work. I merely cleaned up the bottom with an oil stone and ran the spindle checks (Photo 41).

The spindle must be in good condition with no perceptible movement in the vertical or horizontal planes when clamped. A sliding fit is necessary. I cleaned up the taper with a taper reamer. The tailstock base slides had so much wear that I machined the "V" and flat slides (Photo 42).

I then scraped these surfaces with frequent alignment checks. The top surface was scraped and alignment checks frequently performed (Photos 43 and 44). The transverse way and slide should not be scraped. It is a tight fit.

The headstock has already been mentioned. My checks revealed all tests to be well within the tolerances given in *MTR*, except for the alignment with the tailstock. The test showed that the tailstock center was about .040"-.050" lower than headstock center. This is too much to scrape off the "V" and flat sides of the headstock, and I had no way to set the headstock up on the mill with any accuracy.

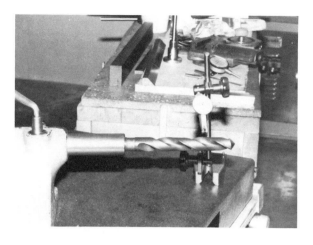

42

41

43

44

45 *TFE Way strip bearing material and epoxy adhesive. The bearing material was cut to size with a utility knife.*

46 *Carriage with the TFE in place and glue curing. You can't see it but there is a piece of quarter-round moulding under the steel on the V-slide.*

Because the other alignment tests were good, I decided to glue way strip bearing material on the tailstock slides to build up the height. This material is a teflon and bronze-filled plastic that is attached to the slide with a two-part epoxy formulation (Photos 45, 46, 47, and 48).

Absolute cleanliness is required when working with this material. It is available in various thicknesses, .015, .030, .060, .090, and .125 × 12" and 24" widths. I cannot tell you where to get it; the material I used was given

to me by the shop that planed the bed. It goes under various names, *TFE, Garlock Way Strip 426, Turcite,* etc. It is very expensive; .060 × 12 × 12" is about $16.00. The epoxy glue is about $19.00 a quart.

The Tailstock Base and Carriage (I also used it on here) must be scraped to fit the bed. This material is much easier to scrape than cast iron or steel, but it gouges easily. The friction between the new surfaces is greatly reduced. It is very abrasive to the scraping tool.

15

47 *TFE 48 hours later with clamps removed. The scraping procedure is to be repeated again.*

48 *Milling clearance groove in "V" slide of carriage.*

49 *Checking squareness of cross slide. This is the final alignment check. All corrective scraping is to be done on "V" slides of carriage.*

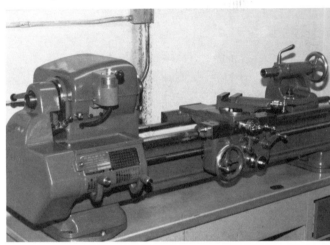

50

51

52

53

54

If you decide to use this material, don't apply it where it will be exposed to impact or metal chips. I understand it tears up easily when abused.

When I scraped the carriage and tailstock slides, I also did the final alignments, with the headstock. (See Photo 49 for the cross slide alignment test.)

The cross slide should face a maximum .0005" concave only per 12" diameter. My test showed no change. For the tailstock center alignment, I used the same test as before: an indicator mounted in the headstock spindle and rotated around the dead center. I had to rescrape the top of the tailstock base to obtain correct alignment.

The lathe, for my purposes, has been reconditioned with respect to the flat bearing surfaces. All that remains is to complete repairs on one gear (replace a tooth) and finish painting the lathe, then assemble.

I completely stripped all painted surfaces of paint, body filler, and other dirt. I used paint stripper, wire brushes and acetone. The acetone is used to thoroughly degrease and

56 *Taper attachment assembly before scraping.*

57 *Checking cross feed screw block ways (horizontal). Notice shim stock.*

clean the surface before painting. A well ventilated room is required. I then applied two coats of rust preventative paint. The color scheme for this lathe is:
Cabinet and drip pan: Pale gray PC75
Door, drawer and lathe: Citation Blue D-5
Inside of lathe bed and headstock bowl:
    Pom Pom Yellow D-6
All paints are manufactured by DeRusto.

For the bare metal surfaces, I attempted to remove all traces of rust, except for deep pits, and polish the pieces to a high shine. I started out with 220 wet and dry paper, progressing to 600 wet and dry. I then used a polishing paste, *Simichrome*, to finish.

I still had to fit a threading dial, and a taper attachment. I also had to mount the three- and four-jaw chucks on their backplates. I will make a steady and follower rest with telescoping jaws and other attachments as necessary.

The taper attachment (T.A.) is not described in *MTR*; however, if carefully thought out no serious problems are encountered. The taper attachment that I obtained for the lathe is the telescoping screw-type (the cross feed nut is not disconnected). The taper attachment is composed of the bed bracket, taper attachment bed, swivel bar, slide block and various other parts (Figure 55 and Photo 56).

After consideration of various orders of scraping, I decided that the bed bracket is the part upon which all alignments are based. The bed bracket has two sets of ways that must be in proper alignment to the bed ways of the lathe: a) the taper attachment bed ways must be parallel to the inverted "V" ways of the lathe bed and b) the cross feed screw block ways must be perpendicular to the inverted

"V" ways of the lathe bed. All planes must be parallel.

The bed bracket is screwed and dowel-pinned to the flat mounting surfaces on the rear of the carriage. The first test I performed was to check the alignments of the cross feed screw block ways. This test was performed with the bed bracket attached to the carriage, using the cross slide with a dial test indicator (DTI) to check the vertical and horizontal ways. Fortunately, this testing showed that scraping was not necessary on the vertical ways, and only about .002″ out on the horizontal ways. If alignment is not present on the vertical ways, the surfaces to be scraped would of necessity be the flat

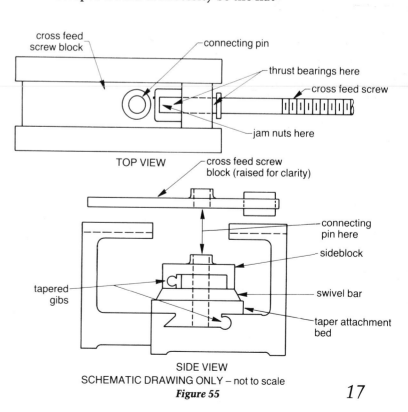

cross feed screw block

connecting pin

thrust bearings here

cross feed screw

jam nuts here

TOP VIEW

cross feed screw block (raised for clarity)

connecting pin here

sideblock

swivel bar

taper attachment bed

tapered gibs

SIDE VIEW
SCHEMATIC DRAWING ONLY – not to scale
Figure 55

17

58 *Checking T.A. flat bed ways.*

59 *Checking parallelism of T.A. bed ways in one direction.*

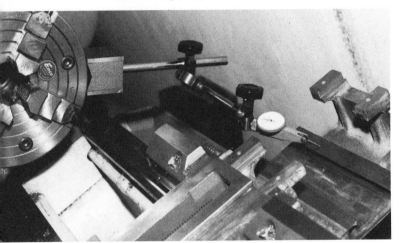

60 *Checking parallelism in the other direction.*

mounting surfaces of the bed bracket. There is not a gib adjustment on the cross feed screw block. The taper attachment bed flat ways were the next surfaces to be checked. All errors were noted, and scraping commenced using the surface plate. There are six flat surfaces on the bottom of the bed bracket, obviously used as reference surfaces on the factory machine setups. I took advantage of these surfaces using feeler gage stock to duplicate the errors (Photos 57 and 58) and to make scraping easier. (You can tell from the photo that this is not an easy piece to scrape and I'm not a contortionist.)

After the flat ways were scraped, the bed bracket was mounted to the carriage, checks were performed on the dovetail ways (Photos 59 and 60) and the bed bracket was dismounted for scraping. This procedure was performed several times before alignment was obtained. The lathe manufacturer usually leaves considerable room for alignment adjustment for field mounting taper attachments. The 13″ Sheldon I own never had a T.A. prior to this

time. I speculate in used machine tools; I removed the T.A. from an 11″ Sheldon I bought for resale. The T.A. was field-mounted and never used on the 11″ lathe. The cross feed screw on the 11″ was the standard screw, not the telescoping type.

The cross slide screw block horizontal ways were scraped and filed into alignment next. No metal was removed from the vertical ways, for reasons already discussed.

The next piece to be scraped is the taper attachment bed. The five surfaces to be scraped include the two flat slides, the guided and gibbed slides that bear on the bed bracket ways, and the flat way that bears with the swivel bar flat slide. The first surface to be scraped on the T.A. bed is the flat way for the swivel bar. The reasons for scraping the flat way first are 1) it will be the reference surface for ensuring parallelism with the flat slides, and 2) it should need minimal attention since this surface does not receive much wear.

All spotting on the flat way is done with a surface plate. Surprisingly, this surface needed considerable scraping due to a warp in the casting of about .0015″. Next, scrape the flat slides using the angle straight edge for spotting, doing frequent checks with DTI surface gage and surface plate to obtain parallelism with the flat way. Then scrape the guided and gibbed slides using the angle straight edge and the guiding way of the bed bracket. The guiding way of the bed bracket has previously been scraped and will indicate if the correct angle is being scraped. I also used the guiding way to spot the gibbed slide of the T.A. bed. Once all the surfaces of the T.A. bed were scraped, I then fitted the tapered gib.

61 *Determining the travel required for the telescoping cross screw.*

The next piece to be scraped is the swivel bar. Again there are five surfaces to be scraped: the flat slide, the flat ways, the guiding way, and the gibbed way. Use the same procedure as the one for the T.A. bed, except that the vertical ways must be perpendicular to the flat ways. I check this with a precision square. Even thought the surface plate is used to spot these surfaces, occasionally spot the flat side against the flat way of the T.A. bed, it for no other reason than insurance.

The slide block is next and has four surfaces to be scraped – the two flat slides, the guided slide and the gibbed slide. Scrape the flat slides first, then scrape the guided slide. Spot the guided slide using the angle straight edge on the guiding way of the swivel bar. Then scrape the gibbed slide and fit the tapered gib.

One part that should need no attention is the swivel pin to swivel on the T.A. bed. If it does not fit correctly, bore out the pin hole in the swivel bar and make a new pin to fit.

The cross feed screw block did not need any scraping, but the hole for the cross feed screw had to be enlarged to permit proper alignment of the cross feed screw. More on this later.

At this point I was satisfied with the work on the taper attachment. I painted and permanently mounted it on the carriage with two screws and two dowel pins. One other essential part to the taper attachment is the bed clamp. When the bed clamp is locked on the lathe bed, the T.A. is operational. It is essential that no distortion be induced in the T.A. through locking of this clamp. Many problems arise when this clamp causes

distortion. The hole in the clamp for the tie rod should be large enough that the tie rod does not come in direct contact with the sides of the hole. Sheldon Machine Company uses a jam nut system to secure the tie rod to the bed clamp; South Bend Lathe uses babbitt. In either method the bed clamp should be locked first, then the jam nuts tightened, or the babbitt poured. I prefer the babbitt method, and may switch if the jam nuts prove to be a problem.

The tedious work is over with, and it is time for the fun stuff to begin. The first order of business is to make a telescoping cross feed screw and a new nut. The originals had about .045" backlash and would be useless with the T.A., since they were the standard type. The biggest problem I had was choosing a design for the telescoping screw. The only manufacturer that I'm familiar with is South Bend, and they use a splined screw. Cutting the slot in the screw would not be a problem; however, making a key for the female portion and having the key hold in a thin wall worried me. While flipping through a Jergen's tool catalogue, I noticed that they stock square hole sleeves, and therein lies the solution. Use a ¼" square hole sleeve for the female portion, and mill a ¼" square male on the screw. This decision meant some minor modification to two pieces, the pinion gear and the cross feed screw bushing. Both had to be bored out to ½" and ⅝", respectively. The cross feed screw is made from Stressproof steel.

A new nut was made from *Meehanite*, and all parts were assembled and checked for smoothness of operation. I discovered at this point that I had permanently mounted the T.A. too soon. I had severe binding of the

19

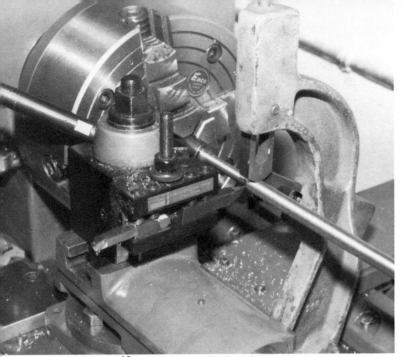

62 *Ready to cut the thread.*

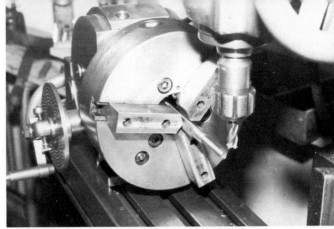

63 *Ready to mill and make the square on the screw. Go slow and easy without a tailstock.*

64 *A view of most of the components for the telescoping cross feed screw. The original cross feed screw can be seen in the foreground.*

screw and nut as the cross slide was fed in. The solution I came up with that involved the least amount of work was to enlarge the bore of the cross feed screw block to allow the screw to shift its position. Not the best solution, but I have not experienced any problems.

In the nine months that the lathe has been in operation, I have experienced no problems with accuracy. In fact, the accuracies achieved have exceeded my expectations. One test, based on a "gentleman's bet" with a friend, was conducted to ensure that the lathe turned round and cylindrical with work mounted in the chuck (a combination of two tests, actually). A 1" diameter bar was chucked in the three-jaw and roughing and finishing cuts (one each) were taken, with .0001" the result over a 4¼" length. The Sheldon test standard is .0003" on a 3" length. The only problem encountered so far, other than replacing a bad motor, was vibration caused by mismatched belts driving the spindle. The belt problem was solved by changing to a banded belt.

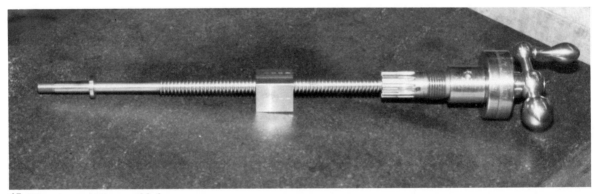

65 *The components assembled.*

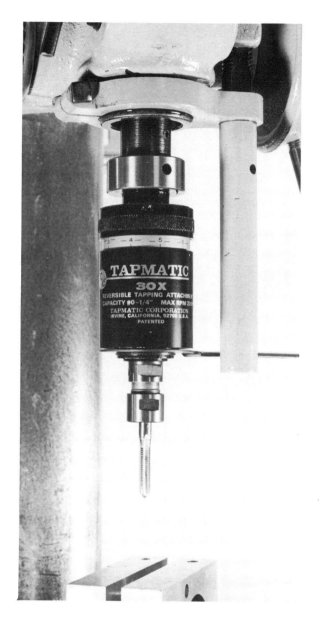

Rapid Machine Tapping Drill Press

by Wm. T. (Ted) Roubal, PhD

Photos by Author

To me, threading holes in metal by hand with a tap held in a tap wrench is downright unpleasant. Some metals aren't so bad to thread – brass for example – but with others it's just a slow process of twist, one two, and untwist all the way, and then repeating the process until the holes are threaded. I get sore hand muscles just thinking about it.

Well, there is a much easier way – using a drillpress-mounted tapping attachment. With the attachment it is possible to maintain a

steady, uninterrupted rotation of the tap, a process which effectively overides the tendency of the tap to grab (as it does in slow hand tapping), and it is possible to thread small diameter holes with the tap rotating at 1300 rpm. As long as there is space for the chips to accumulate, the tap can be driven steadily forward without fear of breakage.

If chip buildup becomes a problem (as in deep hole or blind hole threading), the tap is protected by an adjustment you set prior to tapping which disengages the tap when it encounters too much resistance. The tapping attachment is also constructed such that when the drillpress quill is retracted (changed from downward movement to an upward movement) the tap rotation is automatically reversed (the drillpress continues in its steady clockwise rotation) and the tap is unscrewed at a rotation speed which is greater than the forward rotation. In this manner it is possible to tap all holes – deep, shallow and blind ones – effortlessly within a matter of seconds. Tapping metals now becomes pleasurable. There is a catch, however. It's not just a simple matter of slipping on a tapping attachment and using it in the drillpress. The drillpress has to be modified slightly before the attachment can be used. Therefore, unless you have a spare drillpress upon which to leave the attachment permanently mounted, the tapping attachment loses its appeal. I mounted my attachment on an old, damaged Atlas drillpress that I rebuilt using Sears parts (Atlas used to make Sears drillpresses and spare parts, which are directly interchangeable and are still available from Sears).

My setup is shown in the photo. Against the extension post bolted to the drillpress rides an arm of the tapping attachment. This is part of the mechanism that reverses the tap rotation when an upward pressure is exerted on the tap (downward quill movement is changed to an upward movement). My particular unit is a Tapmatic threading attachment (Tapmatic Corp., 1851 Kettering Street, Irvine, CA), and accommodates taps, sizes 0 to ¼". Attachments for larger taps are available; however, these can't be adjusted to protect taps much smaller than sizes 2 or 3. Attachments are also available to hold threading dies. A good quality thread cutting fluid should be used with machine threading. Tapmatic sells two types. One is used for all metals except aluminum and the other is just for aluminum.

1 *Parting-off semi-finished ring with integral stub.*

2 *Boring tool separates finished ring from waste stub.*

Machining Thin Disks and Rings

by D. E. Johnson, P.E.

Photos by Author

Sooner or later, most home machinists are confronted with the problem of machining relatively thin rings, washers, spacers, collars, and similar disk-like pieces whose faces must be held parallel.

Extremely thin disks, i.e., shims, can be made from shim stock using simple homemade punch setups.

Thicker pieces can be gripped internally and externally in the three-jaw chuck or forced onto a shouldered mandrel with excellent results.

We are concerned here with those in-between requirements for disks or rings whose thickness may range from $1/32''$ or less, to $1/4''$ or more.

If a large number of pieces are required, many tooling methods are available, such as homemade or purchased soft-nosed expanding collets which can be machined to grip the work.

However, we are usually interested in producing only one or a couple of pieces, without special tooling.

The method described here produces disks and rings with faces guaranteed parallel. The small amount of stock wasted is a fair trade for avoidance of special tooling.

Further, the finished surfaces of the work are never subjected to marking or distortion from any work-holding fixture. By running the lathe spindle relatively fast and taking very light cuts, amazingly thin parts can be produced. Use of this method is not limited to round stock; it works equally well on squares and other shapes.

Referring to Figure 1, begin by chucking a suitable piece of stock and turning a stub end of appropriate length and outside diameter **D**, which must be exactly equivalent to the desired inside diameter of the hole in the finished part. Finish surface **A** now since it becomes one face of the part. Drill a hole of

22

any convenient diameter to a depth which will allow the subsequent cutoff operation to intersect the hole.

Using a parting tool, bandsaw, or other method, cut off as in Figure 2 and Photo 1, being sure to allow enough stock for finishing.

In Figure 3 and Photo 2, the work is reversed and held in the chuck by the stub previously formed. Finish the outside diameter and surface **B**. Thickness **T** is machined to the accuracy required at this point. Break edges with a file. A small boring bar is then fed into the hole, being careful not to bore into the chuck jaws. When the boring tool setting is expanded to diameter **D**, the finished part will fall off leaving only a slight burr for cleanup. Feeding the boring tool in at an angle using the compound will produce a countersunk hole.

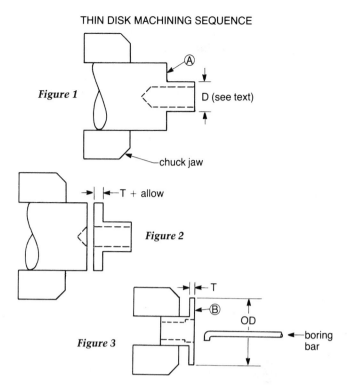

THIN DISK MACHINING SEQUENCE

Figure 1

Ⓐ

D (see text)

chuck jaw

T + allow

Figure 2

T

Ⓑ

OD

boring bar

Figure 3

Swaging Down a Copper Pipe Elbow

by Guy Lautard

A short-run job came in one day that required the diameter of one end of a standard copper pipe elbow to be reduced from ⅝″ ID to ⁹⁄₁₆″ ID. Using a method devised by Bill Fenton, a simple hand swage die was made up as shown below, and the job was done at a profit.

(The segmented "collet" marked the outside of the workpieces somewhat, but the result was entirely to the customer's satisfaction.)

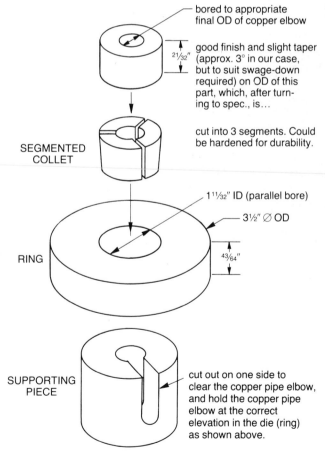

bored to appropriate final OD of copper elbow

2¹⁄₃₂″

good finish and slight taper (approx. 3° in our case, but to suit swage-down required) on OD of this part, which, after turning to spec., is…

SEGMENTED COLLET

cut into 3 segments. Could be hardened for durability.

1¹¹⁄₃₂″ ID (parallel bore)

3½″ ⌀ OD

RING

43⁄64″

SUPPORTING PIECE

cut out on one side to clear the copper pipe elbow, and hold the copper pipe elbow at the correct elevation in the die (ring) as shown above.

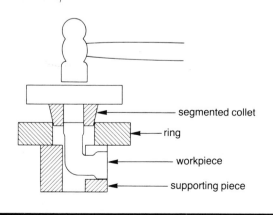

segmented collet

ring

workpiece

supporting piece

Some Pointers on Rotary Table Work

by Guy Lautard

A rotary table is a most useful accessory, particularly on a vertical milling machine. Think of it as adding a circular table motion to the existing x, y, & z axis feeds of your milling machine. Figure 1 shows some aspects of its usefulness. Part circle machining jobs, e.g. radiussing the end of a flat bar (A and B), are one area where it shines. Some types of circular dividing are readily done on a geared rotary table. Spacing out holes on a pitch circle (C) and graduating a micrometer feedscrew dial (D) are two examples of this type of work. Circular slot milling (E), and milling slots whose centerlines are at an angle, are also within the province of a rotary table.

Many jobs are set up on a rotary table using a locating pin – or center pin – which positions the job's center on the rotary table's center. Many times some machining operation is required to be done along some arc centered on a hole in the job. The hole may later be enlarged or eliminated, but the sequence of machining operations can often be planned to take advantage of the possibility of a hole on center. If the hole size does not, or cannot temporarily, suit the size of the center pin, an adapter bushing is made up to act as a "go-between."

In the George Thomas-designed 3¾"Ø rotary table, there is a ¼"Ø reamed hole in the Table's Pivot Pin. A Center Pin of ¼"Ø CRS or drill rod drops into this hole and the workpiece is quickly centered on one or the other of its two ends – one is turned down to ⅛"Ø, the other to ³⁄₁₆"Ø, and it is of a length such that is stands proud of the table surface about ⅜". When neither end of this center pin suits the job at hand, it is a simple matter to turn up a special bushing with a ³⁄₁₆" center hole, or a ¼"Ø spigot which can enter the hole in the Pivot Pin.

If the rotary table has a No. 2 MT (Morse taper) center hole (and this is a common feature on

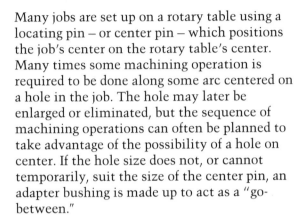

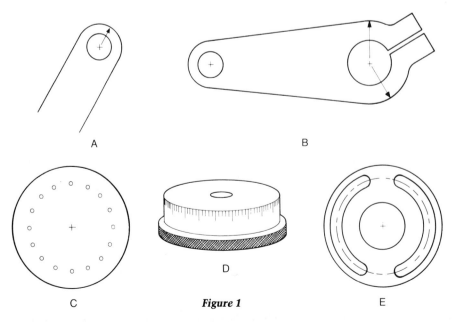

A

B

C

D

E

Figure 1

24

commercial rotary tables of the size we are likely to encounter) the center pin can be made from a No. 2 MT blank end arbor, or some reasonable substitute. Commercial blank end arbors are a standard product, though it usually takes a bit of digging to unearth them. A No. 2 MT shank drill chuck arbor can be purchased and the drill chuck end turned down to some convenient size. My own No. 2 MT center pin was made from a brand new taper shank drill that shattered up the full length of the flutes. A hacksaw cut separated the wheat from the chaff, and I then stuck the taper shank in the No. 2 MT socket in my Myford lathe spindle, faced the end, bored it 0.465", and screwcut an internal ½-28 thread in the end. (I know, that's an oddball thread, but all the adapters which were to go on the end were to be screwcut anyway, so it made no difference.) Three adapters were made as follows:

CENTERING PLUG
Screwcut the end ½-28, knurl a grasping ring, and part off. (later) Replace the No. 2 MT shank in the spindle, screw in the nearly completed Centering plug, face the exposed end, and center drill.

SCREWED ADAPTER PLUGS
Fabricate two more plug blanks as above, one each screwcut 8-32 and ¼-28 (external threads) on the working end while screwed into the taper shank in the same fashion as for the centering plug. These two were for a specific job which had to be, at a later stage in its making, put on the rotary table for graduating (one piece) and having 12 shallow dimples drilled on a 0.512"∅ pitch circle (other piece).

The Center Plug is used to get the rotary table centered with the spindle of the vertical milling machine, thus:

The rotary table is bolted to the machine table but not tightened up. A No. 2 MT shank is dropped into the socket in the rotary table and given a "thwock" with a soft hammer. A centering plug is screwed into ½-28 hole in the top of the taper shank, finger tight. A piece of ⅜"∅ drill rod about 3½" long, with a male 60° conical end, is slipped into a ⅜" collet in the vertical mill's spindle nose. The quill is lowered, and the rotary table moved approximately under the quill center via x and y table feeds. Lower the quill center into the center drilled hole in the centering plug, lock the

quill in down position, and tighten the rotary table hold-down bolts. (Here it helps to have digital readouts on your x and y table axes). Zero your table feeds and shift the machine (and rotary table) so the rotary table center is offset some desired amount, (e.g. ½ the diameter (=radius) of the desired pitch circle diameter for a ring of bolt holes, or whatever), with respect to the machine spindle. Usually only the x axis feed is disturbed to get this desired offset, for obvious reasons, but this would not always be the case.

The centering plug is unscrewed from the ½-28 hole in the No. 2 MT shank, and replaced with a suitable adapter for the job at hand. Most work is bolted down to the rotary table by means of T-slots, T-nuts and clamping bars. Here too, the job's center is centered on the rotary table with the aid of a pin in the rotary table's center hole. A sheet of brass or aluminum should be interposed between job and top of rotary table to protect the working surface of the rotary table.

Another useful adapter is a No. 2 MT shank with a duplicate of your lathe spindle nose on the other end. (Myford has such for their spindle nose.) Using this, a job can be taken, undisturbed, still in the lathe chuck, from lathe to rotary table which has been previously set up on the vertical mill, and the necessary next operation done – marking graduations on a micrometer collar for a feed screw would be an example of this.

It is necessary to know or work out the number of degrees through which the part must turn for a particular curve to be machined. This is so specific to each job as to preclude setting out any "advice" on the matter. As you begin to size up the job and how it will be set up on the rotary table, and how you will go about it, you will either know already the extent of the arcs involved, or you'll darn quick realize you're going to have to sit down and work them out before you cut any metal! Between the degree markings on the periphery of the table, the handwheel on the worm reduction gear, and/or the adjustable stops on the rim of the table, the work is then rolled through the desired arc. Avoid climb milling, and forget not thy feedscrew backlash, and to make due provision thereunto.

1

2

Making the Home Shop Pay

by John W. Oder

Photos by Author

Machining is not how I usually make my living. Being both laid off from my engineering position and having considerable training and experience in machining naturally causes me to fall back on the trade in these hard times.

I had an opportunity to bid on a job involving a fair quantity and requiring a good sized drill press. Having only the usual 15" drill press, I bid the job planning to do it in the 20" x 48" Pratt & Whitney lathe. The job called for one hundred ¾" x 3" x 6" shims from hot rolled 1020 steel, with two 1⅛" holes drilled through each shim. The customer furnished the material already sawed to length. I won the bid at $2.75 per hole. The photos show how I did it.

Photo 1 shows the fixture I made up from a previously used fixture (from an automobile flywheel machining job). It is nothing more than a piece of heat treated 4142 (very, very common in Houston scrap yards), about 7" in diameter and 2" thick. I faced it off true and put in some tapped holes for the strap type clamps and some reamed holes for the locating dowel pins. These dowels position the part in the fixture and some care was expended to get them in the right places. The part was positioned for the first hole by two dowels on its long side and one dowel against its end as shown by the arrow in the photo.

The part, installed in the fixture in position for drilling the first hole, is shown in Photo 2. The

26

3

4

5

6

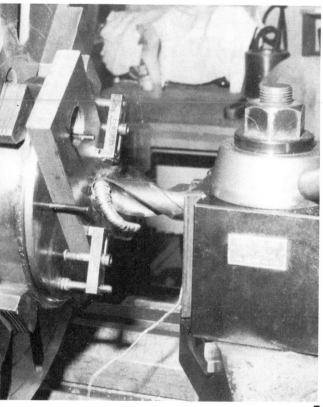

7

... "to fall back on the trade
in these hard times...

...$33.00 per hour is not bad
at all in the garage!"

8

9

part in this case is not against the end locating dowel, because this dowel has already been changed to the position for drilling the second hole in the part. The photography session caught the job in mid stride, so to speak.

The part with the first hole complete is positioned in the fixture for drilling the second hole in Photo 3. Since the hole spacing was fairly critical and the length of the parts varied considerably from the sawing operation, the means shown were resorted to, to assure correct hole spacing. As the arrow shows, the side of the first hole is the locating surface to control the position of the second hole.

Photo 4 illustrates the "spotting" drill. This is a very short ½" drill ground with a split or "aircraft" point. This type of point allows free cutting right to the center. The use of this short, stiff, free cutting drill on this job eliminated any need for center punching or center drilling of the parts prior to drilling them.

The 1⅛" Silver & Demming (½" shank) drill and the method I used to avoid clamping on its small shank are shown in Photo 5. This method also made a much shorter and stiffer setup than the usual drill chuck. Another consideration was the weight, since I would repeatedly be obliged to pick up this assembly in the process of putting it on and taking it off the tool post. The adaptor clamped in the boring bar holder is bored to closely fit both the ½" shank and about ¾" of the butt end of the 1⅛" diameter. I then drilled through both

the adaptor and butt end of the drill (it is soft in this area), tapped from both sides and put in two cap screws to prevent the drill from turning within the adaptor.

The spotting drill is being fed under power into the work for the start of the second hole in Photo 6. This drill was fed all the way through, taking advantage of its free cutting attributes and making the subsequent 1⅛" drill less difficult for the machine to feed through. (The old Pratt has a tendency to lift the front wings of the carriage saddle if you push too hard on a drill mounted on the tool post.)

The 1⅛" drill does its thing on the second hole (Photo 7). Photos 8 and 9 show this from front and rear with a larger field of view. An added attraction was that on the first part, this 1⅛" drill was allowed to cut into the fixture about ⅛". This simple little feature caused the succeeding parts to have only an insignificant burr on the exit side.

172 rpm and .0038 feed in inches per revolution were used throughout this operation, with sulphur base cutting oil applied to the drills with a brush.

The apparent disadvantage of doing a drill press job in the lathe was offset by the ability to change tools with the chuck running (love that Aloris tool post!) and such niceties as gravity chip removal and no layout work (except on fixture) and power feed. I was able to average twelve holes per hour with this arrangement. $33.00 per hour is not bad at all in the garage!

Keep that Universal Chuck Accurate

by Pete Peterka

Drawings by Author

Manufacturers of the three-jaw universal chuck claim a brand new chuck is accurate to within .003″. This means that if a piece of round barstock is chucked and rotated 360°, a dial indicator will show only a .003″ movement. When we consider the construction and machining of the intricate heat-treated parts of this device, our hats are off to the fabricators of these chucks for achieving such accuracy. But, unfortunately, through many years of long, hard use, the chuck does not remain accurate.

Recently, I noticed that mine had developed a .009″ TIR runout. Here is a method of bringing it back to its original setting: Insert a ½″ diameter drill rod into the chuck and tighten. With a dial indicator mounted in the lathe toolpost, determine the point of its

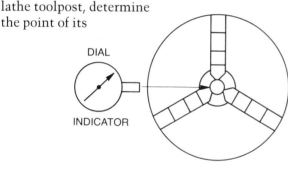

Figure 1

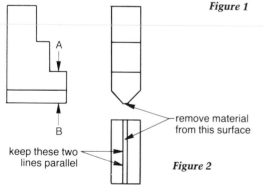

keep these two lines parallel

remove material from this surface

Figure 2

lowest reading. Record the jaw number at this point. Also determine the total runout when the chuck is revolved 360° (Figure 1).

Remove the jaw located near the lowest reading, and remove a little metal from the surface that was in contact with the drill rod. These jaws are heat treated to a high hardness, and the metal must be removed by the use of an oilstone. The amount to be removed is ½ the total indicator reading. To do this accurately, first determine the dimension or measurement between the surface to be stoned and its opposite jaw surface. See Figure 2 showing the reference measured dimension AB. Use a micrometer.

Remove only one or two thousandths of an inch at a time to "play it safe," assemble the jaws into the chuck, and make the original drill rod/dial indicator test. If an appreciable amount of metal must be removed, a belt sander will make this operation easier. Be sure, however, that the jaw is kept perpendicular during removal of the metal. A good way to do this is to keep the two lines bordering the surface being stoned parallel. If these edges are kept parallel, the jaw will automatically stay perpendicular to the chuck face when assembled.

When the stoning is completed, wipe the jaw surfaces and insert into the chuck for the dial indicator test. I brought mine to a TIR of only .001″, which is actually better than the original setting. I wonder how long it will stay that way! (We must realize, too, that the most accurate way to hold work is either by the use of collets or a four-jaw chuck.)

During the assembly and disassembly of the jaws, it is a good idea to blow out the chips and *lightly* lubricate the chuck. A chuck revolving at high rpm slings oil.

Fear Neither Sphere Nor Hemisphere

by John Dean

Photos by Author

Nearly 40 years ago I received a request for several 2" steel balls, but a radius turning attachment was unavailable. The size of the job and an estimate of probable future needs failed to justify the expenditure of work and materials to make a sophisticated device.

One of my students suggested a solution involving no mathematics or engineering, just a practical concept of basic mechanics and geometry, combined with imagination. A simple steel plate would offset the lathe

1

compound to permit its rotation around the pivot point on the cross slide. The plate and the procedure were crude, but the result justified the means.

Many years later a request for 3" balls made it necessary to make a new offset plate having an increased rotation radius. Making the more recently requested ball and socket camera support (Photo 1) will show how it is used.

The offset plate is ⅜" steel, 6" long and 3½" wide. The bottom of one end must duplicate the bottom of the compound, split "V" rings, or whatever, as used on the make and model of the lathe. Photo 2 is of the type that fits my 1932 model, 9" South Bend Jr. The radial channel is to clear the head of the bolt in the cross slide feed.

The upper side of the plate is shown in Photo 3. The compound is fastened in place by the two bolts and nuts. The pivot post is unnecessary but is helpful while attaching the compound.

The plate is placed on the cross slide, with the pivot post protruding up through the hole in the center and the two T-bolts through the

3

2

outer holes. The nuts are placed on the T-bolts and tightened until rotation is stiff but smooth. The assembly may be seen in Photos 4 and 5.

The knurled locater pin at the left in Photo 3 is placed over the cross slide pivot post for use in accurately placing the center of rotation in relation to the work, after which it is removed and laid aside.

In making the ball and socket in Photo 1, the ball is made first. The material for the ball-to-be is mounted in the chuck, and a mark is made at the center of its length. The locater pin is placed on the pivot post and its tip brought to the mark with the carriage and cross slide. This locates the longitudinal center of the ball. The carriage stop is placed against the left side of the carriage and locked to insure return to precisely the same location after the carriage may have been moved to the right.

The fore and aft pivot location is now found by using the cross slide to place the tip of the locater pin into alignment with the point of a dead center placed in the tailstock spindle. The cross slide must not be moved again until the ball is finished; feed control must be entirely by use of the compound. A cross slide lock is helpful if one is provided. The tip of the locater pin may be used in adjusting the height setting of the toolbit, after which it is removed and put aside.

With the carriage positioned against the stop and locked, shaping the ball may begin. Take light cuts and swing the compound smoothly through the full arc from the center to the shank of the ball. In Photo 4 the ball is almost completely formed into the desired 1½″ diameter. The procedure is the same whether the ball is to be the size of a mustard seed or 3″ in diameter.

The lower part of the socket was next. Because of insufficient room under the chuck for the carriage, the socket parts were made on the end of a shaft, to be parted off when finished. The steady rest was used (Photo 5) to provide clearance and insure against misalignment in the chuck jaws. A full hemisphere was desired, so the cross slide pivot was positioned directly under the end of the shaft. The finished ball now becomes a measuring tool. Coated lightly with Prussian blue and placed in the socket, it will indicate when a precision fit has been made.

4

5

Before parting off, 32 threads per inch were cut around the rim to receive the top piece. The bottom of the socket was drilled and tapped ¼-20 to fit on a standard camera tripod.

The top and bottom sections of the socket were made by the same method, except the top was given a larger outside diameter. The throat was counterbored and threaded 32 threads per inch inside to screw onto the lower part. The outside was knurled and parted off slightly to the right of the bottom of the concave, in order to leave a hole large enough for the ball shank to wobble around in while aiming the camera.

The ball shank was turned and threaded ¼-20 to fit the standard bushings on cameras. A camera support washer was tapped ¼-20 and screwed on the shank. The three parts (Photo 6) were then finished for assembly, as in Photo 1.

To use, position the camera as desired, tighten the knurled section of the socket firmly, and you're in business!

6

1 *Pattern follower, and tool bit set up ready to use. Two thumb screws at the right of the saddle provide a drag on the extension link to keep the tool bit from jumping when fed in by hand. A full size template is mounted on taper attachment.*

Turning Ornamental Shapes

by Conrad Milster

Photos by Author

Several years ago, I had the problem of turning several pieces to an identical ornamental shape. The project was part of a grandfather clock restoration. But, although the pieces were wood, the same procedure can be used for metal, and virtually any item which has an unusual shape can be easily made in quantity with accurate results.

The original items in question were three finials with an urn shape. My first thought was to do them freehand, but I gave that up almost immediately. While I have an average skill at machine tools, freehand turning is definitely not on the list. The next thought was to do them as straight machine jobs, but there were too many curves and tool setups needed for that method. The third method was to cut a template and follow this as a guide, but my

initial reaction had been one of reluctance at spending the time in making the template itself.

In the end, however, this latter method was used and turned out to be the easiest by far. Cutting and filing the template out of a piece of ⅛" aluminum proved to be less than a half-hour's work, and several subsequent sets of finials have been made with the greatest of ease using the original template.

The first step is to choose your template material; this can be anything as long as it is strong enough to take the force of a follower pin pressing against it. Brass or aluminum sheet, ⅟₁₆" to ⅛" thick, would be more than strong enough and still not be too difficult to work to provide the final shape. Two factors are important at the layout stage: a center line of

2 *Position of pattern, mounted on the taper turning attachment.*

the pattern on the template, and enough length beyond the actual pattern to provide room for the clamps or screws which will mount the template on the lathe. There is no magnification of the pattern with the method we are discussing, so the pattern must be laid out full size. In order to provide room for the tool bit to finish the work up to and beyond its actual ends there should be a continuation of the final diameter of the job on the template for at least ¼" or so. Another inch at each end should be added for mounting.

The template can be mounted by any method that will hold it near the back of the lathe in a rigid manner. In my case, I found that the two end brackets of the taper turning attachment worked out well and it was held on them by two C-clamps (Photos 1 and 2).

Before firmly bolting or clamping the template in place, we must make another change, this time to the cross feed of the carriage by installing the follower pin. This is the actual "feeler" that will ride on the template, and its position in relation to the work is important.

So that the cross slide may follow the configuration of the template freely, it will be necessary to disconnect the feed screw as if we were actually using the taper attachment. We can also use the extension bar from the taper attachment which bolts to the rear of the cross slide to hold our follower pin. The pin can be made of any material that will easily fasten to the cross slide and be rigid enough not to flex under use. I found that for my particular setup

on a 6" lathe, a piece of 1" aluminum angle, ⅛" thick, was ideal.

With all parts loosely in place there are two key points to check; one, can the follower pin travel the length of the pattern without fouling either chuck or tailstock with the carriage? And two, can the cross slide move enough to cut both largest and smallest diameters without resetting the tool bit? Once these conditions have been met, clamp the template in place. Now is the time to use the center line which we drew when laying out the pattern to insure that the template is parallel to the lathe. A scale or pair of dividers can check the distance between the center line and the ways of the lathe bed. It may be necessary to shim up the template if it's more than ¼" to ½" below the extension bar. The greater the length of the follower pin, the more chance of springing in it.

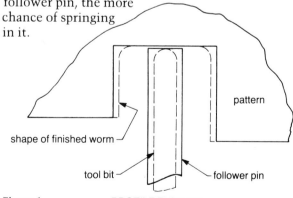

Figure 1   PROFILE TURNING

One critical point is that the shape of the follower pin and that of the tool bit must be identical for accurate results and this is shown

33

3 Roughing out the work. The follower is riding on the pattern, but the tool bit is set to cut work slightly oversize to allow for a finishing cut.

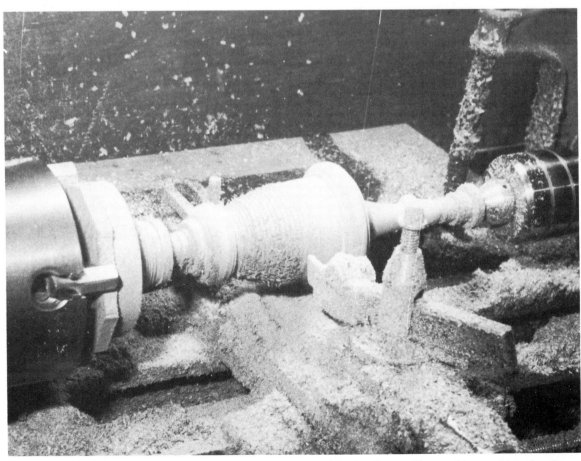

4 Traversing cut along the pattern to take out shoulders (visible to left of tool) caused by roughing cut. Note that the tool bit is moving "downhill," i.e. right to left at this point.

in exaggerated form in Figure 1. If your work has both concave curves and shoulders, you have a problem. The simplest method is to select a tool bit for one or the other and touch up the work with a file when you are done. In my case, I found that a parting tool with a ⅛" wide blade made an ideal match to the ⅛" wide follower pin.

Once all these conditions have been checked, set the compound rest for 90° and back it off most of the way. Pull the cross slide back (you may have to slack off the adjusting screws on the gibs until it slides freely by hand) until the tool bit is clear of the largest diameter of the work, and mount your stock in the chuck. It would be ideal to have your stock rough-turned to a diameter about ⅛" greater than the finished job. If this hasn't been done, do it now by clamping the cross slide in place and using the compound rest feed to control depth of cut. Be sure that the follower pin does not hang up on the template during this operation. With the work rough-turned, insert the tool bit for the profile turning (Photo 3) and place the follower pin on the template's point of largest diameter, slowly advancing the tool bit till it takes a light cut. Check the size of this diameter and set the compound rest feed so that you get a cut leaving your work about .010" in diameter over the correct final size. Carefully advance the tool bit by pushing in the cross slide by hand until the follower pin hits the template and back it out again. Move the carriage slightly less than the width of the tool bit and repeat the procedure, remembering always to work from the jobs largest diameter to its smallest. This procedure is followed for the full length of the pattern and the result will be a piece of work made up of shoulders of different diameters and approximately the finished shape of the work (Photo 4).

It may not be possible to take a full depth cut at the first try and, in that case, simply make several passes back and forth, going deeper each time.

Once the work has been roughed out, you will want to sharpen your tool bit for the finishing cut. This is one reason for leaving our work slightly oversize; we now have a cushion of .010" for resetting the tool bit. In doing this, try to pick a corner which will give an alignment both parallel and at right angles to the center line of the work to insure that your tool bit and follower pin are "in sync," so to speak.

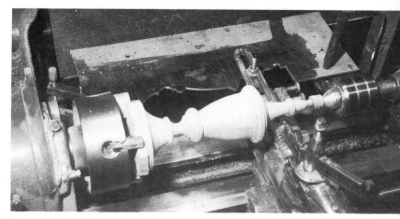

5 *Finished work showing relationship between pattern and work. In this photo, the tool bit and follower have been backed slightly away from pattern and work.*

6 *Finish cut, ready to move tool bit "downhill;" in this case, towards camera. The follower is just visible riding the end shoulder of the pattern.*

Take another light cut off the major diameter, check its size and advance the tool bit the required amount to bring the work to finished size. With one hand, feed or hold the follower pin against the template again at its major diameter while the other hand moves the carriage slowly along the lathe. Keep a gentle pressure on the cross slide; the tool bit should flow smoothly along the work, bringing it to final shape (Photo 5). Be careful not to push on the follower too hard or you run the risk of springing something and distorting the work. Similarly, do not try to work from a smaller diameter up to a larger unless the slope is a very easy one.

If you are turning a shape which tapers off to nothing at the tailstock end, leave enough material intact to support the work while you are finishing it. Then carefully, very carefully, trim off the last of it with as light a cut as possible (Photo 6).

Measuring Pitch Diameter

by Charlie Dondro

Photos by Author

A recent series of articles in *HSM* (November/December 1983 to May/June 1984) described the properties of machine screws and their calculations. This article describes a practical procedure for measuring the pitch diameter of screw threads using the three wire method.

The measuring wires are ordinary sewing needles; they are hardened steel, nickel plated, have a uniform diameter and are inexpensive. Small needles are available in sizes 10, .018" diameter, to 1, which is about .040" in diameter. Larger sizes are called "Yarn Darners." Size 14 measures .056", and 18 measures .071".

Measure all the needles that you have on hand and select groups of three that are as close to the same diameter as possible. An exact diameter is not critical, but the size variation among the group is. I was able to make group selections that varied less than .0001" in the small sizes. Sewing needles, of course, are not as precise as precision-ground measuring wires, but they are entirely satisfactory for home shop use.

A selection of six sets of wires, from .018" to .071", will measure threads from 48 tpi to 8 tpi. However, a larger group will give you wires that are closer to the "best" diameter. A package assortment of 50 needles costs about $1, but don't overlook the possibility of getting at least two or three sizes out of the family sewing basket.

Probably the hardest part of measuring the pitch diameter of screw threads using the three wire method is managing three wires, adjusting the micrometer or caliper and holding the threaded part all at the same time. However, with the proper technique the procedure is not difficult.

For measuring screw diameters from no. 4 to 5/16", roll up two small balls of floral clay. Floral clay is a non-hardening putty-like compound that florists use at the base of a floral design. It can be obtained at a hobby or variety store at low cost. Insert both ends of the wires into the clay and adjust the assembly around the thread to be measured. The clay and wires are light enough to "stay put" on the thread. When the micrometer clamps down on the wires, all the slack is taken up.

For screw diameters between 5/16" and 1½", insert the pointed ends of the needles into a cork at one end only, and fit it over the thread so it is self-supporting. For diameters greater than 1½", use a small diameter aluminum rod as a needle extender and a thin strip of balsa wood to hold the wires.

If you are measuring threads at the workbench, use a micrometer stand to hold the micrometer or caliper. A drill press vise can also be used. Clean the threads to be measured with a discarded toothbrush and kerosene or paint thinner to remove all the chips and cutting fluid. Use a moderate pressure on the micrometer so that the measuring wires seat fully in the threads. Some friction stop micrometers may not apply enough pressure because of their light tension. Use the lower section of the thimble to make the adjustment if this is the case.

When measuring pitch diameters, use the formula in the *HSM* article to select the best maximum and minimum wire size. Convenient tables of wire sizes and additional information on measuring pitch diameters can be found in the *Machinery's Handbook* or *The New American Machinist's Handbook*. Use the formula $PD = M + (.86603 \times p) - (w \times 3)$ to determine the pitch diameter from the measurement over the wires.

Where:
- PD = Pitch diameter
- M = Measurement over the wires
- p = Pitch of thread (1/threads per inch)
- w = Wire size (diameter)

The wire caddy is made from a 3½" plastic screw top household jar, a ½" Masonite base and a pillbox to hold the corks and floral clay. Drill holes in the Masonite to fit the wire group, and fill the holes with clay to secure the wires.

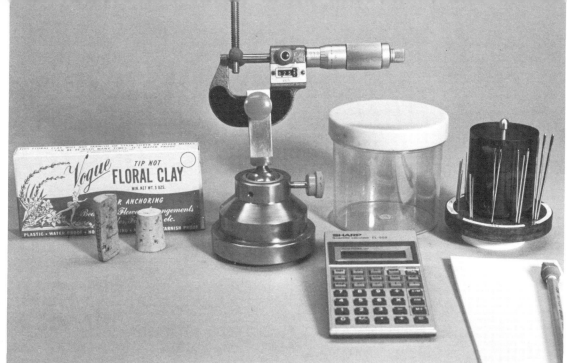

Shown are the tools and equipment needed to measure pitch diameter of screw threads.

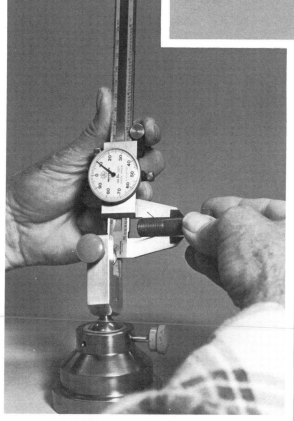

A dial caliper is used for measuring ½ × 20 thread.

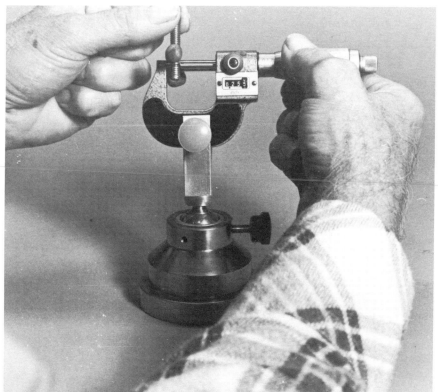

In measuring pitch diameter of ¼ × 20 thread, two small balls of clay hold the wires in place while the micrometer is adjusted.

Square References, their Design, Construction and Inspiration

by Gary F. Reisdorf

Photos by Author

Several articles in *Live Steam* and *The Home Shop Machinist* have addressed or at least mentioned precision measurement in the home shop. All have suggested methods for obtaining a surface plate. Purchasing a granite or cast iron plate and use of a piece of glass were mentioned. One of the former is recommended. Some mention of a square reference was made, but no useful information was provided on how to use or make it, except for an *HSM* article in the March/April 1984 issue.

Commercially available equipment varies widely in its use and accuracy. Squares available for precision measurement are the try square, the solid bevel edge, and the cylinder square (Photo 1). I prefer the solid bevel edge square, because it is lighter than the cylinder square (the ultimate master), as useful as the try square, and generally more accurate. As a note: inexpensive squares are usually seconds and are not very precise. Squares are primarily for inspection, but what if you see a

thin ray of light between your work and the square? How far off is it? How may corrections be made? Or is the square in error?

For machining work square, the machine vise is probably used the most. However, for precision work an accurate *angle plate* is required. It may be used with lathes, mills, drills and surface grinding machines for maximum accuracy. Another type of square machining reference is the toolmaker's cube. Many are not really a "cube," but all for the most part are solid, which yields a very rugged and stable unit. If purchased, angle plates and cubes are very expensive ($100-$300 each). However, these items are relatively easy to construct. By one method or another they may be made as accurate as required.

Several concepts are illustrated; mix and match the features that you require. Size is determined by the following factors: the size of the anticipated work, the available machine

1   *Square references suitable for inspection: the try square, bevel edge solid square, and the cylinder square.*

2   *Clamp a square to the angle plate in question, and zero the indicator held in the transfer stand. Note the reference rail, which references work square to the angle plate edge.*

capacity both to make and use the item, and probably the most important, the available material.

Maximum accuracy may be obtained if surface grinding equipment is available; however, an accurately milled surface will suffice if a lower precision meets your needs.

If possible, use a solid piece of hot rolled steel as the material for all angle plates or cubes. Cold rolled steel has much more internal stress due to its manufacturing process and will not retain its accuracy unless annealed. Weldments also contain stresses, and welds may have hard spots. Bolted constructions usually are not as rigid as a solid unit, and the bolts holding the plate together restrict the location of hold-down holes. Hot rolled solid stock is the best choice, even over castings, because it is uniform, easy to machine and may be casehardened to reduce wear. The use of tool steel is very expensive, and it is tough to machine.

Hardening the surface of the steel helps to preserve the accuracy and precision of the tools. However, it creates other problems. During heat-treating, warpage or other distortion occurs. This necessitates surface grinding to correct these errors. For maximum reliability, the heat-treated steel must be stabilized by sub-zero freezing (-150°F) to complete the metal grain structure conversion from austenite to martensite (See *Machinery's Handbook*, "Heat-treatment of steel and sub-zero freezing of steel").

4 *Mount a foot on the transfer stand, contact the cylinder square, and zero the indicator. (Note the indicator transfer stand – it was inspired by R. S. Hedin's article, "Lathe Milling Attachments" in* HSM, *January/February '83).*

5 *Move to the angle plate in question and contact the foot. Directly read the error on the indicator. This method may be used to easily detect a twisted condition in the vertical surface, by traversing the stand and watching the indicator.*

For uniform results and minimum warpage, I suggest that all hardening be done by a professional heat-treating house. I request liquid carburizing as the process for case-hardening my tools. This uses activated salt baths and is accomplished at a lower temperature than other processes, such as pack hardening and cyanide hardening.

Commercial stabilizing is accomplished with industrial freezers at -105°F. If this is not available in your area, it is possible to use dry

3 *Read the error, if any, at the other end. Of course, the measurements are made on a surface plate, not white paper.*

ice at approximately -110°F. The process I used was to buy 50 lbs. of dry ice and place it in a styrofoam ice chest. Do not crush the ice. Fill the chest nearly full of denatured alcohol to extend the life of the dry ice and to facilitate the heat transfer. Precautions must be taken when handling dry ice and frozen steel to avoid frostbite or other skin damage. Twist wire onto the parts for immersion. Immerse the part for one to two hours, remove and allow it to return to room temperature, without heating. Repeat as many times as possible until the dry ice is gone. Temper the part in the family oven at 200°-250°F for two hours, and allow it to cool to room temperature in the oven overnight.

Because the cube is easy to correct, I recommend that it be made first. The finished project will serve as a master from which all other angle plates will be made. Remember, any error in the finished tool will be reproduced in all subsequent work made with it. Photos 2 through 5 illustrate two methods of *measuring* squareness error. To verify the accuracy of the reference square in Photos 2 and 3, take readings as shown. Reclamp the square after rotating it 180°. Measure the *same* edge of the square previously checked. If the square is okay, the readings will be identical. The indicator will show double any error present in the square.

Start construction on a cube that will be nearly as large as the largest angle plate to be built. Rough machine all surfaces in a machine vise. Mark the sides "A" through "F." Machine side "A" first, place it against the *solid* jaw of the vise with a rod between the work and the movable jaw (Figure 6). Then machine side "B."

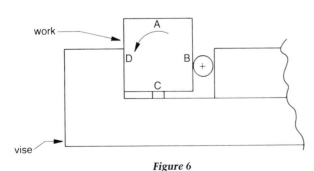

Figure 6

Side "B" is then approximately square to side "A." Repeat the procedure two more times; this will yield four machined surfaces, opposite sides parallel and adjacent sides square. Note: the work will only be as square as the vise. Place side one against the solid jaw, locate side two square to the vise base with a reference square, and tighten the vise (Figure 7). Machine

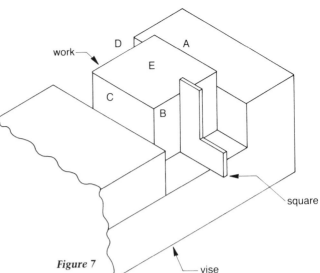

Figure 7

the end square to side one and two. Rotate the block 180° and finish the other end.

Remove all burrs and sharp edges on each surface as you proceed, because burrs will cause error. Now machine any holes, tapped holes, tee slots or vees to suit your clamping requirements. If hardening is required, now is the time. If possible, carburize or nitride maximum depth (approximately .060") and stabilize as previously discussed.

To obtain a master, start by surface grinding all sides of the cube; take a minimal cut to clean up only. This yields a condition of opposite sides parallel. By one of the previous methods, measure the squareness of side "A" with respect to side "B." Study Figure 8, which illustrates the method of correction.*

A 4" cube is being checked with a 6" square. An error of .002" is measured. The correction on the cube is calculated: $\frac{4}{6} \times .002" = .0013"$, the amount of correction required. A cut is made on side "B," removing .0013" of material, except a narrow land is left along the required edge. The cube is then placed on side "B," and side "D" is ground flat. Side "D" and "A" are now square. Side "D" is then used as the base, and "B" is ground parallel. This yields opposite sides parallel and adjacent sides square.

This procedure is repeated with the ends to get them square with sides "A" and "B." A master reference has now been created. Other angle plates or parts may be clamped onto the master and machined. They will, if you work carefully, be as accurate as the original.

*Fundamentals of Dimensional Metrology, Wilkie Brothers Foundation, Ted Busch, Delmar Publishers, Mountain View Avenue, Albany, NY 12205. Copyright 1964, p. 364.

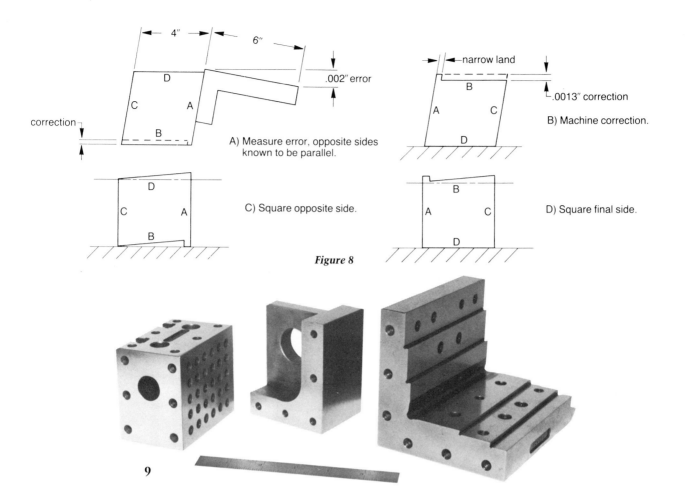

.002″ error

narrow land

.0013″ correction

correction

A) Measure error, opposite sides known to be parallel.

B) Machine correction.

C) Square opposite side.

D) Square final side.

Figure 8

9

When seeking the utmost in accuracy, be very conscious of dirt and burrs, and take shallow cuts less than .0005″, with lots of coolant flooding the work. The maximum error over a distance of a 6″ square for any of my plates or cube is .0003″, which is more than good enough.

Angle plates may then be machined by clamping them to the cube in a manner similar to the one used to clamp the square to an angle plate in Photo 2. Photo 9 shows two angle plates and a cube. A 6″ scale is in the foreground for size comparison.

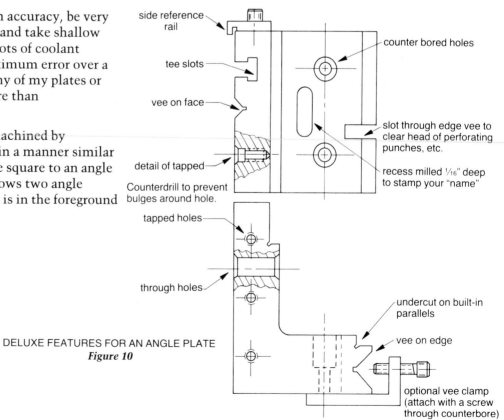

side reference rail

counter bored holes

tee slots

vee on face

slot through edge vee to clear head of perforating punches, etc.

detail of tapped

recess milled 1/16″ deep to stamp your "name"

Counterdrill to prevent bulges around hole.

tapped holes

through holes

undercut on built-in parallels

vee on edge

DELUXE FEATURES FOR AN ANGLE PLATE
Figure 10

optional vee clamp (attach with a screw through counterbore)

Solving a Weighty Problem

by Bill Davidson

Photos by Author

Nearly everyone owning a small lathe has, at one time, dreamed of having a larger one. When that dream comes true, it is accompanied by the reality of transporting and installing the larger lathe in the workshop. The first thoughts about transporting the lathe usually focus on asking two or three friends to help out. Depending on size, a good quality home shop lathe will weigh between 500-1500 lbs., with many older machines weighing even more. Since most workshops are in the basement, there are some very real problems to overcome. These problems are severe enough that several friends with strong backs are not the answer. But, with careful planning, it is surprising how easily the difficult task can be achieved. Without such planning, a careless approach may lead to an unexpected situation that can be an irreversible disaster to man and machine! The following are things to consider, along with a few helpful hints learned through actual experience.

1 *The lathe has been off-loaded from a low utility trailer and moved across a patio using pipe rollers and 4" × 4" timbers.*

TAKING POSSESSION

If you purchase a new lathe from a national distributor, in most cases a trucking company will deliver the lathe to your home. You must arrange to be there when the truck arrives. You must also have present sufficient manpower to off-load the lathe as the driver is usually alone. Techniques described later will be helpful for off-loading.

Mostly likely you will purchase a new lathe from a local distributor. True, many distributors will deliver to your home, and some may even install the equipment. However, there is usually a charge for these services, and it can be very expensive. A less expensive alternative is to pick up the lathe yourself at the place of purchase.

INSPECTION

A new piece of equipment will arrive in a crate. It is prudent to open the crate and give the lathe a quick visual inspection, looking for obvious damage. Take out the manual and specifications; verify that what you have received is what you ordered. Some of the imported lathes from Asia are advertised with large spindle bores, but in fact, are delivered undersized. Specifications may have been the sole reason you purchased a particular brand. If the lathe doesn't meet the basic specifications, it may be useless to you for certain operations. It is much easier to reject the lathe on the seller's dock than after you bring it home.

Don't, however, destroy the crate as you inspect. It provides good protection, and unless it is absolutely necessary, don't remove the crate until the last possible moment when protection is no longer needed.

On the bottom, most crates have strong beams running the length of the lathe. Check to see if the bolts holding the lathe to the crate protrude through the runner; if this is the case, it will be difficult to slide the crate. It may be necessary to build up the runners with extra material. If the runners on your crate are weak or broken, replace or reinforce them now. The runners are essential to the moving process.

If you are buying a used lathe from an individual, you should plan to mount it on a strong skid prior to attempting to transport it.

2 *Note track in front and rear of photo as skid comes through narrow doorway.*

The bed of some lathes cannot easily be separated from the base. In this case, when building a skid, be sure it is wide enough at the base to stabilize the topheavy lathe – *but will still fit through the door.* If the used lathe is in someone's basement, be sure to estimate the amount of work and risk involved in removing the lathe before finalizing the price.

LOADING

On a level concrete floor, it is easy to lift one end of the crate or skid with a long pry bar or lever dolly. Insert a piece of pipe as far under the skid as possible. Now, by placing a small block of wood under your bar, lift again, thereby allowing the pipe to move further toward the center. Be ready to insert additional pipe until the lathe is fully supported in a level manner. Usually, three pieces of pipe adequately support the lathe. It is now possible to move the lathe with ease. A change of direction can be achieved by nudging the side with a pry bar. Be careful not to slide off the ends of the pipe rollers. As you move the crate forward, lay pipe that is no longer needed by the rear of the crate out in front, in this manner keeping the lathe evenly supported on the rollers.

Most distributors have a loading dock. If the height of the dock matches your vehicle or trailer, you have no problem. If it doesn't, you must use movable timbers to make a gently sloping ramp, allowing you to roll the lathe in a controlled fashion. Be sure the ramp is secure as the timbers may have a tendency to slide. If the ramp is steep, use a winch or ropes to control the crate. It is wise to use the winch, etc., for loading and off-loading, even though it

may be slower than manhandling. Maintaining absolute control of the crate at all times is critical. In avoiding the unexpected, you can't be too careful.

You will also face the problem of no loading dock at home. Rigging a temporary ramp from the back of a truck to the ground can be done – but not easily. And, starting the crate onto the ramp from the back of a truck can be difficult.

A very practical solution to this entire dilemma is quite readily available. A low profile, wide-tire utility trailer fits the bill. These trailers are used for hauling snow-mobiles, golf carts, or lawn tractors. They usually have a tilting bed and are equipped with a hand-cranked winch. This makes for easy on- and off-loading of the lathe using the skid and roller technique.

TRANSPORTING

After the lathe is loaded, be sure it is securely tied down before transporting. Use the pry bar to remove the pipe rollers. The lathe must be adequately scotched to prevent movement in any direction. Stabilize all four corners with rope, or preferably, chain and toggle-type tensioners. Remember – if you have to make a quick stop, you want the lathe to stop, too!

The lathe must be properly positioned on the trailer for good balance of tongue vs. axle weight. Pick a route home that will allow you to drive safely at a reduced speed. One final suggestion is to contact your insurance agent to determine if you have insurance coverage for this activity. If not, check to see if it is possible to obtain a rider.

OFF-LOADING AND MOVING

After arriving safely at home, the fun begins. If you are very fortunate, you will be able to attach the trailer to a garden tractor and pull it around to your walk-in basement. Even in the absence of a tractor, a well-balanced trailer is easily handled by two people to move the lathe close to the entrance provided the ground is reasonably level. If you're not so lucky, use the reverse of the loading procedure and carefully roll the skid-mounted lathe on to a track constructed of 4" × 4" or other adequate timber. This track will allow you to go over grass, doorstoops, around corners, and across carpet with relative ease (Photos 1 and 2). Short pieces of timber work well as they are easy to handle and make it possible to turn tight corners. Once you are on concrete flooring, the track will not be necessary. Use the roller pipes directly on the floor. As you go from the track to the floor, use the pry bar to prevent a sudden drop.

DOWN THE STAIRS

If you must go down stairs, you are facing one of the more challenging situations. You should have already inspected the stairway, determined if it will adequately support the weight, and if not, made necessary modifications (Photo 3). Remember, it must support the weight of the lathe, skid, and two or three helpful neighbors all at the same time.

Check to be sure the skid is sufficiently strong to handle the weight at a single point when the lathe starts over the stairs and tilts from the level position to the angle of the staircase. You may consider using two winches, or comealongs, in order to keep the lathe under control at the vulnerable moment when it rotates. It is possible to use a single winch, but some long "handles" should be added to the rear of the crate, giving controlling leverage.

It is probably best to have the headstock end of the lathe go down the stairs first. However, space or turning requirements may rule out

5 *Skid-mounted lathe being winched down staircase. Note temporary track. Pipe rollers are not used during this portion of the operation.*

this approach. If the protective crate has been removed, watch carefully for protruding handle or levers. Also, if convenient, remove the tailstock and other detachable accessories in order to reduce weight (Photo 4).

Once on the stairs, the skid can be slowly winched down the temporary track which must be securely anchored to prevent sliding (Photo 5). At the bottom of the stairs, the lathe will rest at a rather steep angle. You can resume with the temporary track method. However, if space permits, the use of a rented engine hoist simplifies this step, and solves the very difficult problem of "How do you get the lathe on the stand?"

LIFTING

Such a hoist is available from most tool rental agencies at a modest charge. They can be disassembled without tools, carried piecemeal

3 *A steep staircase temporarily reinforced with timbers held by clamps. Originally, stairs were held in place only by four nails.*

4 *The lathe is being lowered with the headstock end down to maintain maximum control on the steep staircase. Removable parts have been stripped to reduce weight.*

6 *The engine hoist can be disassembled without tools. In its disassembled state, the hoist can be transported in a station wagon or large passenger car.*

into your basement, and reassembled (Photos 6 and 7). They are on rollers and have a hydraulic jack on the boom. These two features give you the flexibility needed for lifting, positioning, and setting the lathe on its stand in the proper location. Even owners of workshops with overhead I beams capable of lifting the lathe with a chain hoist may find merit in the engine hoist method because of the great portability.

Make sure the hoist has the necessary capacity and the hydraulic control valve is in good condition. Before lifting your lathe, it is a good idea to lift a heavy object with the hoist and set it down. This will give you some experience with the control valve which you will need when lifting and lowering the lathe.

8 *Showing forged lifting ring. Wooden blocks placed between the ways prevent movement.*

7 *Engine hoist reassembled in the basement. Casters under boom end pivot for easy maneuvering. Most hoists of this type are rated between 1000-1500 pounds capacity.*

Before lifting the lathe, carefully consider the type of lifting arrangement you intend to use. A single lifting point is generally less satisfactory than a multiple point setup achieved with a lifting harness. Be careful with a harness, however, to avoid damaging the lead screw or feed rod as you sling the lathe.

A single point consists of an eye bolt. Be sure it is strong enough and mounted between the ways in such a manner *that it will not move* in any direction (Photo 8 and Figure 9). Cover the ways near the lifting point with rags or other protective material to prevent an accidental nick.

Lathe manufacturers frequently supply a drawing showing the lifting point (Figure 10) and give some general instructions. *Warning –* most manufacturer's diagrams show the center of gravity along the bed. They do not take into account the motor. If it is mounted on the rear, as the lift begins, the lathe can abruptly tip in

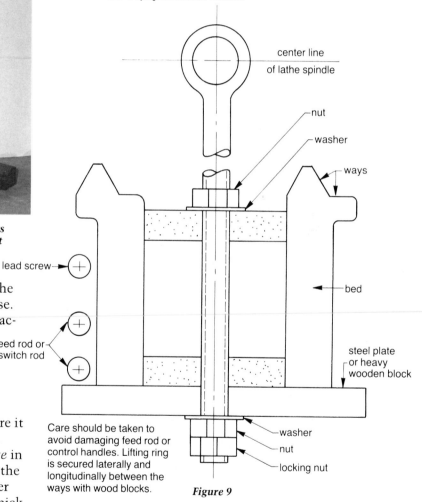

Figure 9

The lifting ring must not be able to move in any direction. Wooden blocks are used to make it fast. Also use wooden spacers longitudinally in the bed. Be sure the bottom beam clears the feed rod on the front of the bed.

the direction of the motor. Be sure to consider this when rigging the lifting ring. If you don't want to remove the motor, then use some type of harness to stabilize the off-center weight. It

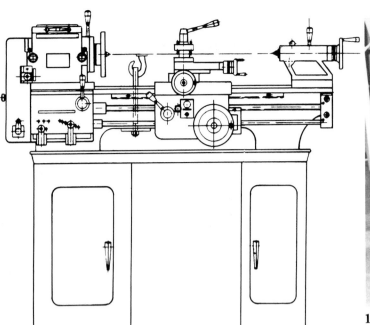

Figure 10
Lifting diagram supplied by lathe manufacturer.

12 *Shows lathe being lowered off stairs using a lever dolly. Note cable attached to rear of lathe controlling the rate of descent.*

is, however, possible to reduce this effect by having your lifting ring at, or above, the center line of the lathe. Balancing the lathe is achieved by moving the carriage toward the tailstock until the weight is equally distributed (Photo 11). Lock the carriage in place. Check to see that the tailstock is securely fastened in place, also.

11 *The lathe is being lifted from crate. The lathe is balanced by moving the carriage toward the tailstock. Once the lathe is balanced, lock all moving parts. Participants should wear safety shoes with steel toes.*

As you *slowly* begin lifting the lathe off the stairs, the lathe will shift until it is suspended directly under the end of the boom. As it seeks this position, it may cause the hoist to move. Be ready! An alternate method is to use a lever

dolly to lift the leading end of the lathe while slowly playing out the winch (Photo 12).

Move the lathe off the stairs to a level area, and set it down for removal of the remaining crate and loosening from the skid.

SETTING UP

You are now ready to lift and move the lathe to the stand. Measure the holes in the stand and lathe bed. Be sure they correspond. Position the stand where you want it, leaving ample clearance from walls and obstacles for leveling, maintenance, etc. Level the stand as much as possible at this point.

Lift and position the lathe over the stand (Photo 13). Don't forget the chip pan! This is usually a separate item which gets set aside and is easily forgotten. Place drill rod stock through the holes in the lathe bed and stand to serve as a guide when lowering the lathe onto the stand. Because of clearance problems, this may not be possible, and you may have to use the mounting bolts to perform this function (Photo 14). Be careful, however, as it is easy to damage the threads as the holes are being aligned. Watch your hands – fingers damage more easily than threads. Very carefully lower the lathe onto the stand. This is where practice with the control valve pays off.

A friend recently installed a 12″ × 36″ lathe in his garage. Setting the lathe on the stand was accomplished by using the boom of a wrecker. In attempting to use this method, be sure there is adequate overhead clearance and that the hoist controls on the wrecker's winch are sufficiently sensitive for the task.

13 *Shows lathe being lifted over the stand with the engine hoist. Note lack of overhead clearance.*

14 *Lathe being lowered into position. Mounting bolts are serving as guides to line up holes.*

Make sure the stand is adequate, stable, and the lathe is bolted down before removing the hoist. Bench lathes with rear mounted motors, even when mounted on the manufacturer's stand, can be severely topheavy. You may have to consider some type of stabilizing mount to a nearby wall or post (Photo 15). Now's the time to address these points while the lathe is highly mobile and easily repositioned.

Leveling is so important that it will not be addressed in detail in this article; however, keep in mind a typical workshop level does not have the accuracy required to level a lathe. Obtain access to a machinist level with a sensitivity of at least 0.001" per foot.

Purchasing a large home shop lathe represents a major investment. Transporting and installing it yourself means you are solely responsible for the consequences. A serious injury or dropped equipment can turn a lifelong dream into a nightmare. When you have safely and successfully installed your lathe, you can be proud of the fact that you have solved a "weighty problem."

LIST OF MATERIALS

4 – pieces of pipe > 2" diameter – long enough to span the crate or skid. (If you must turn sharp corners, several pieces of longer pipe will be useful.)

4 – heavy timbers (4 × 4) 4 feet to 8 feet in length.

1 – pry bar, or lever dolly (rental – $5 per day).

1 – forged eye bolt.

15 *A lathe stand with a stabilizing mount to a stone wall. Note how mounting bracket is constructed to avoid putting stress on the lathe stand, which would affect accuracy.*

1 – comealong or chain hoist. (A second device may be desirable if a steep stairway needs to be negotiated.)

1 – portable engine hoist (available at local tool rentals – $15-$17 per day).

And sufficient chain or strong rope to secure and control the lathe during transport, off-loading and positioning.

Most of these items, including the lift, are standard items for a maintenance shop in a manufacturing facility. If you are employed by such a company, they frequently have a signout procedure that will allow you to use these items over a weekend.

OPTIONAL

1 – tilt bed trailer.

1 – lifting harness.

Getting the Most from Your Center Gage and Other Threading Gages

by Edward G. Hoffman

Threading is one of the most basic tasks a machinist performs. Whether the threading operation is performed with taps and dies or on a screw cutting lathe, there are several tools the machinist can use to make threading easier and more accurate. The three most common thread and thread cutting gages the machinist uses are the center gage, Acme thread gage, and the screw pitch gage. To insure the desired results in any threading operation you should become familiar with these threading gages and how they are designed to be used.

CENTER GAGE

The center gage is, unfortunately, one of the more neglected tools in a machinist's tool box.

Most hobby machinists have a general idea of some of the uses and applications of this gage, but, unfortunately, most do not fully understand just how versatile and useful this small tool can really be.

While normally thought of only for lathe threading work, the center gage can be used as an inspection tool to check just about any 60° form – both internal and external, flat or conical. But, in most shops, the center gage is usually used strictly for lathe threading operations. Here, this tool is employed as both a gage to inspect the shape and geometry of the 60° threading tool and as a setup tool to properly set and align the threading tool in a lathe. Figure 1 shows several typical applications of the center gage and how it is generally used as a grinding gage and setup tool for both external and internal threading operations.

To achieve the best results and maximum benefit from your center gage, you should thoroughly understand each of its features and how they are intended to make any threading job easier. For the most part, most home machinists know how to use the gaging surfaces of this tool, but for those unfamiliar with these applications, each will be described briefly. The large external V shape, or point, is used to check any 60° internal form, such as a

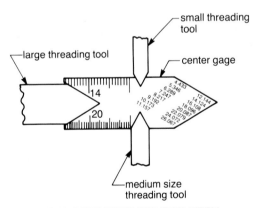

CHECKING THE FORM AND GEOMETRY
OF THREADING TOOLS

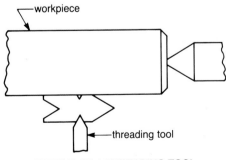

SETTING UP A THREADING TOOL
FOR EXTERNAL THREADING OPERATIONS

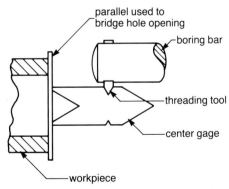

SETTING UP A THREADING TOOL
FOR INTERNAL THREADING OPERATIONS

Figure 1

60° internal center, cup center or 60° crotch centers. The large internal V is typically used for checking external lathe centers or as a grinding and inspection gage for grinding very large threading tools. The two V notches on the sides are also used as a grinding and inspection tool for smaller 60° threading tools.

The chart shown on the center gage represents the depth of the thread, expressed as a double depth. Some center gages have the values listed for "Sharp V" threads, while others have the double depths of the American National thread form. These values represent the depth of the thread on both sides of the shaft, or bolt. So, to find the actual depth of the thread measured from the crest to the root, on one side, this value should be halved. There are a few reasons for expressing this value as a double depth. One reason is that the root diameter of the thread is easier to calculate. Since the root diameter is equal to the major diameter minus twice the depth, by simply subtracting the double depth from the major diameter the root diameter is easier to calculate. Measuring the root diameter is one way to determine where the threads are cut to the correct depth. In fact, several years ago, before the advent of "precision" manufacturing, many times the root diameter of a thread was preset with a set of outside calipers and the thread was cut until the root diameter matched the caliper setting. Today, however, we have much more accurate methods of inspecting thread sizes. Another reason for expressing the depth as a double depth is the graduations on a lathe. Most lathe cross slides are graduated in units of diameter reduction rather than radius reduction. That is, for each .001″ graduation the cross slide is advanced, the tool only moves .0005″. This results in a removal of .001″ from the diameter of the part. Expressing the thread depth as a double depth is simply another way of expressing the depth of the thread. In this case, the depth is based on the diameter of the part rather than the radius.

To fully understand the reason why some center gages have the double depth values for "Sharp V" threads and why others have the values for the American National thread forms, you'll have to understand the differences in these two, as well as the other, 60° thread forms. Today there are several different types and forms of 60° threads in common use. A few of these variations are the Unified thread, ISO Metric thread, American National thread, National Pipe thread, and the Sharp "V" thread. While the Unified thread and ISO

Metric thread forms are the most commonly used today, the other forms are still found in some applications. The primary difference in these thread forms is in their depth and the size and style of the root and crest, Figure 2. Since most commercial threads are cut with dies, these thread forms and their different root and crest shapes are relatively easy for commercial manufacturers to produce by simply matching the shape of the threading dies to the required thread form. This is not quite as simple when cutting threads on a lathe.

When threading on a lathe, the thread form most generally produced is the "Sharp V" thread. This is due to the shape and configuration of the threading tool. The "Sharp V" thread form, while having the same outside diameter and number of threads per inch as the Unified thread, or the same pitch as an ISO Metric thread, does not conform to the recognized standard form, or shape, of these thread forms. Consequently, the other thread dimensions, such as the depth, of these threads are also different. For example, the depth of a "Sharp V" thread having 10 threads per inch is .0866″, while the depth of a Unified thread of the same number of threads per inch is .0613″. This difference is caused by the basic shape of the thread. A "Sharp V" thread has a sharp V-shaped root and crest while the Unified thread has either a flat or rounded root and crest. This difference can, again, be seen in Figure 2.

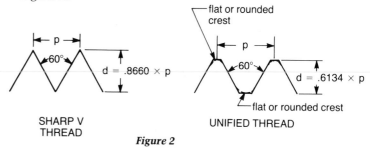

SHARP V THREAD

UNIFIED THREAD

Figure 2

While the "Sharp V" thread does not conform to the exact thread form specifications for the Unified, ISO Metric, American National, or pipe thread, this type of thread will work in every application where the other thread forms are used. Even though the thread form is slightly different, the "Sharp V" thread form can be machined to the same pitch as any of the other threads. The pitch of a thread is the distance between the same points on adjacent threads. The number of threads per inch is the number of individual threads in one inch. Do not get these terms confused. The difference between these terms is shown in Figure 3. To find the pitch when the number of threads is known, simply divide the number of threads per inch into 1. Likewise, to find the number of threads per inch when the pitch is known, divide 1 by the pitch value.

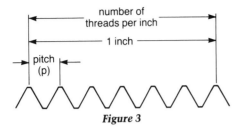

Figure 3

Another useful feature of the center gage is the graduated scales found along each edge. These scales are used to check the pitch of the thread. When cutting threads on a lathe, the first pass is usually a marking pass where the tool just skims the surface. The pitch of the thread is then checked to make sure the lathe is properly set up and the correct thread pitch is being machined. By using the graduated scales on the center gage, the pitch of many of the more common thread sizes can be easily checked. The four scales most commonly found on a center gage are 14, 20, 24, and 32 threads per inch. By comparing the marked workpiece against these graduations, it is very easy to determine if the correct number of threads per inch are being cut. The 14 graduations per inch scale can be used to check both 14, 7, and 3½ threads per inch. The 20 graduations scale can be used for 20, 10, 5, and 4 threads per inch. The 24 graduations scale on the other side of the center gage can check 24, 12, 8, 6, and 4 threads per inch. And the 32 graduations scale can inspect 32, 16, 8, and 4 threads per inch.

When using the center gage to check and set up a threading tool, the threading tool is first ground to the required 60° angle and checked with one of the V-shaped notches. Once the threading tool has the proper 60° form, the tool should be deburred with an oilstone. Once the tool is properly ground and honed to remove the burrs, it is mounted in the lathe and the tool is aligned with the workpiece using the center gage. The compound rest for this threading operation should be set at approximately 29½° for roughing and 30° for finishing. The threads are cut by taking successively deeper cuts with the compound while maintaining the same cross slide position. The threads should be machined to a depth equal to half the double depth shown on the center gage, if measured from crest to root, or to depth equal to the double depth if measured

from the amount of diameter reduction. This depth may be checked with a thread micrometer, an outside micrometer and three wires, or cut to suit the mating part.

ACME THREAD GAGE

The Acme thread gage, like the center gage, is a tool that is primarily used as a grinding and setup gage for threading operations. The Acme thread gage, as its name implies, is used for Acme threads, rather than Unified or ISO Metric threads. The Acme thread, shown in Figure 4, has a 29° thread angle and a flat root and crest.

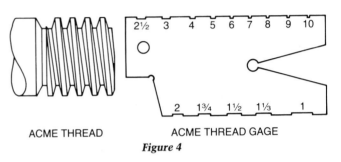

ACME THREAD   ACME THREAD GAGE

Figure 4

Typically, this gage is used in much the same way as a center gage. The large V-shaped notch in the end of the tool is used as a gage to check the form and geometry of the 29° Acme threading tool. The 14½° shoulder at the other end is used as a setup gage for aligning the threading tool with the workpiece for cutting Acme threads, Figure 5. The notches along each edge of the tool are used as a gage for grinding the end of the threading tool to the proper width to suit the pitch of the thread being cut.

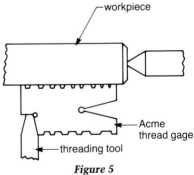

Figure 5

In use, the threading tool is first ground to a 29° angle and checked with the large V notch. Once the threading tool has the proper 29° form, the end of the tool is compared against the notch on the side of the gage which corresponds to the number of threads to be cut. The end of the threading tool is then ground flat to fit the notch. Once the tool is properly ground, it is mounted in the lathe and the notched shoulder is used to align the tool with the workpiece to be threaded. The compound rest for this threading operation should be set at 14½° and the threads are cut in the same manner as that used for 60° threads. An alternate method of cutting Acme threads is to set the compound perpendicular to the workpiece and feed the tool directly into the workpiece at a 90° angle rather than the 14½° angle previously mentioned. The thread should be machined to a depth equal to half the pitch plus .010″. This depth may be checked with a micrometer, vernier, or cut to suit the mating part.

SCREW PITCH GAGE

The screw pitch gage, Figure 6, is mainly used to check the number of threads per inch on a Unified thread, or the pitch of an ISO Metric thread. Depending on the type gage used, either the number of threads per inch or the pitch of the thread will be marked on each individual leaf of the gage. In addition to its primary purpose, the screw pitch gage may also be used for a less obvious application. In this application, the screw pitch gage can be used to aid in grinding a threading tool to the

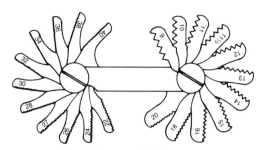

SCREW PITCH GAGE

Figure 6

exact form required for a specific thread. By selecting the proper gage leaf for the desired number of threads and grinding the threading tool to exactly fit one of the "V" notches in the gage, the thread produced can very closely approximate any of the standard 60° thread forms. Before trying this, however, make sure you have a screw pitch gage which matches the thread form you wish to cut. Screw pitch gages are commercially available for the Unified, ISO Metric, and American National thread forms as well as some of the less frequently used types of threads.

A Cutting Tool For Machining Aluminum

by James R. Lewis

Photos by Author

Any illustrations I have seen of aluminum being machined on a lathe or a shaper show a cutting tool designed for cutting steel or cast iron being used. Although a cutting tool with this configuration will work, it tends to leave the machined surface rather rough. Aluminum, whether wrought or cast, is a soft, gummy material that is prone to chip welding; that is, bonding itself to the cutting tool, thus creating a built-up mass that forms a new, but not too reliable, cutting edge.

With a cutting tool formed for aluminum as illustrated in Figure 1 and Photos 2, 3 and 4, chip welding may not be completely eliminated, but it occurs less readily because the blocky, flat ledge of the standard cutting tool is eliminated. Moreover, if kerosene-based cutting fluids or soluble cutting oils are in constant use, chip welding is almost non-existent, and glass-smooth surfaces are easy to produce. The shape of the tool can be as rounded or as pointed as the work requires so long as the steep back rake angle is maintained.

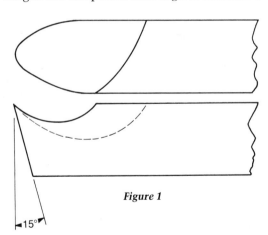

◄15°

Figure 1

This tool configuration is satisfactory only for aluminum and aluminum alloys. On extruded (wrought) aluminum of the 2011-T3 or 2024-T4 designations, a glass-smooth, shiny surface can be produced just by decreasing the rate of tool feed into the work. This smoothness can be maintained even while removing

more than 100 thousandths from the diameter (Photo 5). Satisfactory results are even easy to achieve with the 6061-T6 alloy, which is high in silicon and therefore much more abrasive to the edge of the cutting tool.

2

3

4

5

LATHE ACCESSORIES

Temporary Self-locking Stub Mandrel

by Philip Duclos

Photos by Author

1

Occasionally, the only way a piece of work can be machined properly is to mount it on a lathe mandrel. Who in the world owns a complete set of lathe mandrels? I pride myself on having a very well-equipped home workshop and, thanks to this simple little trick, I've never had to buy a single lathe mandrel.

This temporary (discard after use) stub mandrel derives its grip on the workpiece by the wedging action of a pin between a flat on the mandrel and the inner surface of the hole in the workpiece. The stronger the force of the cutting action of the lathe, the tighter the grip becomes. However, if your mandrel is small in diameter in relation to the outside diameter of the workpiece, a heavy machining cut on the work could actually create enough force to flatten the little locking pin and allow it to slip. In

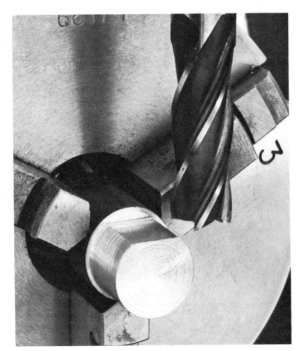

cases like this, take light cuts when machining – or use a hardened pin made from drill rod.

To make a stub mandrel, select a piece of round steel rod slightly larger in diameter than the bore of the piece to be worked. Clamp it in the lathe chuck and machine it to a length about equal to the thickness or length of the workpiece (Photo 1). In this case we are making a stub mandrel to fit a roughed-out gear blank.

Carefully machine the diameter of the stub so that the workpiece will *slide* onto it snugly without binding. The next operation is to mill – or file by hand – a flat section on the stub (Photo 2). The depth of this flat is controlled by the diameter of the little locking pin. You should maintain, roughly, a ratio of about 12 to 1 between the diameter of the stub and the diameter of the pin.

The pin can be made from a *straight* piece of wire or a portion of a nail, brad, pin or needle, depending on the size you'll need for your particular mandrel. In other words, if the diameter of your stub mandrel is .500″, you'll need a pin that's about .040″ in diameter. Select the proper size material for your pin and make the length of it about equal to the length of the flat section on the mandrel.

If you file the flat section by hand, try to make the surface as *parallel* to the axis of the mandrel as possible. As you file the flat section, occasionally lay the pin on the flat and mike the diameter over the shaft and pin (Photo 3). The flat section is deep enough when the reading is about .002″ smaller than the bore of the workpiece. Now slip the workpiece onto the stub mandrel and check to make sure the

2

pin will slide freely into the slot (Photo 4). If it won't, it means your pin is bent or burred on the ends.

When everything fits properly, and you have the workpiece mounted on the stub and the locking pin in place, simply rotate the lathe spindle by hand until the flat section on the stub is roughly in a vertical position *away* from you (towards the back of the lathe). Now hold the lathe spindle to keep it from turning and twist the workpiece clockwise by hand. You'll feel it lock almost immediately. You're now ready to machine the work. When it's time to remove the workpiece, simply twist it by hand in a counterclockwise direction until you feel the locking pin loosen; then slide the workpiece *straight* off.

4

With this setup you can machine both the outer end of the work and the diameter. If it's necessary to machine the back side of the work, simply remove it and reverse it on the mandrel. By letting the workpiece hang out about $\frac{1}{16}''$ beyond the shaft, it's easy to machine a chamfer on the sharp edge of the exposed bore hole. If your work calls for a long stub mandrel, it's usually not necessary to mill a flat section the whole length of the shaft (Photo 5). Also, you can center drill the end of the mandrel and support it with the tailstock for more rigidity.

5

A Toolpost Grinder

by John Dean

Photos by Author

If you have many toolposts to grind, you'll need a toolpost grinder. You can build one easily of scrap. If you use high quality scrap, and work carefully, you can expect 75 years of service from it, and that's a long grind. The one in the photos has 50 years of experience. The motor, pulleys and belts have been updated twice, but the arbor shows no detectable wear.

The shafts and plate steel were from outdated farm machinery, the bearings taken from the generator of a 1925 model Chandler car, and the quills made of crankcase bolts from a WW-I, 12-cylinder airplane engine. If there are no Liberty engines in your scrap pile, you can turn quills from ¾" shafts. Include a few blank extras for unforeseen future needs.

1

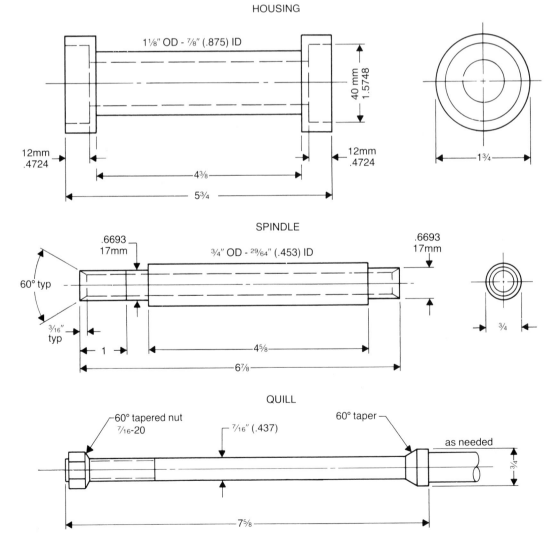

HOUSING

1⅛" OD - ⅞" (.875) ID

40 mm 1.5748

12mm .4724

12mm .4724

4⅜

5¾

1¾

SPINDLE

.6693 17mm

.6693 17mm

¾" OD - ²⁹⁄₆₄" (.453) ID

60° typ

³⁄₁₆" typ

1

4⅝

6⅞

¾

QUILL

60° tapered nut ⁷⁄₁₆-20

⁷⁄₁₆" (.437)

60° taper

as needed

¾

7⅝

What! No Chandler generator either? Your bearing dispenser can help you. You are likely to come home with a pair of sheilded MRC bearings, No. 203-SZZ, so the drawings give the dimensions for them.

The most useful feature is that the quills may be inserted from either end of the spindle, greatly increasing the scope of possible setups. A reversible motor has often been appreciated. Variable speed motors, used with, or without, suitably sized stepcone pulleys, makes possible the use of tools other than grinding wheels. Photo 1 offers some suggestions. Effective use of small milling cutters, slitting saws, files or rag wheels may require reduced speeds.

Suitable motors of less than 1/6 hp often have speed lower than 1725, making computation of pulley ratios necessary. Maximum speeds are not critical; motors with 3450 rpm may be used. The 3" Norton wheel in Photo 2 is rated at 8280 maximum rpm. Hand grinder tools are designed for 30,000 rpm.

2

If you enjoy worrying about safety, design some guards.

Tailstock Die Holder

by Harold Timm

My old friend and I made a tailstock die holder some time ago. The holder was made from 1½" round stock. After chucking one end in a three-jaw chuck, the other end was center drilled. A center was used at the outer end to assist in a steady work piece. The various diameters were turned. After cutting off, the part was reversed in the chuck and the several holes bored and turned.

The milled slot is necessary to aid in removing some tight dies. A 10-32 bolt tapped into the holder completes the unit.

I have since made two others to allow different sized dies. The holders were made roughly proportional to the different die sizes. These holders have been very useful, allowing an old duffer like me to thread dowels and pipes at right angles to the material. I have used this one for sizes from 0-80 to ⅛" NPT.

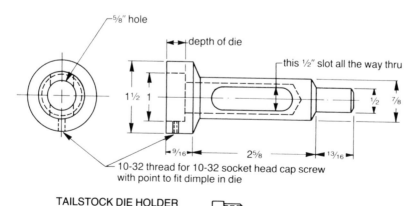

TAILSTOCK DIE HOLDER
FOR 1" BUTTON DIE

Lathe Chip Shield

by Jim Berger

Photos and Drawings by Author

I learned early in my home shop experiences that hot chips on the face, neck, or arms was an unpleasant experience, since most turning in the home shop is done "dry." Full face shields are stuffy and inconvenient (I can't smoke my trusty pipe), so I had incentive to build a chip shield. Somewhere along the way I've seen commercially made lathe shields mounted on a rod, but I wanted to be able to move the shield quickly out of the way after making a cut. The design I hit upon has a horizontal hinge pin, so I can "flip the lid" back against the rest when inspecting the work or if I don't need the shield for slow work, such as threading.

The 12" Craftsman or Atlas lathe conveniently has two 3/8-16 tapped holes at the rear of the carriage, which I used for mounting the shield. Mounting it on the carriage has an advantage of always being over the cutting area, regardless of the end of the lathe bed on which you happen to be making a cut.

Before drilling these two mounting holes in the rear mounting bar, you should check to make sure you have adequate clearance between the left vertical member and the head stock, chuck, and belt release lever when working next to the chuck with the carriage.

The main parts are aluminum bar and angle for ease of fabrication; also, aluminum lends itself nicely to damaskeining (engine spot polishing) for a nice finishing touch. This is done by chucking a typewriter eraser (or similar type abrasive eraser) in a drill press and lightly bringing the spinning eraser down on the surface of the aluminum part. Move the part slightly so the spots overlap approximately by a quarter circle. If done with enough pressure, the spots will be permanent.

Although I used 1/8" thick Plexiglas for my shield, you might consider the more popular .100" thick glazing storm door Plexiglas, available at most hardware stores.

Leave the covering paper on the Plexiglas and use a fine-tooth blade of 14 or more teeth per inch in your jigsaw or bandsaw to cut out the shield, using slow speed (if you have multiple-

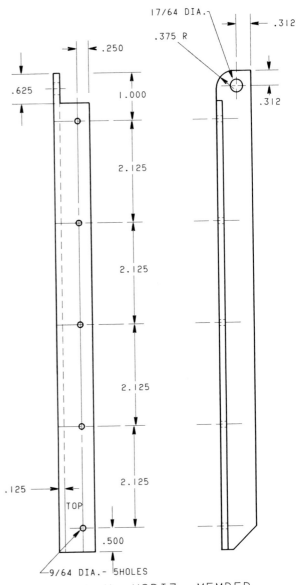

L.H. HORIZ. MEMBER
3/4 X 3/4 X 1/8 ALUM. ANGLE

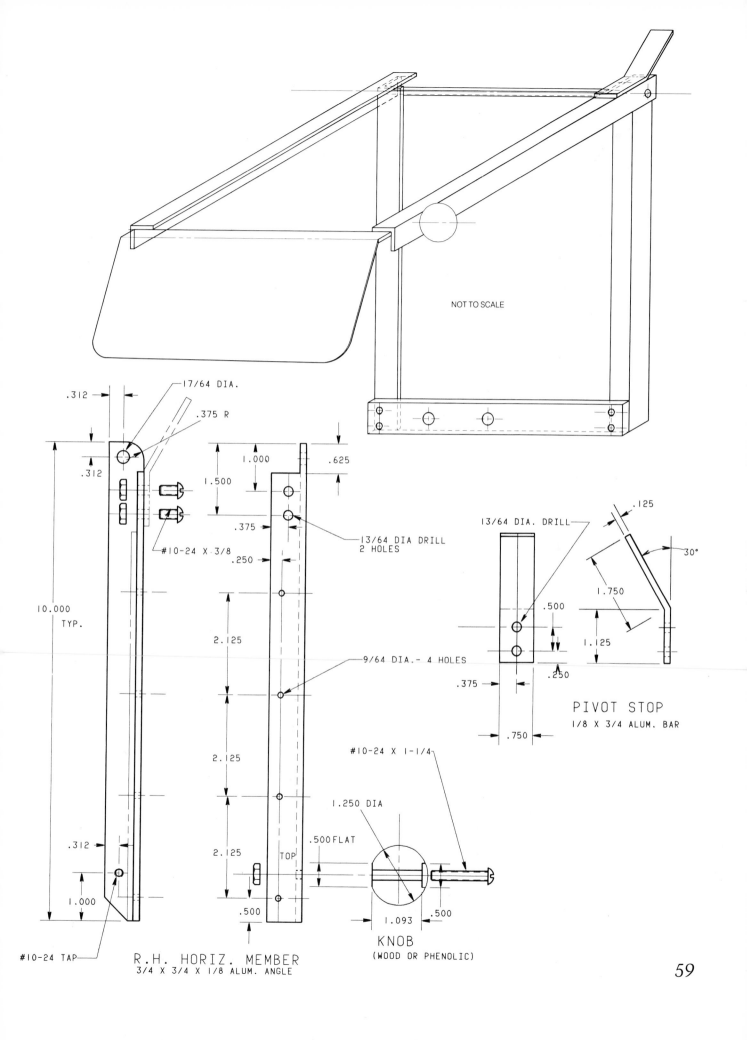

NOT TO SCALE

17/64 DIA.

.375 R

.312

.312

13/64 DIA. DRILL

.125

1.000

.625

1.500

.375

13/64 DIA DRILL
2 HOLES

.250

30°

1.750

.500

.250

#10-24 X 3/8

10.000
TYP.

1.125

2.125

9/64 DIA.- 4 HOLES

.375

PIVOT STOP
1/8 X 3/4 ALUM. BAR

.750

2.125

#10-24 X 1-1/4

.312

2.125

TOP

1.250 DIA

.500 FLAT

1.000

.500

.500

1.093

.500

#10-24 TAP

R.H. HORIZ. MEMBER
3/4 X 3/4 X 1/8 ALUM. ANGLE

KNOB
(WOOD OR PHENOLIC)

59

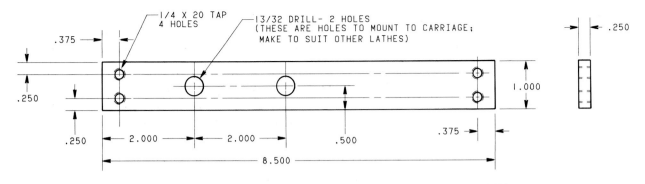

1/4 X 20 TAP
4 HOLES

13/32 DRILL- 2 HOLES
(THESE ARE HOLES TO MOUNT TO CARRIAGE;
MAKE TO SUIT OTHER LATHES)

.375

.250

.250

1.000

2.000

2.000

.500

.375

.250

8.500

MOUNTING BAR (SHIELD TO CARRIAGE)
1/4 X 1 ALUMINUM. BAR

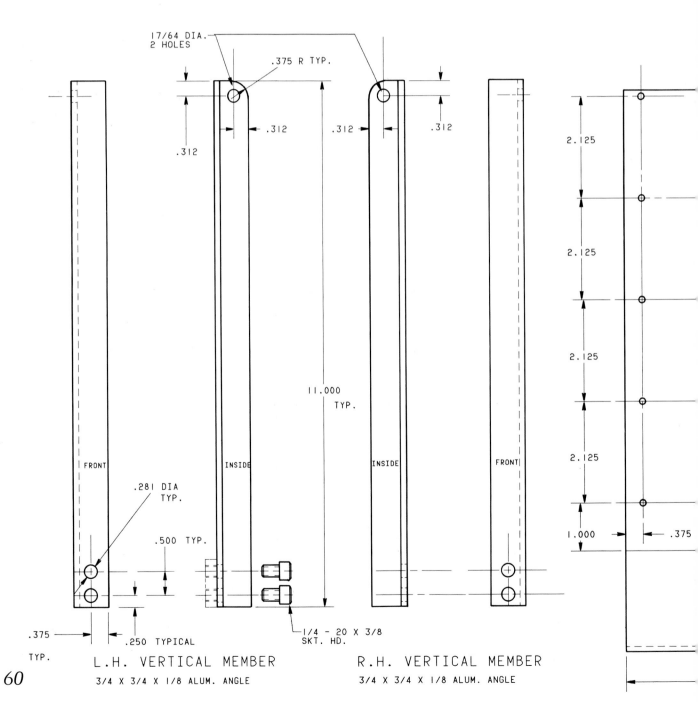

17/64 DIA.
2 HOLES

.375 R TYP.

.312

.312

.312

.312

.312

11.000
TYP.

FRONT

INSIDE

INSIDE

FRONT

.281 DIA
TYP.

.500 TYP.

1/4 - 20 X 3/8
SKT. HD.

.375

.250 TYPICAL

TYP.

2.125

2.125

2.125

2.125

2.125

1.000

.375

L.H. VERTICAL MEMBER
3/4 X 3/4 X 1/8 ALUM. ANGLE

R.H. VERTICAL MEMBER
3/4 X 3/4 X 1/8 ALUM. ANGLE

60

groove sheaves on your equipment), and a light feed to avoid melting the material along the cut and clogging the blade teeth.

Drill and assemble the aluminum frame parts first, and mount the assembly on the lathe carriage. Using two small C-clamps and backup pads of soft wood or similar material, clamp the unbent Plexiglas in place under the horizontal members. The mounting holes are then marked using the two horizontal members as templates. Before removing the Plexiglas, mark a line with a felt tip pen at the proper bend line, and check your line-of-sight down on a part chucked in the lathe. It may be necessary, due to the operator's height or the lathe bench height, to move the bend line forward or back so you won't be looking through the slight distortion of the bend line.

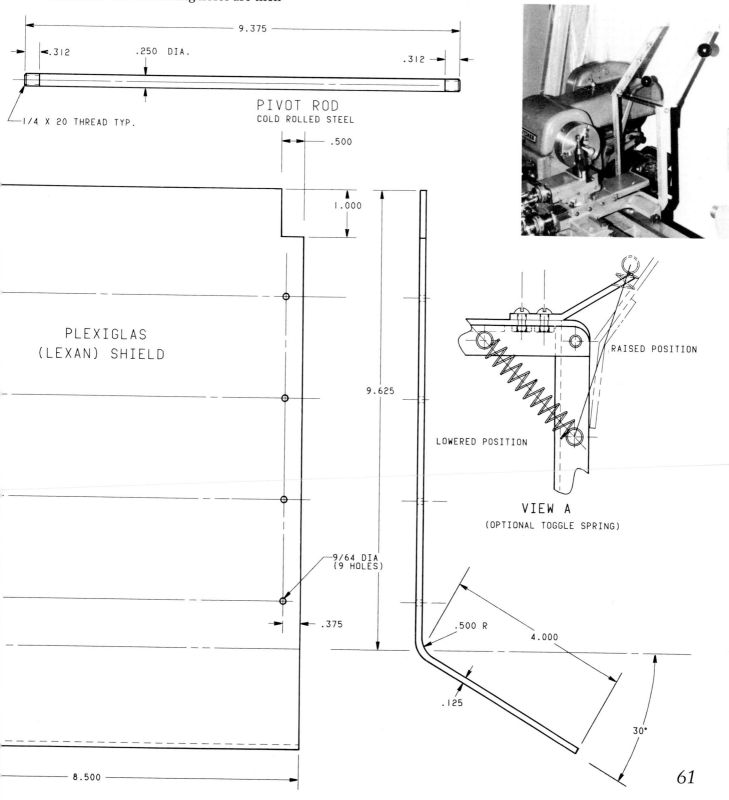

PIVOT ROD
COLD ROLLED STEEL

1/4 X 20 THREAD TYP.

PLEXIGLAS
(LEXAN) SHIELD

9/64 DIA
(9 HOLES)

RAISED POSITION

LOWERED POSITION

VIEW A
(OPTIONAL TOGGLE SPRING)

61

Drill the screw mounting holes in the Plexiglas using a soft, clean board beneath to avoid scratching the Plexiglas. The standard lip included angle of 118° will work okay if light pressure is used, although I'm sure there must be a better recommended angle by the plastic suppliers. Unfortunately, I wasn't able to find anything in my sources.

To bend the shield, I clamped it approximately ¼" behind the correct bend line between two smoothed boards using C-clamps and overhanging the work bench edge. Using a propane torch with a very soft flame, I played the flame back and forth across both the top and bottom surfaces at the bend line, never letting the flame touch the Plexiglas, or else bubbles might appear in the surface.

Patience is the word here – when the Plexiglas is ready, the edge will begin to droop slightly. The bend angle isn't critical, but you can make a cardboard angle template to occasionally check the progress of the bend.

Since this is all freehand, you might try bending some scrap pieces just to get the feel of the proper amount of heat and bending pressure required.

In the "down" position, the horizontal members rest on the top of the vertical members, so accurate location of the top edges of the vertical members with respect to the .265" diameter pivot holes is fairly critical, to assure the horizontal members and shield rest in a horizontal plane for best appearance.

When flipped back, the shield rests with the pivot stop against the back of the right hand vertical member. The 30° bend allows it to just clear my micrometer tool case, which is mounted behind the lathe – check for any obstructions you might have along the carriage's travel.

Vibration hasn't caused any problems of the shield shaking, but there is a fairly simple solution that should hold it firmly in place. An extension spring can be added to the right hand members to toggle over the pivot center (see View A).

Windex does a good job of cleaning the shield, but I've learned to cover all my shop machines with thin, clear plastic sheets to keep dust off. An advantage of plastic sheets over cloth is they don't draw dampness, an important factor when considering the cost of these expensive machine tools.

A Large Steady Rest from the Scrap Pile

by J. O. Barbour, Jr.

Photos by Author

On a recent trip to my No. 1 salvage source, I noticed three very interesting items in the stainless steel scrap.

There were two rings 10¼" OD × 8¾" ID made from ½" stainless plate, and a rather odd-shaped piece of ¾" ss plate.

"There," said an inner voice, "lies a perfect unmade oversized steady rest, just right for your lathe."

After a bit of successful negotiation, an exchange of opinions on the weather, and a short drive back to the workshop, the fun began.

The odd-sized scrap of ¾" plate was milled to 2" wide × 8" long, step-milled to fit inside the lathe bed, and a ¹⁷⁄₃₂" hole drilled in its center.

A small flat was milled on each ring to properly center the rings with the center in the tailstock.

My own scrap pile supplied three pieces of ⅞" ss hexagon stock, which were cut to 1½" length, faced on each end, and bored and threaded to ⅝" NC.

Now, the only new items that had to be purchased were next in line.

A 24" piece of ⅝" bronze continuous thread rod was cut into three 8" pieces, which were machined as follows:

One end was faced and machined with a short taper. The other end was also faced and chamfered to facilitate silver brazing.

A full-sized brass nut was run down flush with the chamfered end of each rod and silver brazed. The three half nuts were run on to serve as lock nuts.

The three rods were screwed through the 1½" long ss nuts and, after a little balancing act with three C-clamps, a level and a square, the nuts were lined up with the witness marks (previously stamped on the rings) and the end of the screws correctly centered with the tailstock center.

All components were tack welded with #316 ss rod, again checked for accuracy, and final welding completed.

The clamp plate was made from a piece of 1" × 2" × 6¾" flat H.R. stock, step-milled to fit the lathe bed, and drilled to match the steady rest base plate.

The final item, a ⅝" × 3" bolt, was machined from ⅞" ss hex stock, with the head sized to lock between the rings, and the steady rest was ready to receive any diameter up to 8".

It has proven to be a very rigid and serviceable accessory, and it would be well worth the effort, even if you had to torch cut the rings from steel plate and machine them.

1 *Top view.*

2 *Left side view showing table.*

A Milling Machine for Your Lathe

by John Snyder

Photos by Author

Ialways wanted and needed a milling machine, but the cost was too much, so I decided to design and build my own to attach to my old 12″ treadle lathe (Pat. Sept. 21, 1880 and Feb. 15, 1887), which has since been motorized. I could then use the compound, cross slide, and power-driven carriage for the table.

Photo 1 looks down on the milling machine, showing the arrangement of motor, belts and pulleys.

Photo 2 is a left side view, showing the plate mounted on the compound used as a table.

Photo 3 is a front view, showing the angle vise mounted on the cross slide. I used this mill to partly make the vise.

Photo 4 is a right side view, showing the arrangement of the adjusting screw, bevel gears, graduated dial, and locking device handle.

Photo 5 partly shows the arrangement for attaching the mill to the lathe.

Photo 6 shows the mill head in raised position; it will be out of the way when running the lathe.

I got all of my steel from junk yards, the two 45° bevel gears from an old ringer washing machine, and the ½-hp reconditioned motor for $20.00. My total cost for everything was about $125.00.

The weight of the column is over 60 lbs. The total weight of the mill head is 90 lbs. I counterbalanced this by fastening a ⅛ wire cable, showing in the photos, up through the shop attic, over a pulley, and hanging on 94 lbs. of steel. The heavier weight adds a little drag to the head when feeding down to counteract the weight and backlash.

The Column (Detail 45) must be round, straight, have a thick wall, and have a fairly good finish. Before welding angle iron pieces to tubing of Det. 15 (Head Guide), make left-, right-hand, and front Panels (Dets. 10, 11 and 12) and, together with the Quill (Det. 55),

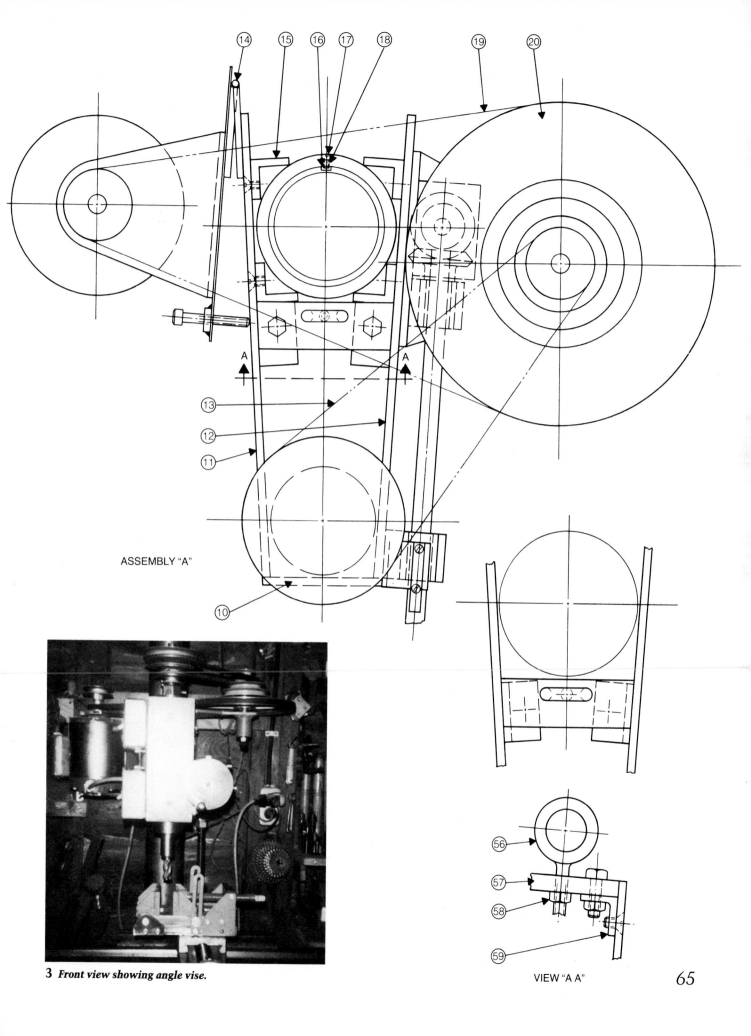

ASSEMBLY "A"

3 *Front view showing angle vise.*

VIEW "A A"

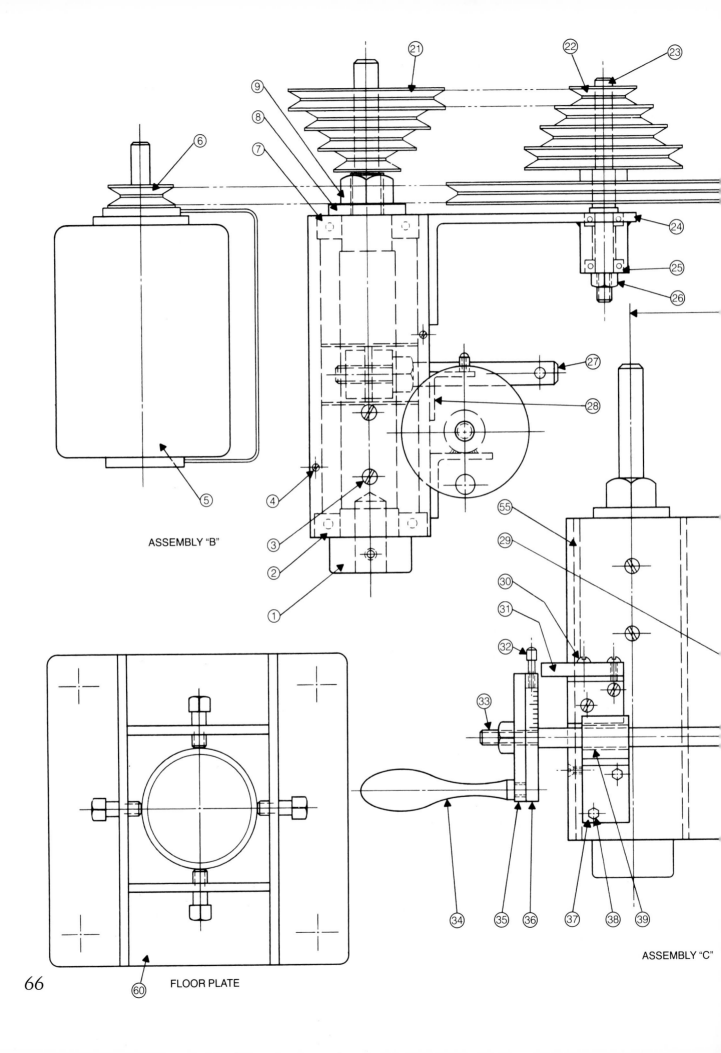

ASSEMBLY "B"

ASSEMBLY "C"

FLOOR PLATE

66

temporarily put them together with tubing in order to place angle iron pieces at the proper angle. The center distance between the quill and tubing is 9⅛″ (see assembly drawings). Next, weld Clamping Blocks (in Det. 15) in the correct position as shown. Let the unit cool by itself after welding. Drill and tap the clamp blocks as shown. Set up and bore the ID to a free slip fit to the column, then saw on each side of the clamp blocks, half way around the tubing. Cut into and between the blocks, from one saw kerf to the other. Locate, drill, and countersink for No. 8 flathead screws, five holes as per the drawing.

I cut the keyway in the column on my lathe. I clamped the column in the chuck, supported the opposite end on a bench, and indicated it in with the carriage both ways. Photo 7 will show the attachment I made, mounted on the cross slide, to hold a ¼″ endmill. It is made from a 41 to 1 worm reduction unit, driven by a 1725 rpm motor, and an 8″ pulley to a 1½″ pulley. I put a handle on the 104-tooth thread gear, and moved the carriage by hand with ease. If you cut a keyway by this method, be sure the endmill is square and in line with the centerline of the column.

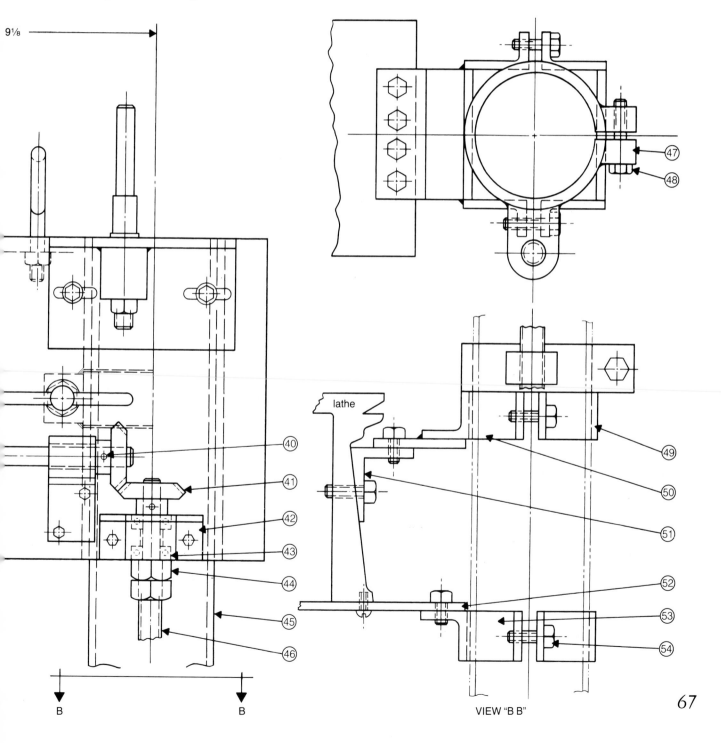

VIEW "B B"

67

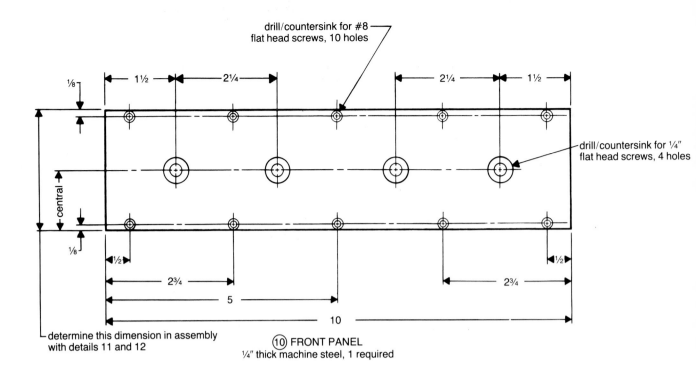

drill/countersink for #8 flat head screws, 10 holes

drill/countersink for ¼″ flat head screws, 4 holes

1½   2¼   2¼   1½

⅛

central

⅛

½   ½

2¾   2¾

5

10

determine this dimension in assembly with details 11 and 12

⑩ FRONT PANEL
¼″ thick machine steel, 1 required

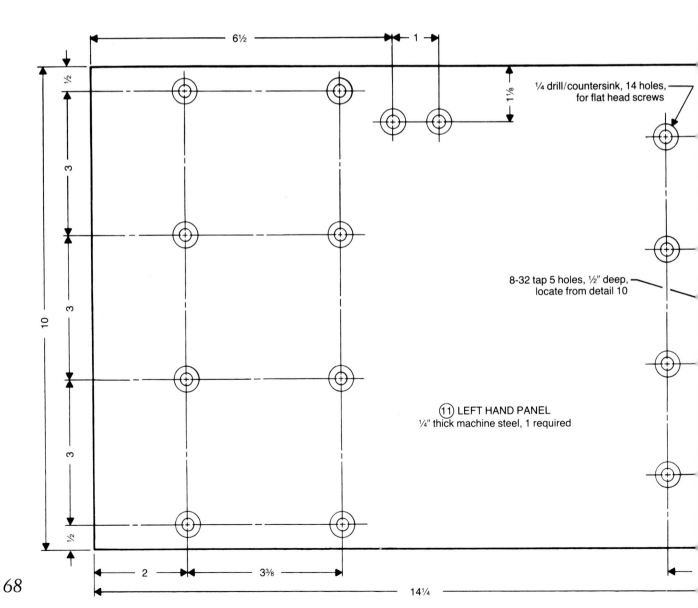

6½   1

½

1⅛

¼ drill/countersink, 14 holes, for flat head screws

3

3

10

8-32 tap 5 holes, ½″ deep, locate from detail 10

3

⑪ LEFT HAND PANEL
¼″ thick machine steel, 1 required

3

½

2   3⅜

14¼

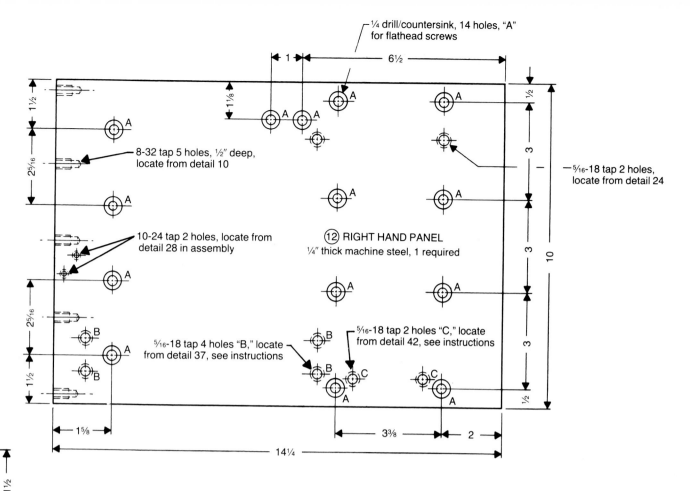

¼ drill/countersink, 14 holes, "A" for flathead screws

8-32 tap 5 holes, ½" deep, locate from detail 10

10-24 tap 2 holes, locate from detail 28 in assembly

⁵⁄₁₆-18 tap 4 holes "B," locate from detail 37, see instructions

⑫ RIGHT HAND PANEL
¼" thick machine steel, 1 required

⁵⁄₁₆-18 tap 2 holes, locate from detail 24

⁵⁄₁₆-18 tap 2 holes "C," locate from detail 42, see instructions

LATHE MILLING MACHINE PARTS LIST

DETAIL	NO. REQ'D.	ITEM & DESCRIPTION	SOURCE
1	1	Spindle – 2¾ dia. × 16" long crs	
2	1	Ball Bearing – ID 1.7717, OD 3.3465, width .7480, #6209-2NSL	Grainger's
3	32	Flathead Screw – ¼-20 × ¾" long	Std
4	10	Flathead Screw – 8-32 × ⅝" long	Std
5	1	½ hp Electric Motor – 1725 rpm	Std
6	1	½ × 2" dia. Vee Pulley – bore to suit motor	Std
7	1	Ball Bearing – ID 1.5748, OD 3.1496, width .7087, #6208-2NSL	Grainger's
8	1	Washer – 2½" dia. × ¼" long crs	
9	1	1-8 Hex Nut	Std
10	1	Front Panel – ¼ × 4 × 10⅛" machine steel	
11	1	Left-hand Panel – ¼ × 10⅛ × 14⅜" machine steel	
12	1	Right-hand Panel – ¼ × 10⅛ × 14⅜" machine steel	
13	1	½" Vee Belt – approx. 33" long	Std
14	1	Motor Bracket – make to suit	
15	1	Head Guide – welded con'st. (see Det.)	
16	1	Key – ⅛" × ⁹⁄₃₂" × 10⅛", keystock or crs	
17	5	Flathead Screw – 8-32 × ½" long	Std
18	2	Flathead Screw – ⅛" dia. × ½" long	Std
19	1	½" Vee Belt – approx. 50" long	Std
20	1	½" Vee Pulley – ⅝" bore × 10" dia., with hub	Std
21	1	4-step Vee Pulley – 2"-3"-4"-5" dias., ¾" bore	Std
22	1	4-step Vee Pulley – 2"-3"-4"-5" dias., ⅝" bore	Std
23	1	Idler Shaft – 1" dia. × 7½" long crs	
24	1	Idler Pulley Bracket – welded con'st. (see Det.)	
25	2	Ball Bearing – ID .5906, OD 1.3780, width .4331, #6202-2NSL	Grainger's
26	3	½-13 Hex Nut	Std
27	1	Clamp Screw – ⅝" dia. × 7⅜" long crs	
28	1	Marker Bracket – ⅛ × 1½ × 1½ × 1⅝" long angle iron	
29	1	Clamp Screw Handle – ¼" dia. × 4" long crs	
30	4	Round-Head Screw – 10-24 × ½" long	Std
31	1	Marker – ⅜ × ⅜ × 2⅝" long crs	
32	1	Socket Head Cap Screw – 10-24 × ¾ long	Std
33	1	Adjusting Shaft – .625 + .000 – .001" dia. crs	
34	1	Handle – 1" dia. × 3⅞" long crs	
35	1	Dial Plate – 4¼" dia. × ⅞" long crs	
36	1	Dial – 4¼" dia. × ½" long crs	
37	2	Bracket – welded con'st. (see Det.)	
38	21	Hex Head Cap Screw – ⁵⁄₁₆-18 × ¾" long	Std
39	2	Bronze Bushing – ⅝" ID × ¾" OD × 1¼" long, #2X774	Grainger's
40	2	Dowel Pins to fit bevel gears	Std
41	2	45° Bevel Gears – approx. 1⅞" dia. × 1" long, with hub	
42	1	Adjusting Screw Bracket – welded con'st. (see Det.)	
43	2	Ball Bearings – ID .625, OD 1.5748, width .4724, #6203-10ZZM	Grainger's
44	1	¾-10 Hex Nuts	Std
45	1	Column – 3⅜ ID × 3⅞" OD × 72" long tubing or equal	
46	1	Adjusting Screw – ¾-10 × 27½" long, threaded rod	Std
47	1	Adjusting Screw Guide – welded con'st. (see Det.)	
48	1	Hex Head Cap Screw – ⅜-16 × 2" long	Std
49	2	Clamp Cap – welded con'st. (see Det.)	
50	1	Top Clamp – welded con'st. (see Det.)	
51	1	Lathe Bracket – ¼ × 2 × 2 × 6" long, angle iron	
52	1	Plate to suit lathe – see Assembly	
53	1	Bottom Clamp – welded con'st. (see Det.)	
54	6	Hex Head Cap Screw – ⅜-16 × 1" long	Std
55	1	Quill – 3" ID × 3½" OD × 10⅛" long, tubing or equal	
56	1	Eye Bolt or Hook – ⅜-16 × 2"	Std
57	1	Counterbalance Cable Plate – ⅜ × 1½ × 4¼" crs	
58	3	⅜-16 Hex Nuts	
59	2	Counterbalance Bracket – ⅛ × 1¼ × 1¼ × 2" angle iron	
60	1	Floor Plate – welded con'st. (see Det.)	
61	1	⅛" dia. wire cable for counterbalance, to suit	Std
62	1	Endmill Adapter for ⅜" shank crs	
63	1	Endmill Adapter for ½" shank crs	
64	1	Endmill Adapter for ⅝" shank crs	

69

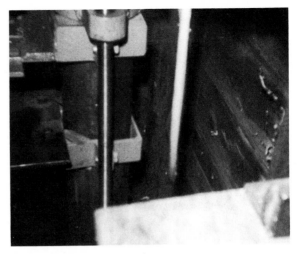

5 *Attaching the mill to lathe.*

4 *Showing right side arrangement of adjusting screw, bevel gears, graduated dial, and locking device.*

6 *Shows mill in up position.*

Make the Key (Det. 16) from ⅛″ steel. The width must be a good slip fit in the keyway column. Assemble the column, key, and head guide, and locate the holes in the key from the latter. Disassemble and drill and tap for an 8-32 thread. Reassemble and screw the key to the head guide. Now, be sure that it slides freely on the column; then dowel the two together. To assure that the key will not move or come loose, I welded both ends of the key to the head guide.

Machine the Quill (Det. 55), as per the drawing, to hold the bearings. Bearing bores must be in line with each other. I purchased all bearings and bushings from W. W. Graingers, Inc., whose outlets are located in almost every state, and who also sell vee belts and pulleys. However, they are wholesale only, so you must be in a business, or have someone who is get them for you. They have good prices.

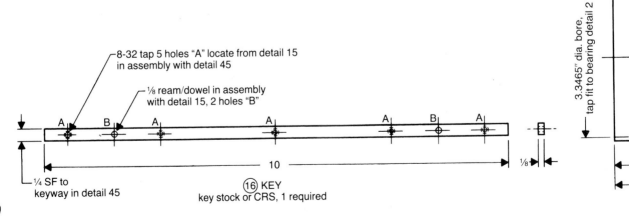

8-32 tap 5 holes "A" locate from detail 15 in assembly with detail 45

⅛ ream/dowel in assembly with detail 15, 2 holes "B"

10

¼ SF to keyway in detail 45

16 KEY
key stock or CRS, 1 required

3.3465″ dia. bore, tap fit to bearing detail 2

.748

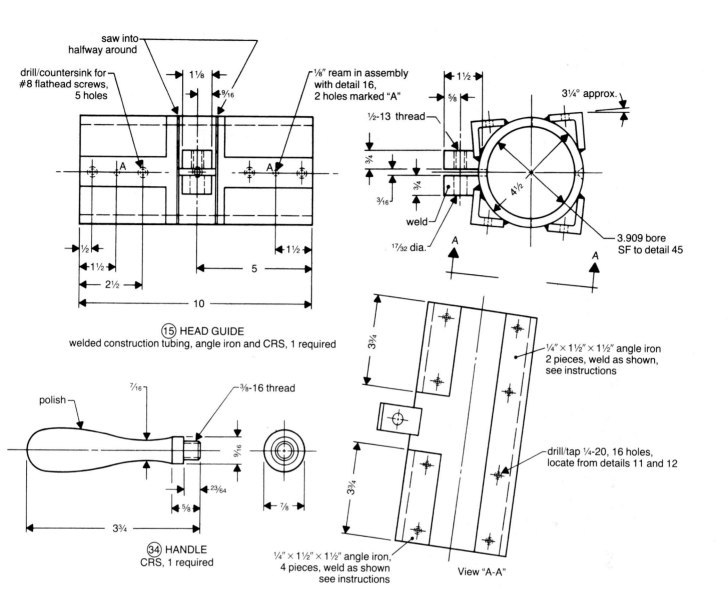

saw into halfway around

drill/countersink for #8 flathead screws, 5 holes

1⅛

⁹⁄₁₆

⅛" ream in assembly with detail 16, 2 holes marked "A"

A — A

½

1½

2½

5

1½

10

⑮ HEAD GUIDE
welded construction tubing, angle iron and CRS, 1 required

1½

⅝

3¼° approx.

½-13 thread

¾

¾

³⁄₁₆

weld

4½

¹⁷⁄₃₂ dia.

A

A

3.909 bore
SF to detail 45

polish

⁷⁄₁₆

⅜-16 thread

⁹⁄₁₆

²³⁄₆₄

⅝

⅞

3¾

㉞ HANDLE
CRS, 1 required

3¾

3¾

¼" × 1½" × 1½" angle iron
2 pieces, weld as shown,
see instructions

drill/tap ¼-20, 16 holes,
locate from details 11 and 12

¼" × 1½" × 1½" angle iron,
4 pieces, weld as shown
see instructions

View "A-A"

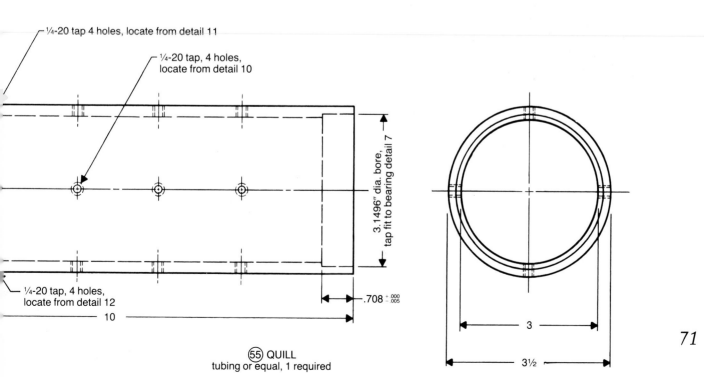

¼-20 tap 4 holes, locate from detail 11

¼-20 tap, 4 holes,
locate from detail 10

3.1496" dia. bore,
tap fit to bearing detail 7

¼-20 tap, 4 holes,
locate from detail 12

10

.708 ⁺·⁰⁰⁰ ₋·₀₀₅

3

3½

㉕ QUILL
tubing or equal, 1 required

Now, finish making the left, right, and front Panels (Dets. 10, 11, and 12), and assemble them with Dets. 15 and 55, maintaining a center distance of 9⅛″ between Dets. 15 and 45. Do not forget to drill a ⅞″ or 1″ diameter hole through the right-hand panel (Det. 12). Locate from, and in line with, the ¹⁷⁄₃₂″ diameter hole in the clamp block. This is a clearance hole for the Clamp Screw (Det. 27).

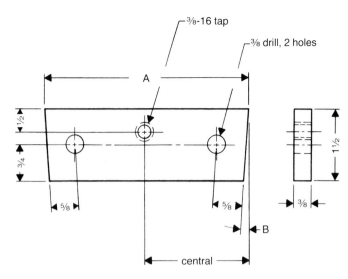

Determine dimension "A" / angle "B" in assembly with details 11, 12, and 15.

㊼ COUNTERBALANCE CABLE PLATE
CRS, 1 required

7 *Shows attachment I made to cut keyway on lathe.*

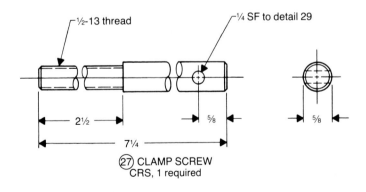

㉗ CLAMP SCREW
CRS, 1 required

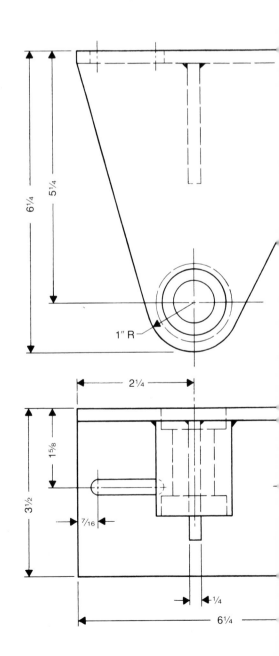

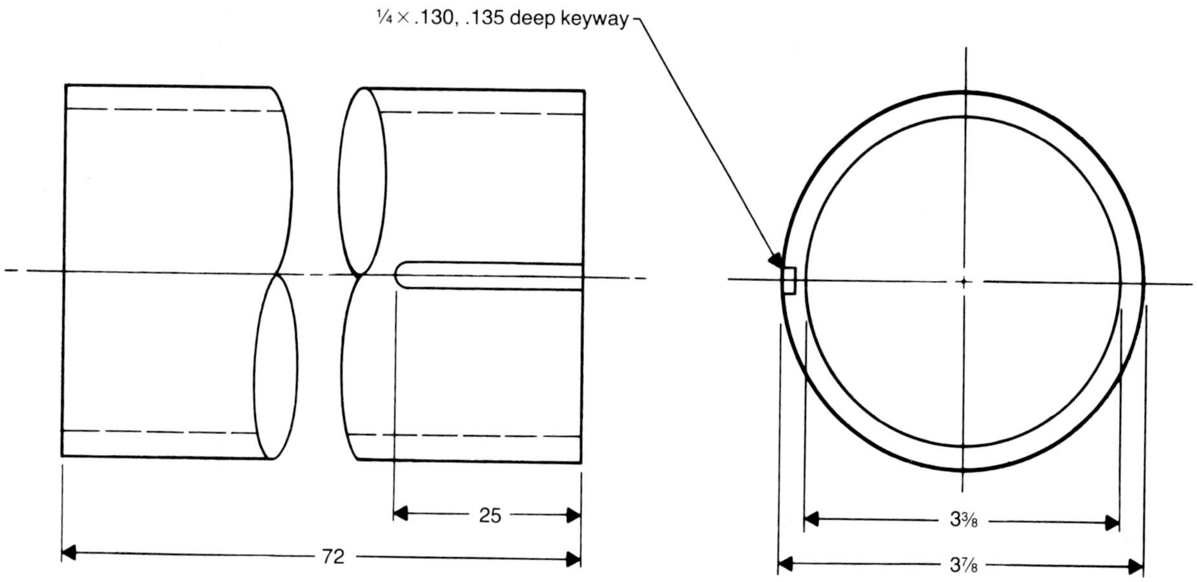

¼ × .130, .135 deep keyway
25
72
3⅜
3⅞

(45) COLUMN
pipe or tubing, 1 required

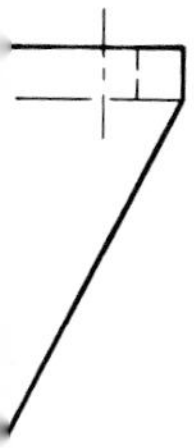

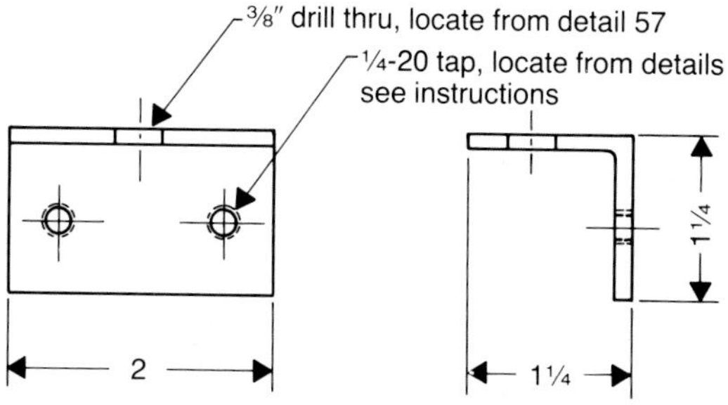

⅜″ drill thru, locate from detail 57
¼-20 tap, locate from details 11 and 12
see instructions
2
1¼
1¼

(59) COUNTERBALANCE BRACKET
⅛″ angle iron, 2 required

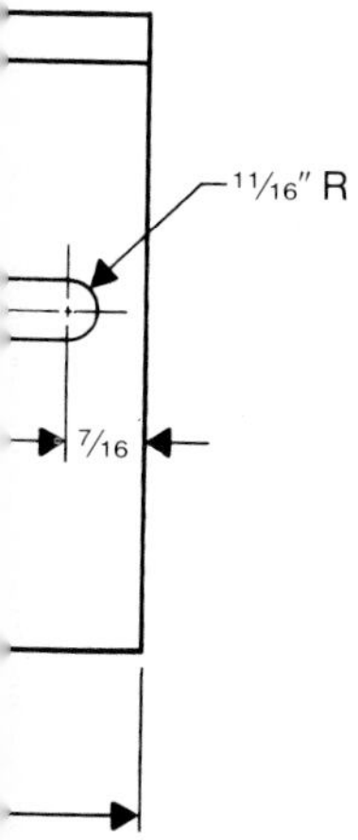

11/16″ R
7/16

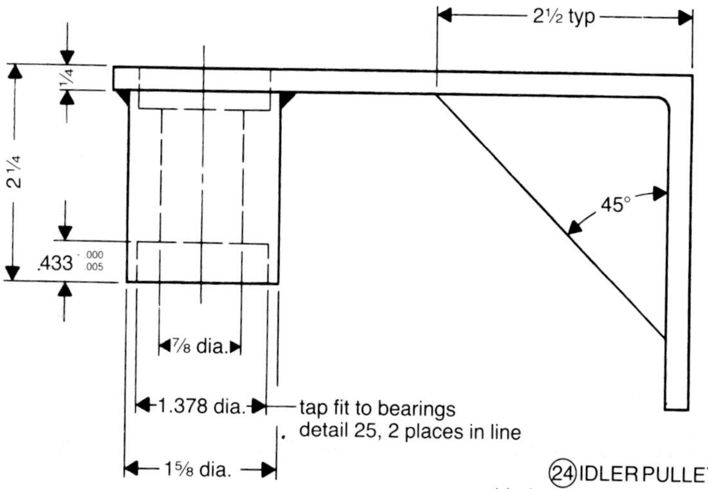

2½ typ
¼
2¼
45°
.433 .000 .005
⅞ dia.
1.378 dia.
tap fit to bearings
detail 25, 2 places in line
1⅝ dia.

(24) IDLER PULLEY BRACKET
welded construction – angle iron / CRS, 1 required

Now make and install Counterbalance Brackets (Det. 59) and the Cable Plate (Det. 57). The top of the cable plate should be flush with side panels, and the back edge against the tubing of Det. 15 (see Assembly "A").

Make the Idler Pulley Bracket (Det. 24), as per the drawing, and install Bearings (Det. 25). Locate to drill two 5/16-18 tapped holes in Det. 12. The top of the bracket should be flush with Det. 12. (See Assembly View "B" and "C," but do not install at this time.)

Make two Brackets (Det. 37), and install bronze Bushings (Det. 39).

Make the Adjusting Shaft (Det. 33). It must turn freely in the bronze bushings in Dets. 39.

Make the Adjusting Screw Bracket (Det. 42), and install the bearings (Det. 43).

Make the Adjusting Screw (Det. 46) from 3/4-10 threaded rod. The .625" diameter end must be a free slip fit in the bearings.

Locate and install the bracket to the right-hand panel, the centerline to be on the centerline of Det. 15 (see Assembly "C").

Make the Adjusting Screw Guide (Det. 47), but do not drill and tap the 3/4-10 thread at this time.

1/2-13 thread

locate in assembly with bevel gear

1

12¼

.625 +.000 -.002

(33) ADJUSTING SHAFT
CRS, 1 required

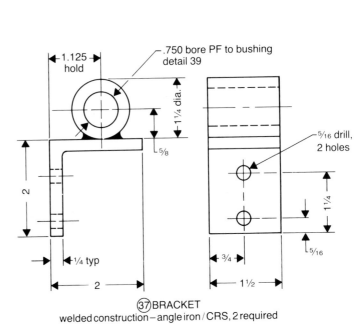

1.125 hold

.750 bore PF to bushing detail 39

1¼ dia.

5/8

5/16 drill, 2 holes

2

1¼

¼ typ

2

3/4

1½

5/16

(37) BRACKET
welded construction – angle iron / CRS, 2 required

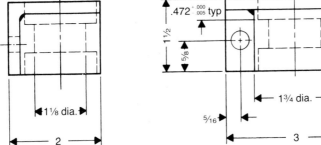

1.125 hold

1⅛ dia.

2

tap fit to bearing detail 43
2 places, in line

1.5748 dia.

3/8" drill, 2 holes

.472 +.000 -.005 typ

1½

5/8

1¾ dia.

5/16

5/16

3

(42) ADJUSTING SCREW BRACKET
welded construction – ¼" angle iron / CRS, 1 required

Temporarily assemble the mill head on the column, and bring the adjusting screw guide on the column up to the adjusting screw bracket. Make a suitable pin to slip through the bearings to mark and locate the ¾-10 tapped hole in that bracket. Remove, drill and tap the ¾-10 thread, square it with a 3⅞" diameter bore and reinstall on the column.

Locate one bevel gear on a ⅝" diameter adjusting screw and drill for a proper dowel pin. Do not assemble. Install two ¾-10 hex nuts (Det. 44) on the adjusting screw, below ⅝" diameter, and thread the screw through the screw guide (Det. 47). Push the ⅝" diameter screw through the bearings, and install the bevel gear with the dowel. Now snug the ¾-10 hex nuts up against the bracket. Position the adjusting screw guide and tighten with a hex head bolt (Det. 48), in a position that the screw may turn freely. Now assemble the other bevel

gear to the ⅝" end of the shaft (Det. 33), and install the shaft through the two Brackets (Det. 37). Now locate this assembly by meshing the two bevel gears together in such a way that there is no end-play in the adjusting shaft and so that it turns the adjusting screw freely with no binding. Locate holes, drill and tap, and install bolts (see Assembly "C").

Make Dets. 34, 35 and Dial 36, and install them on the Shaft (Det. 33). I cut the 100 graduation lines on my lathe, using a 20-tooth thread gear mounted on the lathe spindle and a stop pin, using every tooth = .005". Then I divided one space into five equal parts, very carefully using dividers. I then realigned the marking tool to one divider mark, and indexed all around, repeating until all 100 lines were cut. Make the Marker (Det. 31), and marker bracket (Det. 28), and install on the right-hand panel as shown in Assembly "C".

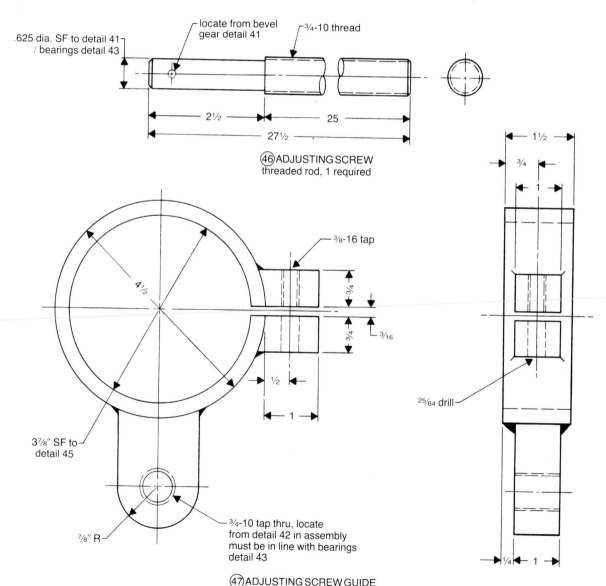

.625 dia. SF to detail 41 / bearings detail 43

locate from bevel gear detail 41

¾-10 thread

2½   25

27½

(46) ADJUSTING SCREW
threaded rod, 1 required

4½

3⅞" SF to detail 45

⅜-16 tap

¾

¾

³⁄₁₆

½

1

1½

¾

1

25⁄64 drill

7⁄8" R

¾-10 tap thru, locate from detail 42 in assembly must be in line with bearings detail 43

¼   1

(47) ADJUSTING SCREW GUIDE
welded construction – tubing / CRS, 1 required

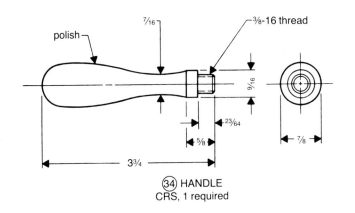

polish

⁷⁄₁₆

⅜-16 thread

⁹⁄₁₆

²³⁄₆₄

⅝

3¾

⅞

(34) HANDLE
CRS, 1 required

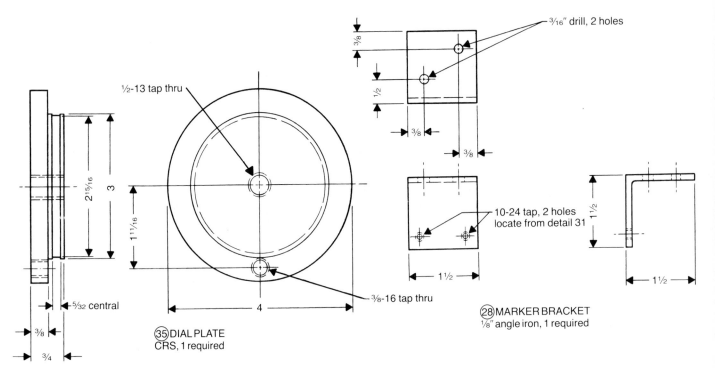

½-13 tap thru

³⁄₁₆" drill, 2 holes

⅜

½

⅜

⅜

2¹⁵⁄₁₆

3

1¹¹⁄₁₆

10-24 tap, 2 holes
locate from detail 31

1½

⅜-16 tap thru

1½

⁵⁄₃₂ central

⅜

¾

4

(35) DIAL PLATE
CRS, 1 required

(28) MARKER BRACKET
⅛" angle iron, 1 required

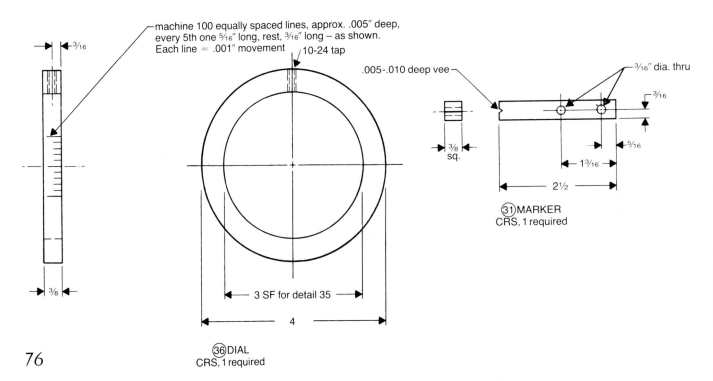

³⁄₁₆

machine 100 equally spaced lines, approx. .005" deep,
every 5th one ⁵⁄₁₆" long, rest, ³⁄₁₆" long – as shown.
Each line = .001" movement

10-24 tap

.005-.010 deep vee

³⁄₁₆" dia. thru

³⁄₁₆

⅜
sq.

⁵⁄₁₆

1³⁄₁₆

2½

⅜

3 SF for detail 35

4

(31) MARKER
CRS, 1 required

(36) DIAL
CRS, 1 required

76

Install Bearings (Det. 2 and Det. 7) into the quill. Make the Spindle (Det. 1) and Washer (Det. 8). Install the spindle through the bearings in the quill with the washer (Det. 8) and snug up with the Nut (Det. 9) (see Assembly View "B").

Make the clamp screw (Det. 27). Thread a ½-13 hex nut, on the threaded end, up against the ⅝" diameter. Install the screw into the clamp blocks and install the Handle (Det. 29). See Assembly View "C."

Make the Idler Shaft (Det. 23); install through the bearings in the idler pulley bracket

(Det. 24), and snub up with a hex nut (Det. 26). Assemble the bracket to Det. 12, as shown in Assembly "B" and "C."

Loosen Bolt 48 on the adjusting screw guide, and turn the screw until it is disengaged. Remove the guide from the column. Remove the pin from the bevel gear on the end of the adjusting screw and pull the adjusting screw out of the bracket. Remove the mill head from the column, and set it up on the blocks in an upright position.

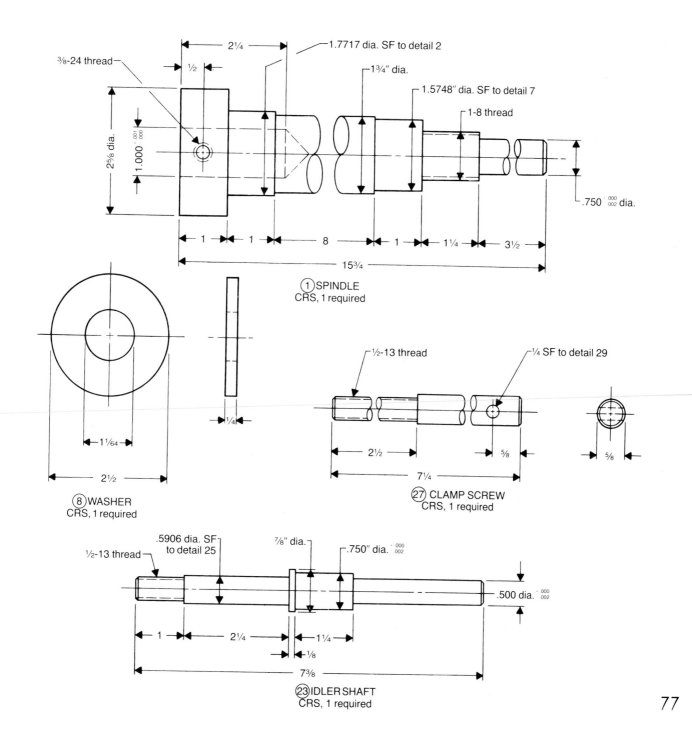

① SPINDLE
CRS, 1 required

⑧ WASHER
CRS, 1 required

㉗ CLAMP SCREW
CRS, 1 required

㉓ IDLER SHAFT
CRS, 1 required

Install Pulley 21 on the spindle (Det. 1 – refer to Part I, May/June 1984), Pulley 20 on the Idler Shaft (Det. 23) and Pulley 22 on top of Pulley 20. Install a 2″ diameter pulley on your motor, and refer to Photos 1 and 2, and Assembly Drawings "A" and "B," for location and arrangement of motor and belts.

Now make Clamps (Dets. 49, 50 and 53). Dets. 51 and 52 must be made to suit your lathe. Also make the floor plate (Det. 60).

Place the floor plate on the floor behind your lathe, and the column behind the lathe into the floor plate. Locate and install clamps on

both the lathe and column. Square up the column both ways with the lathe fairly close and bolt the plate to the floor. Then tighten the clamps. Slip the adjusting screw guide onto the column, and install the adjusting screw into the guide quite a ways. Install Eye Bolt 56 into the counterbalance plate.

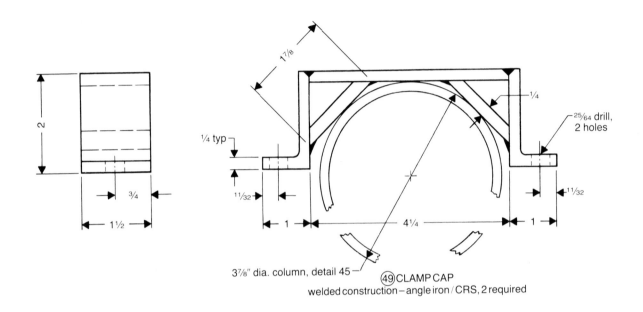

3⅞″ dia. column, detail 45

㊾ CLAMP CAP
welded construction – angle iron / CRS, 2 required

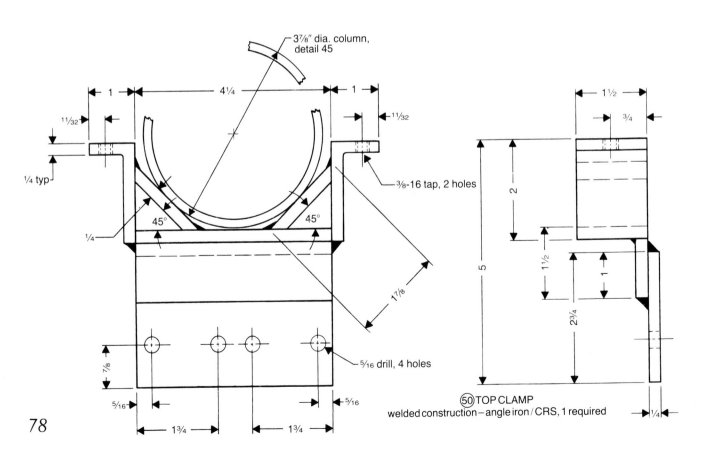

㊿ TOP CLAMP
welded construction – angle iron / CRS, 1 required

You are now ready to install the mill head on the column, and you will need help on this operation. Grease the keyway, column and ID of tubing with light grease. I raised mine with a block and tackle. You must be very careful to line up the key with the keyway, and as you lower the head, the adjusting screw must go through the bearings. Then the bevel gear can be reinstalled. Snug up the two ¾-10 hex nuts. Continue lowering the head until the adjusting screw guide rests on top of clamp Dets. 49 and

50, and tighten. Lock the head with the clamp screw and remove the hoisting device.

Install the cable, the necessary pulley or pulleys, and counterbalance weight. Attach the indicator to the spindle, unclamp the head, lower it to the lathe, reclamp, and indicate 360° to lathe. Adjust the floor plate screws and shim the lathe clamps where necessary. Then reclamp.

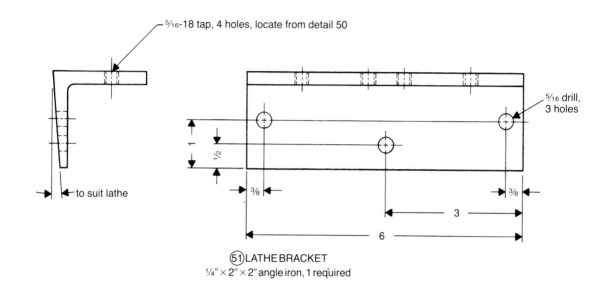

⑤①LATHE BRACKET
¼″ × 2″ × 2″ angle iron, 1 required

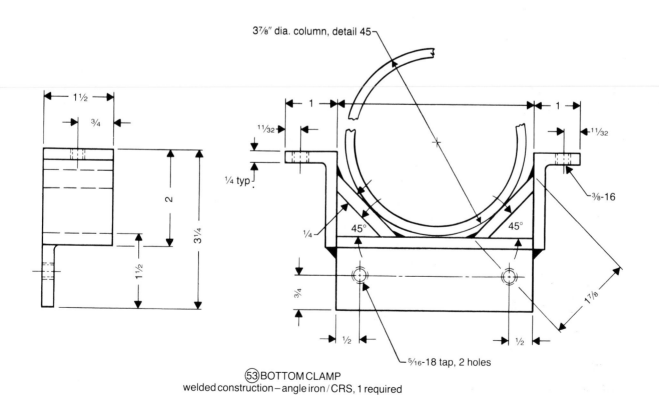

⑤③BOTTOM CLAMP
welded construction – angle iron / CRS, 1 required

79

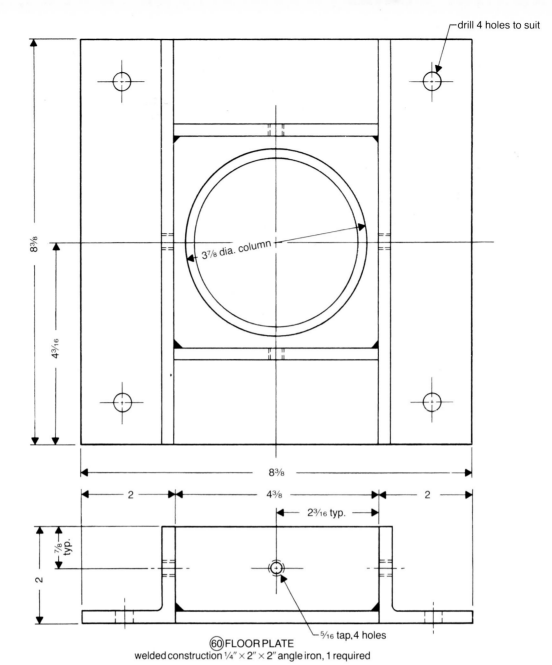

drill 4 holes to suit

8³⁄₈

4³⁄₁₆

3⁷⁄₈ dia. column

8³⁄₈

2   4³⁄₈   2

2³⁄₁₆ typ.

7⁄₈ typ.

2

60 FLOOR PLATE
welded construction ¼″ × 2″ × 2″ angle iron, 1 required

⁵⁄₁₆ tap, 4 holes

1.000 dia. SF to detail 1

1¹⁄₁₆

⁵⁄₁₆

7°

"C"

"B"

"A" SF

⅛″ × 45°

2

2¼

4³⁄₈

1¼

END MILL ADAPTER

	"A"	"B"	"C"	REQUIRED	MATERIAL
62	³⁄₈	⁵⁄₈	⁵⁄₁₆-18 tap	1	CRS
63	½	⅞	³⁄₈-16 tap	1	CRS
64	⅝	⅞	³⁄₈-16 tap	1	CRS

Endmill adapters (Dets. 62, 63 and 64) are what I have made so far, but I will also add one for a drill chuck. I did put a light inside the mill head, and you may want to, also.

You can run a belt directly from the motor to the spindle for high speeds, which I have done when forming molding designs on wood for clocks, or other items.

Center Test Indicator

by Frank Brockardt

Wiggler bars are, in my estimation, time consuming, cumbersome and not the best mechanics. I have a center test indicator which I find more suitable to my needs.

The test bar is made from either cold rolled steel or drill rod. The pointed end should be turned true, as it may be desirable to use it in setting up work that has a center-drilled hole in it.

The rod does not have to rotate with the work to get a true setup.

The slight pressure from the spring at the tailstock end keeps the rod seated in the work as the work is brought to center with chuck jaw adjustment.

Wiggler rods setup methods provide no following pressure as the work is moved to true center.

Before proceeding with machine work, make sure that the face of the work indicates true and that the test rod indicates true.

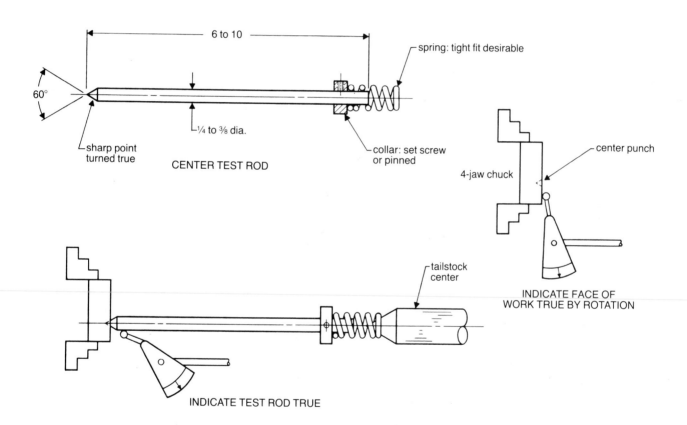

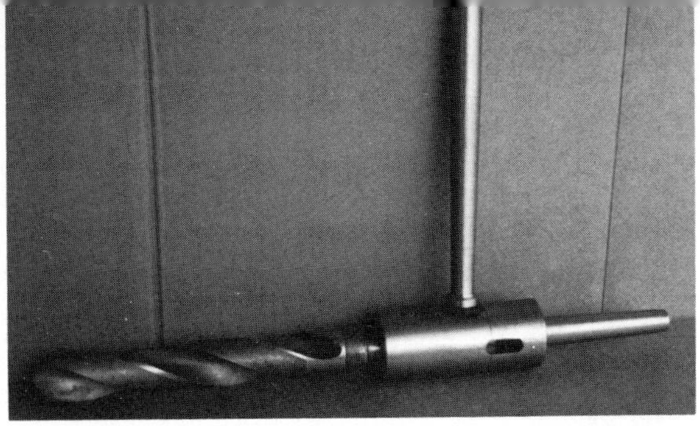

A Drill Holder for Your Lathe

by George A. Peavey

Photo By Author

As every lathe operator knows, in a lathe, a taper shank drill is held in the tailstock only by the taper. The flat end tang of the drill does not mate with anything. It is difficult to prevent a drill from turning in the socket. To overcome this problem, I made the drill holder shown in the photograph. It has a no. 2 Morse taper socket and a no. 2 Morse taper tail. The two tapers are on the same center line. The slot (shown) accepts the drill tang.

I install the drill in the holder before placing the holder in the tailstock. When installing the drill, I twist it as much as the tang will permit; then I tap the end of the drill with a lead hammer to set the drill in the socket. The tail of the holder is then inserted into the tailstock, and the handle is rested on top of the compound rest. This drill holder does a good job and I am very happy with it.

The drawing shows some of the dimensions for the holder I made. The Morse taper dimensions can be found in almost any engineering or machinist book. I made the body quite heavy to be sure there was enough material for the ½″ diameter thread for the handle. The spot face on my holder is 1″ in diameter because that is the size of my mill.

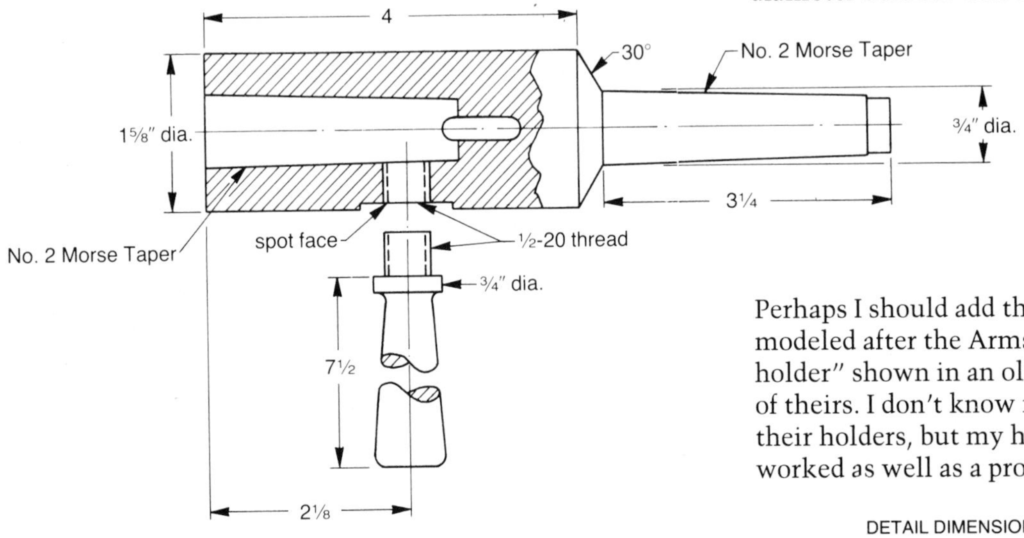
4
30°
No. 2 Morse Taper
1 5/8″ dia.
3/4″ dia.
3 1/4
No. 2 Morse Taper
spot face
1/2-20 thread
3/4″ dia.
7 1/2
2 1/8

A couple of my drills had a no. 3 Morse taper shank. I turned them down to a no. 2. Of course, no. 1 Morse taper shank drills are used with a sleeve. My lathe is a 10″ Logan.

Perhaps I should add that my holder is modeled after the Armstrong "safety drill holder" shown in an old C-39 (1939?) catalog of theirs. I don't know if Armstrong still sells their holders, but my homemade holder has worked as well as a professionally-made one.

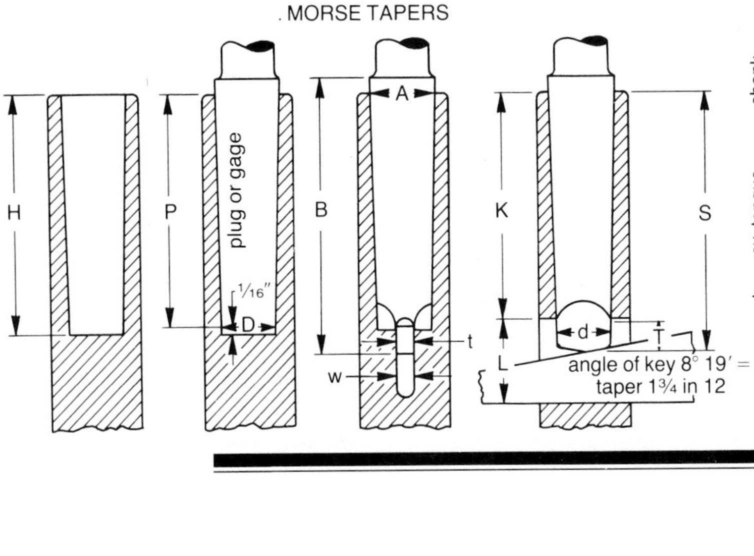
. MORSE TAPERS
H
P
plug or gage
1/16″
D
B
A
t
w
K
d
T
L
S
angle of key 8° 19′ = taper 1 3/4 in 12

DETAIL DIMENSIONS

	number of taper		0	1	2	3	4	5	6	7
	diam. of plug at small end	D	.252	.369	.572	.778	1.020	1.475	2.116	2.75
	diam. at end of socket	A	.3561	.475	.700	.938	1.231	1.748	2.494	3.27
shank	whole length of shank	B	2 11/32	2 9/16	3 1/8	3 7/8	4 7/8	6 1/8	8 9/16	11 5/
shank	shank depth	S	2 7/32	2 7/16	2 15/16	3 11/16	4 5/8	5 7/8	8 1/4	11 1/
	depth of hole	H	2 1/32	2 3/16	2 5/8	3 1/4	4 1/8	5 1/4	7 3/8	10 1/
	standard plug depth	P	2	2 1/8	2 9/16	3 3/16	4 1/16	5 3/16	7 1/4	10
tongue	thickness of tongue	t	5/32	13/64	1/4	5/16	15/32	5/8	3/4	1 1/8
tongue	length of tongue	T	1/4	3/8	7/16	9/16	5/8	3/4	1 1/8	1 3/8
tongue	diameter of tongue	d	.235	.343	17/32	23/32	31/32	1 13/32	2	2 5/8
keyway	width of keyway	W	.160	.213	.260	.322	.478	.635	.760	1.13
keyway	length of keyway	L	9/16	3/4	7/8	1 3/16	1 1/4	1 1/2	1 3/4	2 5/8
keyway	end of socket to keyway	K	1 15/16	2 1/16	2 1/2	3 1/16	3 7/8	4 15/16	7	9 1/2
	taper per foot		.625	.600	.602	.602	.623	.630	.626	.62
	taper per inch		.05208	.05	.05016	.05016	.05191	.0525	.05216	.052
	number of key		0	1	2	3	4	5	6	7

Modifications to a Maximat V-8 Lathe

by Dave Marshall

Photos by Author

Having given the matter a great deal of thought, it was late 1976 when I finally purchased a Maximat V-8. Like many other purchasers, I liked the built-in milling facility, and I soon found that the machine could handle most jobs with ease. There were, however, three things that bothered me.

First, the nut to secure the tailstock – the wrench and the compound slide operating hand wheel always seemed to be in conflict. Similarly, there was an interference problem between the wrench and the screws, when tightening or loosening the nut securing the four-tool turret. The third problem involved the four-tool turret itself, which would not accommodate my favorite cutoff tool and had limited tool size capacity. Finally, I decided to attempt to rectify these problems. Having carried out the modifications and used them for over a year, I thought others might be interested in adding these changes to their machines. Incidentally, the lever clamp modification for the tailstock is really not as formidable as it might seem from the photographs.

First, it is necessary to drill or bore a ¾" hole through the vertical section of the tailstock to accept the Sleeve (Part 1). It is important that the centerline of this hole and the vertical centerline of the hole for the clamp bolt intersect. This requires care in measurement and marking out procedure, as well as care in setting up to perform the machining. In my case, I was fortunate to obtain access to a Bridgeport milling machine to drill the actual hole. The tailstock was bolted to a large angle plate mounted on the table; packing was used under the tailstock to prevent any movement.

After drilling a pilot, I discovered that there is a strengthening rib in the hollow casting. The casting and the base were not separated for this operation, so the tailstock would not require re-aligning when mounted back on the lathe. Otherwise, the rib would have been spotted before drilling the pilot hole. I decided to continue drilling the hole and finish with a

reamer. An alternative would be to drill to, say, ½" diameter and finish to size by boring. If you elect to drill the hole, it is recommended that this be done in stages and finished to size with a ¾" reamer. After finishing the hole, countersink about 1/16" deep on the back side to ensure the flange on the sleeve will seat properly to the casting. Those who wish may also counterbore the back to accept the flange, but in this case it was not necessary.

1 *The modified tailstock with cover fitted.*

The sleeve should be turned to size, preferably from bearing bronze, though an alternative would be to use steel and fit two bronze bushings. The finished sleeve should be a good fit through the casting. After drilling and counterboring the holes in the flange, the casting can be drilled and tapped for three no. 4-40 x ¾" socket head cap screws, the holes being spotted through the flange to ensure correct location. The ⅛" depth of the counterbore ensures that the head of the screws will be below the surface of the flange. A word to the novice – do not forget to remove the burrs or sharp edges from the holes in the flange, because they will prevent smooth operation when complete. Similarly countersink or drill the locations for the tapped holes with a clearance-sized drill to not more than $\frac{1}{16}$" deep to prevent the burr raised by tapping from interfering with the correct seating of the flange. We used to be taught to counterbore the tapping hole clearance-size for a depth of two threads (in this case .050"), but $\frac{1}{32}$" to $\frac{1}{16}$" will be satisfactory. If you choose to leave the sleeve fitted at this point, you will find it necessary to use either a standard 8 mm nut or shorten the existing one in order to be able to use the tailstock.

The Shaft (Part 2) is a straightforward turning job from mild steel. A short length of $\frac{1}{2}$" diameter ground shafting will simplify its production even further. The $\frac{1}{16}$" offset for the eccentric has proved more than adequate, but, with the Bushing (Part 3) in place, the shaft as shown is effectively prevented from sliding along its axis. The eccentric can be turned in the four-jaw chuck or thread the $\frac{1}{4}$" diameter portion of the shaft with a split circular die held in the tailstock die holder. If you don't have one, then screwcut the thread to a little over half depth and finish with the die in an ordinary diestock. The bushing is a simple turning exercise from bearing bronze and should require no further explanation. After removing all sharp edges, degrease the bushing and the eccentric end of the shaft with acetone. When dry, fit together with a drop of red *Loctite* (stud and bearing mount) and set aside to allow it to harden.

While we are waiting for the *Loctite* to harden, we can turn our attention to the Strap (Part 4). This is the only item that the novice is likely to have trouble with, so this will be discussed in a little more detail. To start with, we require a piece of cold rolled steel $\frac{1}{2}$" x $\frac{3}{4}$" about $1\frac{1}{4}$" long. Coat one of the $\frac{3}{4}$" wide faces with layout blue and scribe the long centerline. Then scribe the other centerline for the $\frac{1}{2}$" diameter hole $\frac{5}{8}$" from one end. Center pop the intersection of the two lines and set the piece in the four-jaw chuck with this center mark running true. Centerdrill and drill through using a small pilot drill, about no. 30 will do. Then drill $\frac{31}{64}$" diameter and finish to size with a $\frac{1}{2}$" reamer, using slow speed and plenty of cutting oil. Remove from the chuck and file the end

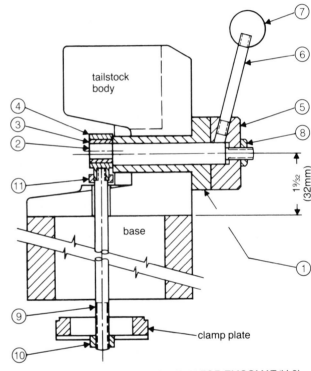

TAILSTOCK LEVER CLAMP ASSEMBLY FOR EMCOMAT 'V-8'

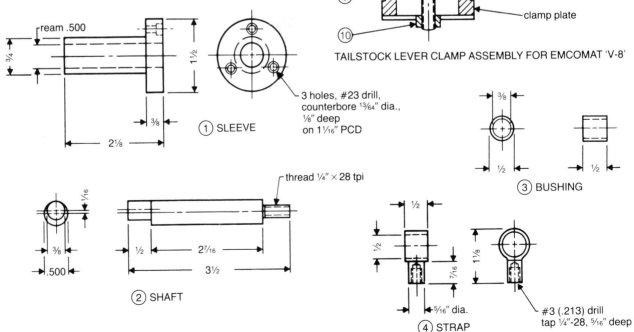

furthest from the hole smooth and coat with layout blue. Mark out and punch the center of this face and replace in the four-jaw chuck using brass packing pieces across the ½" hole, ensuring that about ⁹/₁₆" projects from the chuck jaws. Set the center pop to run true and turn to ⁵/₁₆" diameter for ½" length. Centerdrill the end and drill 5.5 mm or no. 3 for a depth of ⁷/₁₆" counterbore ¹⁷/₆₄" diameter ⅛" deep. Face off the end to leave the ⁵/₁₆" diameter ⁷/₁₆" long and tap the hole ¼-28 thread. Remove from the chuck and either file or machine the outside of the ½" hole to ⅝" diameter. The machining can be done by milling using a rotary table or by shaping, as so aptly illustrated and described by Kozo Hiraoka in *Live Steam* Magazine.

Finally remove all burrs and sharp edges caused by machining or filing operations and set to one side until you make the Clamp Bolt (Part 9) and the Square Nut (Part 10). If you do not wish to make the square nut, you can use a regular ⁵/₁₆-24 thread nut.

The next items to make are the Adjusting Plate (Part 5) and the Operating Lever (Part 6). Both of these are straightforward turning jobs from mild steel, with the exception of the tapped hole at an angle of 15° in the adjusting plate. Do not drill this hole until you have fitted everything together so you can find the right location on the circumference of the plate. The angle and the length of the operating lever are designed to miss both the clamping nut for the

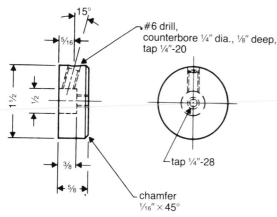

⑤ ADJUSTING PLATE

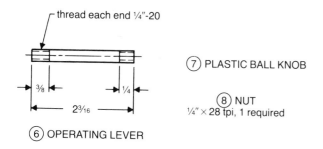

⑥ OPERATING LEVER

⑦ PLASTIC BALL KNOB

⑧ NUT
¼" × 28 tpi, 1 required

2 *Cover removed showing Parts 2, 3, 4 and 11.*

3 *Rear view of tailstock showing Parts 5 and 6.*

tailstock barrel and the vertical column of the milling head. Select the location of the hole for the operating lever so that it is about 10° on the headstock side of vertical when the clamp is released. Drilling and tapping of this hole is easily accomplished with the adjusting plate held in the machine vise at 90° to the axis of the latch and the milling head tilted to 15° from the vertical.

If you have a sliding tap holder to fit the drill chuck, then tapping this hole is very simple. My sliding tap holder consists of a Jacobs drill chuck with a screwed mount fitted to a ¾" diameter sleeve to slide on a ⁵/₁₆" diameter rod. The drill chuck accepts 0 - ¼" diameter and has been used successfully to tap holes down to ¹/₁₆"

85

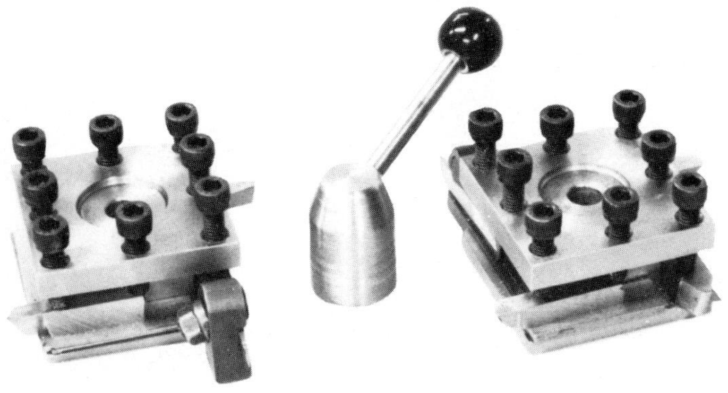

4 ***Four tool turrets and clamp.***

diameter without tap breakage. On larger holes such as this, it is used to start the tap squarely in the hole, and the tapping is finished by hand. The ball on the end of the operating lever is a standard ¾" diameter phenolic ball with a ¼-20 tapped insert. These are readily available from regular advertisers in both *Home Shop Machinist* and *Live Steam* Magazines.

We now come the the Stop (Part 11). This was necessary to limit the vertical travel of the clamp and prevent the clamp plate sliding sideways under the ways. To make this item, take a piece of ¼" x ½" cold rolled steel and finish the ends to a length of ⅞". Mark out and drill two no. 43 holes on ⅝" centers as shown on the center of the ¼" wide face. Next, drill and ream 5/16" diameter centrally on the ½" wide face. The piece is now set in the bench vise with the center of the ½" wide face approximately 1/64" above the vise jaws and cut in half with a hacksaw using the vise jaws to guide the blade. While this method may sound primitive to some readers, it is quick, simple and effective. Use a smooth file to clean up the rough edges and open the no. 43 holes in one half to no. 30. Tap the holes in the other half 4-40 and assemble with two no. 4-40 socket head cap screws.

Because the cast clamp plate as supplied had sharp edges where it was intended to slide between the ways, it had a tendency to catch. Therefore, I decided to modify it slightly, and the two milled sliding surfaces were milled .030" deeper. The edges and ends were then given a slight radius to ensure no sharp edges were left that could catch along the bed.

After a final trial setup has been made to check how smoothly everything operates, don't forget to put a smear of grease on the rotating parts and degrease the threads where the two nuts are to fit. After checking the adjustment, apply green *Loctite* (wick and feed) to the lock nut. Use the same grade of *Loctite* to secure the 5/16" nut after removing the tailstock assembly from the lathe, taking care not to move the nut from the setting position. Replace the tailstock on the lathe and clamp it in position with the operating lever. Now fit the clamp and, using feeler gages, set it to allow .015" vertical travel. As can be seen in Photo 1, a sheetmetal guard has been fitted to keep out swarf and dust. This is not detailed but can be easily formed from a piece of 20-gage aluminum sheet and secured with two no. 4-40 socket head cap screws.

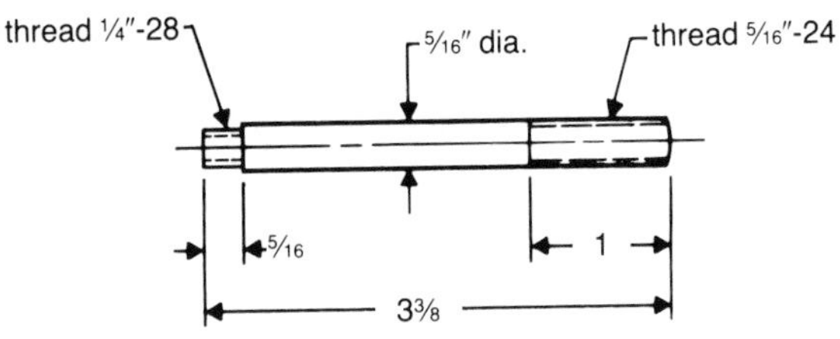
thread ¼"-28
5/16" dia.
thread 5/16"-24
5/16
1
3⅜

(9) CLAMP BOLT

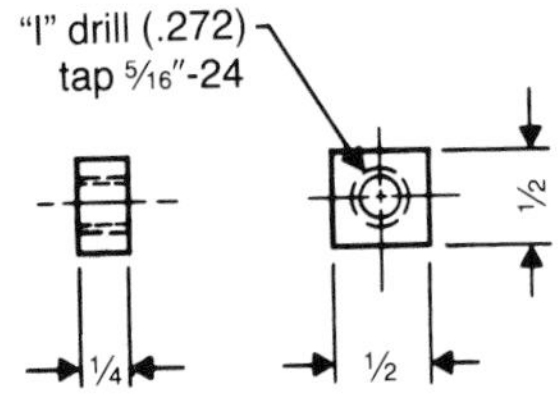
"I" drill (.272)
tap 5/16"-24
½
¼
½

(10) SQUARE NUT

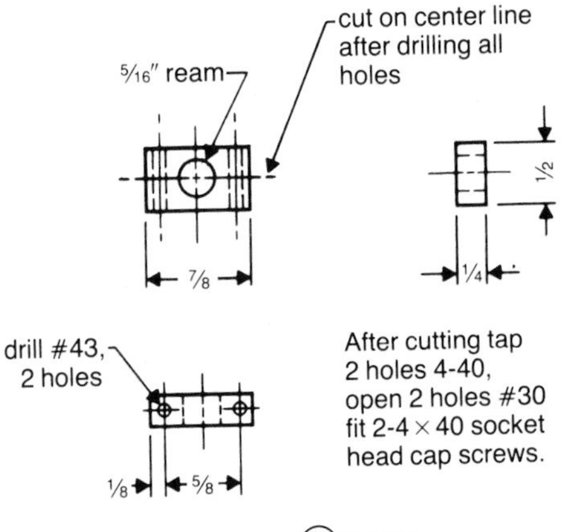
5/16" ream
cut on center line after drilling all holes
⅞
½
¼
drill #43, 2 holes
⅛
⅝
After cutting tap 2 holes 4-40, open 2 holes #30 fit 2-4 × 40 socket head cap screws.

(11) STOP

The toolpost clamp shown in the photographs replaces the nut supplied with the machine and allows adjustment without using a separate wrench. It also can be used with the clamp plate-type toolpost supplied with the machine.

The Toolpost Nut (Part 16) is turned from mild steel to the dimensions given and tapped M8-1.25 to suit the clamping stud fitted to the compound rest. The tapped hole for the Handle (Part 15) is done on the machine as previously described after trying the nut in place to select the correct circumferential location. A ¾" ball is then fitted to the end of the handle to complete the toolpost clamp. Should anyone think that the ball is merely an ornament, try omitting it at first. After tightening and loosening the clamp a few times, it will become apparent that the handle can leave a very sore spot on the palm of the hand, even without the threads. Don't forget that the handle should lie between the lathe centerline and the operator and point toward the tailstock end of the lathe. This is to prevent interference with the tailstock or the workpiece.

As readers may have gathered at the beginning, I am a firm believer in the four-tool turret-type tool post. This is a result of 30 years of experience and, while the later examples of quick-change toolposts have much to recommend them, I still believe the older four-tool-type is easier to manufacture for the home shop machinist.

5 *Four tool turret and clamp on lathe.*

The toolpost about to be described is capable of accepting a wide range of tool sizes and, as shown in Photos 4 and 6, will accept a slightly modified Eclipse no. 633S cutoff tool holder. The blade for this is hollow ground and only ⁵⁄₁₆" high x ¹⁄₁₆" thick, making it an ideal tool for home and model use. To the best of my knowledge, this is the smallest cutoff tool made and was originally designed for the now famous Myford lathes.

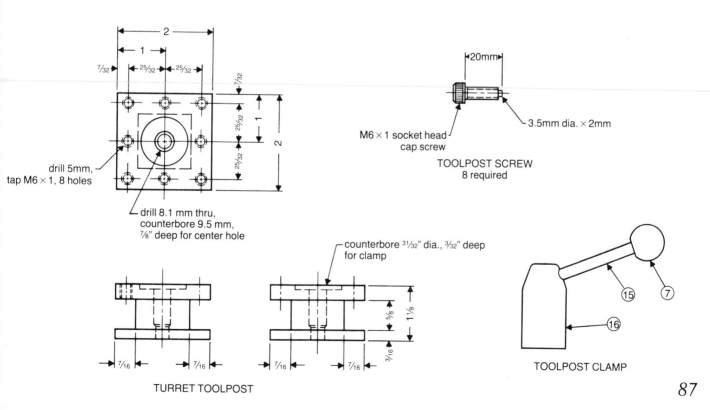

TURRET TOOLPOST

TOOLPOST SCREW
8 required

TOOLPOST CLAMP

6 *Cutoff tool in turret an hex key.*

To proceed with our toolpost, we require a piece of cold rolled steel 2″ square and a finished length of 1⅛″. For this toolpost to function properly and provide the greatest support for the cutting tools, it is most important that the base be as flat as possible, because it relies on the friction between itself and the top of the compound slide to resist movement while machining is being carried out. While the friction is created by the action of the clamp, if the base is not flat, the clamping force will distort the top of the compound slide. Machine the base very carefully and, if possible, have the base lapped by machine to ensure it is truly flat. I was fortunate to have a friend who was able to do this operation for me; otherwise, I would have settled for a machined surface. Lay out the center of the top of the toolpost and set

it to run true in the four-jaw chuck with the base firmly seated on the step of the jaws. Proceed to drill the center hole 8.1 mm and counterbore 9.5 mm or ⅜″ diameter for a depth of ⅞″. This will provide a register to fit the step on the bottom of the clamp stud. At the same setting, bore out the ³¹⁄₃₂″ diameter x ³⁄₃₂″ deep recess to accommodate the toolpost clamp, and finish machine the top face.

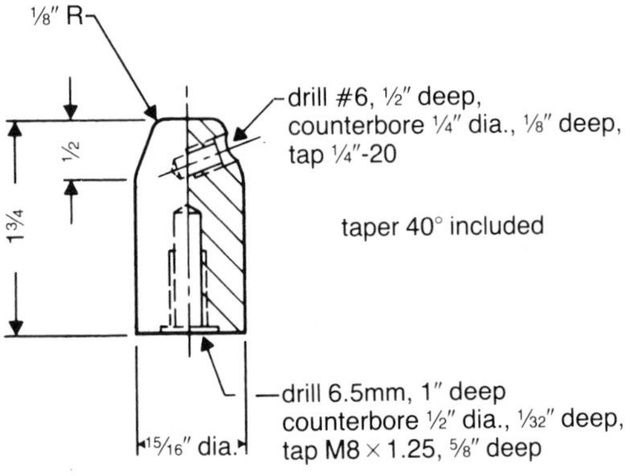

Next, mark out and mill the slot on each side for the tools. Mill these with a ⅜″ or ½″ endmill first, centering the cutter on the slot, and then finish to the ⅝″ dimension. If this operation is carried out on the machine, do not attempt too heavy a cut. Take your time and you will end up with a good job. Some time can be saved by drilling out most of the material with a ⅜″ diameter drill before attempting to mill the slots. As shown in Photo 6, the hex key supplied with the machine clears the toolpost clamp. At present, I am contemplating making a tee-handled hex key to replace the more common type. Of course, these can be purchased, but money saved can always be used elsewhere in the shop.

After removing any burrs or sharp edges, lay out and drill for the eight screws. I apologize to those who object to metric threads, but I already had a similar toolpost by Emco and wished to use the same hex key, so I fitted M 6-1 socket head cap screws.

Anyone who so wishes may substitute ¼-20 by drilling the holes no. 7 and using the appropriate tap. The dog turned on the end of the screws is simply to ensure that any burr raised on the ends will not interfere with their removal. The two turrets shown in Photo 4 are equipped one for steel and one for brass, allowing a quick changeover from one to the other. The previously mentioned modification to the cutoff tool holder consists of milling .031″ from the base using a carbide cutter and cutting to length to fit the turrets.

⅛″ R

drill #6, ½″ deep,
counterbore ¼″ dia., ⅛″ deep,
tap ¼″-20

taper 40° included

drill 6.5mm, 1″ deep
counterbore ½″ dia., ¹⁄₃₂″ deep,
tap M8 × 1.25, ⅝″ deep

½

1¾

¹⁵⁄₁₆″ dia.

⑯ NUT

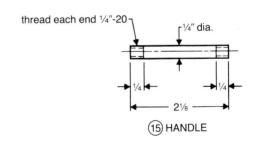

thread each end ¼″-20

¼″ dia.

¼

¼

2⅛

⑮ HANDLE

1

Construction & Use of the Lathe Carriage Stop

by D. E. Johnson, P.E.

Photos by Author

A solidly constructed and lockable carriage stop, used with inside measuring tools, greatly facilitates many common lathe operations. This is among the first items of tooling the beginner should consider making for a newly-acquired lathe.

The primary use of the carriage stop is to accurately locate various features such as fins, grooves, and shoulders to be formed along the length of turned work. Even internal grooves can be located simply and with confidence. Probably the most common lathe operation is some form of turning to a shoulder, and the carriage stop makes this work surprisingly fast and accurate with only a light cleaning cut required.

The carriage stop is handy for aligning the pivot of ball-turning fixtures with the center of the balls to be machined. Further, the carriage stop is almost indispensable for accurately advancing the vertical milling slide toward the milling cutter. Yes, many of us have the type of vertical slide designed to mount on the compound and use the compound feed screw for advance. After some experience with the compound-mounted-type milling attachment, it is my view that, for a couple of reasons, the compound is not really the best place to mount this gadget. This subject will be discussed further in a forthcoming article.

Back to the carriage stop. Here's another slightly different design with a couple of added features to complement those already shown in *HSM*. It's a good beginner's project in that construction will provide practice in most of the common lathe operations, such as turning, facing, drilling, single point threading, knurling, and a little simple milling that can be done without a milling attachment. Construction does not demand extreme accuracy, so disappointment should be minimized for the beginner. There are two opportunities to make things for press fits, but if you err on the loose side, just knurl the pressed-in part to expand it, or use a spring-pin retainer.

As shown in Photo 1, the major parts consist of a threaded spindle passing through a tapped hole in the body, a handwheel press fit to the spindle, a lock-wheel identical to the handwheel except it's threaded, a clamping plate, and a socket head cap screw.

Figure 2, a combination detail and assembly drawing, is dimensioned to fit the popular

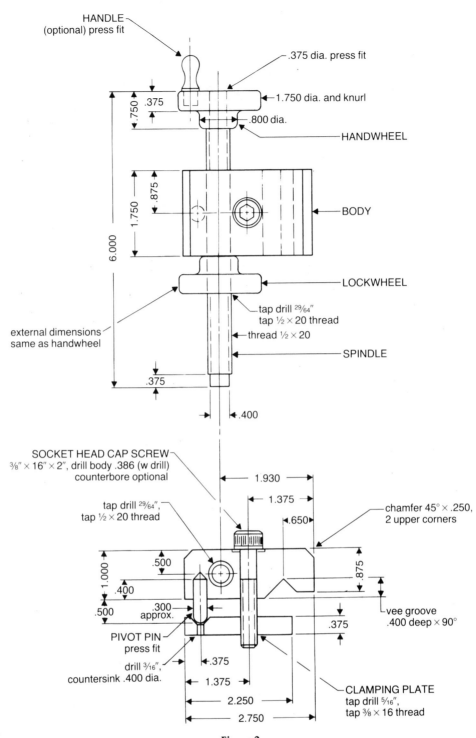

HANDLE
(optional) press fit

.375 dia. press fit

1.750 dia. and knurl

.800 dia.

HANDWHEEL

.750

.375

.875

1.750

BODY

6.000

LOCKWHEEL

external dimensions
same as handwheel

tap drill ²⁹⁄₆₄"
tap ½ × 20 thread

thread ½ × 20

SPINDLE

.375

.400

SOCKET HEAD CAP SCREW
³⁄₈" × 16" × 2", drill body .386 (w drill)
counterbore optional

1.930

tap drill ²⁹⁄₆₄",
tap ½ × 20 thread

1.375

.650

chamfer 45° × .250,
2 upper corners

1.000

.500

.400

.875

.500

.300
approx.

vee groove
.400 deep × 90°

PIVOT PIN
press fit

.375

.375

drill ³⁄₁₆",
countersink .400 dia.

1.375

2.250

CLAMPING PLATE
tap drill ⁵⁄₁₆",
tap ³⁄₈ × 16 thread

2.750

Figure 2

South Bend Model 10K lathe. These dimensions will require adjustment for other machines.

Most South Bend lathes (and others) have a cast boss on both headstock and tailstock sides of the carriage for contact with the carriage stop. The spindle is seen contacting one boss in Photo 3. This carriage stop is fully reversible; sometimes it is more convenient to reference the tailstock side of the carriage.

$$\frac{1 \text{ inch}}{.025''/\text{Rev}} = 40 \text{ TPI}$$

Now, if we use 20 TPI for our carriage stop spindle, it will move twice as far as the micrometer spindle per revolution; i.e., .050". It's convenient to remember this thing is "geared" twice as fast as a micrometer. The little handle on the handwheel helps keep track of the turns.

1 full turn = .050"
½ turn = .025"
¼ turn = .0125"

3

A quarter turn (i.e., .012″) is about as accurate as the spindle can be set simply by counting full and partial turns of the handle, but this method is sufficiently accurate for many jobs. For greater accuracy, I use various items of inside measuring equipment, such as feeler gages, ball and telescoping inside gages, and inside micrometers, measuring between the carriage stop spindle and the boss on the carriage. The objective usually is to set the end of the stop spindle in a new position an exact distance from the boss while the carriage remains locked in a known fixed position, such as after just finishing a cut.

For example, let's say a shoulder is to be formed on a bar exactly 1″ from the end. Lock the carriage and face the end of the bar. Set, say .995″ on a telescoping gage and adjust the carriage stop spindle this distance from the carriage boss. Lock the carriage stop, unlock the carriage and begin the cut toward the stop. When the required diameter is reached, back

off the carriage stop slightly and take the .005″ finish facing cut. This eliminates all the guesswork in stopping the tool when forming shoulders. Using the same technique, the vertical milling slide can be advanced toward the milling cutter for successive passes at whatever depth of cut is desired using a set of .005″-.050″ feeler gages to space between the spindle and boss.

A note of caution: Never run the carriage up to the carriage stop with the longitudinal power feed. Always disengage the power feed and manually advance the carriage snugly to the stop.

A Toolpost Problem Solver

by John Dean

Photos by Author

When using carbide bits, we may want more than normal toolpost rigidity, or we may want to use a larger or smaller bit, use a forming tool, or position the bit higher or lower than the toolpost rocker will permit, and the conventional tool holder just won't work. These two washers will "wash" away our troubles.

The lower washer is ¹⁄₁₆″ thick, 2½″ in diameter, and the center hole fits freely around the ¹⁵⁄₁₆″ toolpost.

The upper washer is ¼″ thick, 2½″ in diameter, and the hole made to fit sloppy enough on the toolpost to allow adequate amounts of tipping and tilting of the toolbit by adjusting the four ¼-20 bolts tapped through it.

The ³⁄₈ × ½ × 3½″ gib clamps the toolbit firmly in place.

Micrometer Attachment For Lathe Lead Screws

by John P. McDermott, Jr.

Photos by Author

I recently needed a ball-end handle for a project, but I had never taken the time to build a fixture for this kind of work. I remembered reading an article in *HSM* about a method of producing balls that didn't require any tooling, so I began to search through past issues of the magazine. I found what I was looking for in the September/October 1983 issue. Guy Lautard's two-part article, "Balls and Bull Noses," contains all the information that is required to turn out a simple ball handle. His method requires a lead screw micrometer on the lathe in order for the efficiency of the technique to be maximized. Unfortunately, my lathe wasn't equipped with such a device and, therefore, I was faced with the choice between making a ball-turning fixture from among the several designs available or designing and fabricating a lead screw micrometer attachment to fit my Atlas 12" lathe. I chose the latter course because I figured it would be more fun and if I was successful, I'd have an accessory that was more useful in general lathe operations.

I began the designing process by looking the lathe over to see what was the most practical and feasible approach. I first considered making an attachment to fit on the left end of one of the gear shafts that protrudes from the quick change gearbox. This would be possible by replacing one of the collar washers with the micrometer attachment and fastening it to a shaft by a roll pin, but the attachment would have to be awkwardly long in order to clear the change gearbox cover, which pivots open in a leftward direction. A better approach seemed to be to find a way to fasten the attachment to the right end of the lead screw. The only practical way to do this would be to design the attachment to replace the cone lock nut on the end of the lead screw, thus establishing one of the mandatory design elements. Another consideration was to design the accessory in such a way that there would be no protruding, rotating parts to catch clothing or hands when the half-nuts were closed and the lead screw turning under power.

The individual parts of the micrometer attachment are shown prior to assembly.

One of my principles is never go to the supply store if the materials on hand can be made to do the job, so the contents of my scrap box were taken into consideration. After discarding several approaches, I settled on the design shown in the drawings and photos. In use it has proven very satisfactory, and it can be dismounted easily after use or left in place permanently without interfering with any standard lathe function. Before going into details of construction I must make a disclaimer; I don't claim that the design is original. I am certain some other practitioner has used the same principle at some time for this or another lathe. However, none of the sources available to me makes reference to any

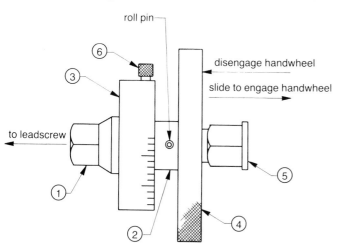

LEADSCREW MICROMETER ASSEMBLY.
(see part drawings for end and top views)

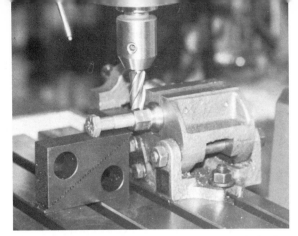

This setup is for milling hex flats for Part no. 1, the lead screw extension.

such attachment or feature. Undoubtedly, it could be adapted to other makes of machine.

I began construction by making the Lead Screw Extension (Part 1) from mild steel shafting. It's a simple and straightforward turning job, even if it looks a little complicated. The only tricky part might be machining the hex portion, but this too is simplified if all the turning, drilling, threading and tapping is completed before milling or filing the flats for the hex portion. I screwed a new ½-20 bolt tightly into its threaded hole, and the head of the bolt served nicely as a register surface for establishing the location of the hex flats. Part 1 should have smoothly finished surfaces for the sake of both function and appearance, although a mirror polish job is probably gilding the lily a bit.

Make the Micrometer Hub (Part 2) next. I used a piece of the mild steel shafting that I used for Part 1. Again, the construction is simple, but care was taken to assure correct dimensions and a good finish, because this part is the one on which the micrometer dial itself turns. The roll pin hole was drilled later in the construction.

Part 3 (the Micrometer Dial) is the most difficult and interesting part in the project. It will be a great deal easier to make if you

happen to have a dividing head and some stock of suitable dimensions on hand. Unfortunately, I had neither so I had to improvise. I wanted to use aluminum for this part in order to keep down the weight and turning forces on the lead screw. I didn't have any of the right size, and sources of supply in my area couldn't provide any, except in substantially larger quantities than I needed. I did have some ¼" scrap aluminum plate, so I decided to laminate two thicknesses together to get the size the design called for. I roughed out two circles a little larger than finished size and epoxied them together using *Duro* two-part cement. It is important that the surfaces laminated together be cleaned of dirt and oil and roughened with abrasive cloth to provide a base for a good bond.

After allowing ample time for the epoxy to cure, I located and drilled a ½" hole in the approximate center of the laminated disk and mounted it on a stub mandrel. (If you don't have such a mandrel, try making one like that described in Grant W. Wood's short article in November/December 1982 issue of *HSM*. It is quick and easy to make and works pretty well.) I turned the rough disk round, then faced both sides parallel. The outside dimension of the disk isn't critical, but it should be fairly close to that given in order to retain the maximum contact surface for the epoxy.

Next, I wrapped the circumference of the disk with a single layer of pressure-sensitive tape to prevent marring, mounted the assembly in the

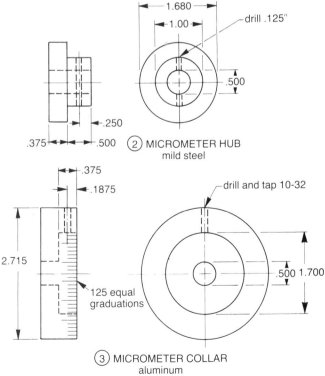

② MICROMETER HUB
mild steel

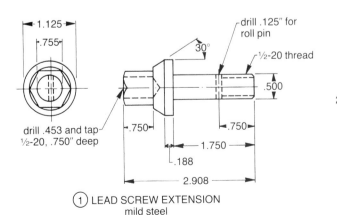

① LEAD SCREW EXTENSION
mild steel

③ MICROMETER COLLAR
aluminum

three-jaw chuck and bored out the recess to the depth indicated to receive the micrometer hub (Part 2). The recess was bored carefully, to make sure that the bottom was smooth and flat. Also, the sides had to be parallel to the axis of the bore and deep enough to take the full depth of the major diameter of Part 2. The diameter of the recess was machined so that the hub makes a smooth running fit within it, with no play. After removing the protective tape, the collar was remounted on the mandrel and any marks made by the chuck jaws were turned off. Polishing of this part was done at this point.

This is where I began to have *fun*! The lead screw on the Atlas lathe is 8-pitch, making it necessary to divide the micrometer collar into 125 equal divisions in order for the collar to read in thousandths and the lathe carriage to move one thousandth of an inch for each division the micrometer attachment is turned. As mentioned before, I don't have a dividing head, so another method of splitting the collar into 125 equal parts had to be found.

Turning to good ol' *HSM* again, I found a workable method in "Micrometer Dial for the Tailstock" by W. C. Grosjean in the July/August 1983 issue. This involves dividing a strip of paper, which in length is equal to the circumference of the lathe chuck, into the desired number of divisions. The paper strip is then fastened around the circumference of the chuck, a strip of thin metal is fastened to a convenient spot on the head stock to act as a witness mark, and the chuck is rotated by hand to each division on the paper in turn. As the chuck is moved to each division in its turn, a division mark is engraved onto the metal collar (held on a mandrel) by a sharp, pointed tool bit mounted on its side in the carriage tool post. The engraving is accomplished by first advancing the tool bit to touch the work, moving the carriage clear, advancing the tool bit .005"-.007", and then racking the carriage toward the headstock slowly until the division mark is as long as desired. A carriage stop on the lathe bed is most helpful. Sounds easy doesn't it? It is, except for marking that strip of paper into 125 equal divisions – that's a bear! The only way I know is to use a simple draftsman's divider, trial and error, and a lot of patience (the *really fun* part). This method of dividing a circumference works well, however, and yields a surprisingly accurate result.

Part 4 (the Handwheel) was fabricated next, using the same material as the micrometer

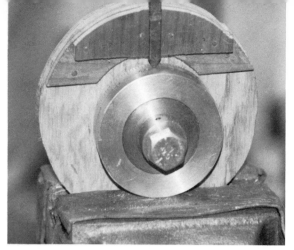

Stamping the numbers was accomplished with the use of a plywood jig.

Engraving the graduations on the micrometer collar was done with this lathe setup.

collar and the same laminating and machining techniques. The knurling was done on the circumference before removing the piece from the mandrel. Note: all machining of these epoxy laminated parts should be done slowly or, if it's available, coolant should be liberally applied to prevent excessive heat buildup resulting in subsequent delamination. The central hex hole in this part was filed out by hand. The filing can be made an easier task if the hex is marked out and the corners center-punched lightly before the ½" center hole is drilled. The filing of the hex hole was delayed until Part 5 was completed, since the two parts interact and must be fitted. The two parts should mate with an easy, sliding fit in all positions.

The Clutch Nut (Part 5) was made from mild steel bar stock and all turning, drilling, and threading were completed before the hex flats were machined. Again, the head of a machine bolt was used to establish register surfaces in the same manner used in the fabrication of Part 1. All surfaces on this Part were smoothly finished.

I made Part 6 (the Lock Screw) from drill rod and left it soft. A common Allen head setscrew of suitable size could be substituted. Part 7 (the Witness Mark Plate) was made from a scrap of aluminum angle, but any bent sheet metal would also serve. This part fastens to the lathe bed with one of the lead screw bearing bracket bolts and is left permanently in place.

The micrometer attachment is mounted, with the handwheel engaged. Sliding the handwheel toward the micrometer hub disengages it.

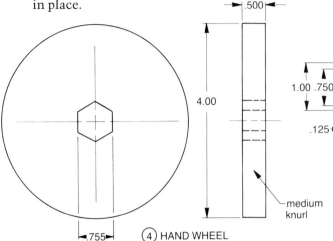

(4) HAND WHEEL
aluminum

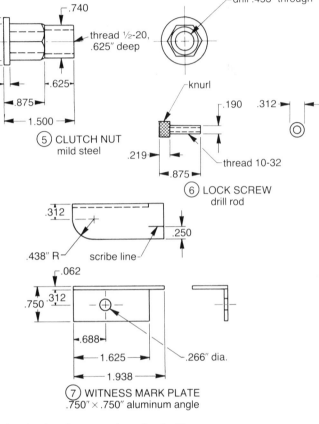

(5) CLUTCH NUT
mild steel

(6) LOCK SCREW
drill rod

(7) WITNESS MARK PLATE
.750" × .750" aluminum angle

The last operations before assembly and installation were to drill the hole for the roll pin and to number every fifth graduation on the micrometer dial. I cut a circle out of bond paper of a size to fit in the recess of the micrometer dial (Part 3) and made a ½" hole in the center as a first step toward drilling the roll pin hole. This paper shim serves to assure rotational clearance between Parts 2 and 3. I slipped the micrometer dial, including the shim, over the lead screw extension, and slid the micrometer hub on behind it. A spacer of suitable length went on behind the hub, and a ½-20 nut was screwed on to clamp everything together so the roll pin hole could be drilled through Parts 1 and 2 simultaneously. I dismantled this preliminary assembly after drilling and discarded the paper shim. The micrometer dial graduations were numbered with an ordinary number stamp set. I made a crude holding jig for the micrometer collar from scrap plywood to help make the numbering more uniform.

The Parts were assembled as a unit in the following order: 1, 3, 2, roll pin, 4, and 5. The last should be snugged up firmly. The lock screw was screwed into its hole in the micrometer dial, and the attachment was mounted by replacing the lead screw cone lock nut with the completed attachment. Accuracy was checked by positioning a dial indicator on the lathe bed in contact with the carriage. I

checked to be sure that the half-nuts were closed and the quick change gearbox levers were disengaged. Rotating the lead screw with the handwheel caused the dial indicator needle to move .001" for each graduation passed on the micrometer dial, in either direction.

My first attempt to make a ball-end handle using Guy Lautard's method was very successful. With the ball stock mounted in the three-jaw chuck, the lathe running, and the lead screw stationary, I slid the handwheel of the attachment to the right to engage the clutch nut. Now the lead screw could be turned incrementally to follow Lautard's tables and directions with ease. I have subsequently found the attachment most useful in other lathe operations. If you don't already have such a device for your lathe, it's worth the time and trouble to make one.

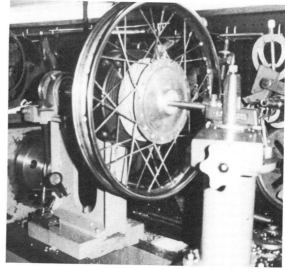

1

2

Double the Capacity of Your Lathe

by J.O. Barbour, Jr.

Photos by Author

The raised headstock for my 10″ Atlas lathe was not a planned addition – it just happened.

Several years ago when diesel automobiles were becoming quite popular, I decided I needed one. After looking at sticker prices, I decided I really didn't need one after all, but it might be fun to build one.

To build a diesel car, the number one priority is a diesel engine – so I found a beautiful surplus four-cylinder 36 horsepower diesel engine. It had been removed from a marine generator unit. Now what? The engine connects to the transmission – right – so back to the salvage yard and then home with a great five-speed syncro-mesh manual transmission with overdrive, complete with flywheel and clutch assembly.

So how do you connect the diesel engine to the transmission? You make an adapter housing. Question? How do you machine a 12¾″ OD steel tube with a 16″ OD flange welded on one end, and an internal flange welded inside the other end, on a 10″ swing Atlas lathe? You get off your duff and make a raised headstock!

As you can see in Photo 1, it is of very simple but sturdy construction. The main support is a

section of 35 lb. 10″ I-beam 8″ long with a section removed from its center to lighten it and admit the hold-down bolt. A ¼″ × 2½″ plate is welded on each end for greater rigidity.

Four pieces of 2″ × 2″ × ⅜″ angle 1¾″ long are welded to the top flange of the beam and drilled and tapped for ⅜″ setscrews for cross adjustment of the spindle bearings. The bottom flange of the beam is step-machined on a milling machine to center on the lathe bed.

The bearings are standard 1½″ industrial ball bearing pillow blocks, bolted to the top flange of the beam. The spindle is machined from a scrap piece of 2″ diameter stainless steel shafting and threaded on one end for a threaded chuck. The opposite end is machined and keyway milled to accommodate a "V" pulley.

The drive shaft is made from a short scrap of crs shaft, machined with a number three Morse taper on one end to fit the Atlas headstock with a "V" pulley fitted and keyed to the opposite end.

The compound rest is raised to its proper position by welding flanges on a section of 2″ extra heavy pipe and machining to fit.

The "V" belt was fitted, a test bar chucked, a

97

cut taken, a few adjustments made before a final check with a dial indicator and presto – we were all set to machine the adapter or anything else up to 24″ in diameter.

The transmission housing was then machined to size, and the diesel car project was back on schedule. I later made risers of 6″ H-beam to support the Atlas tailstock and steady rest.

Last year I sold the Atlas and purchased a 12″ swing lathe. To fit the unit to the new 12″ lathe, I made the adapter plate you see in Photo 2. It was step-milled from 2″ thick steel plate to fit the wider bed of the 12″ lathe and increased the swing on the new lathe to 28″.

A new riser for the compound rest on the 12″ lathe was made from 3″ extra heavy pipe with ½″ thick flanges welded on each end and machined. Risers made from 8″ H-beam for the tailstock and steady rest of the 12″ lathe have also been completed and are plainly shown in Photo 3.

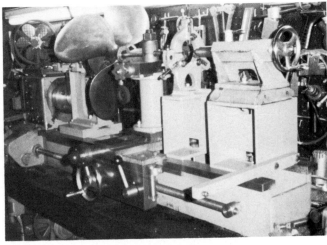

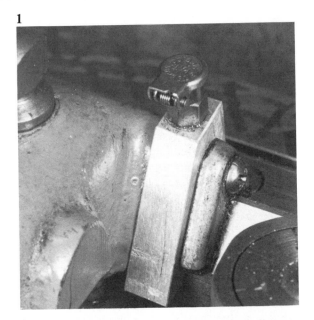

3

The raised headstock can be set up for turning and boring large diameters in just a few minutes and is a very useful attachment.

The diesel car is alive and well and averages approximately 50 miles per gallon.

Lathe Carriage Oiler

by N. H. Bennett

Photos by Author

1

Carriage oilers on a lathe are necessary to wipe off the ways as the carriage moves. They also wipe off most of the oil placed on the bed if the carriage isn't internally oiled. The oiler shown in Photo 1 will admit oil to the ways behind the wiper. The material can be aluminum, brass or plastic 5/16″ thick. The vee should match the way closely and, as in Photo 2, a small relief is cut or filed at the top of the vee to allow oil to pass into the carriage relief. The mounting hole is also drilled oversize to allow oil to pass around it. The tap drill for the oiler's ¼-28 threads is drilled through the vee.

A further note about lathe beds. When lapping, sanding or grinding on a lathe, always cover the bed. I use a layer of aluminum foil covered with paper towels. When finished, carefully remove and dispose of. Grinding or sanding grit left on the bed will imbed in the carriage and lap the bed every time the carriage is moved.

2

1

2

Build Your Own Faceplate

by Marlyn Hadley

Photos by Author

It became apparent to me, soon after I started making steam models, that in the process of making eccentrics in a four-jaw chuck there is a lot of waste time involved. To somehow cut down on wasted time, I designed and built a face plate, shown in Photo 1, which is capable of holding and offsetting without unclamping the workpiece. I made the adjustable part with a V to clamp round pieces and by reversing it, I can clamp pieces on the flat end. With an angle plate bolted to the face, the machining of the cylinder fit on the bed plate of a Stuart #9 is easy. A regular face plate with an angle plate can do this, but with this special plate, the adjustments take so much less time that it is worth the time spent making it (Photo 2). The clamping cap screws can be loosened just enough so that the block can be tapped into alignment with a plastic hammer. In offsetting

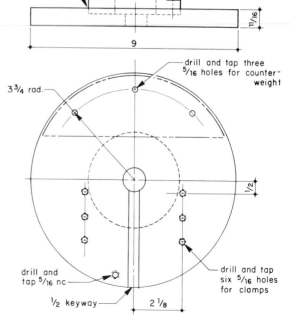

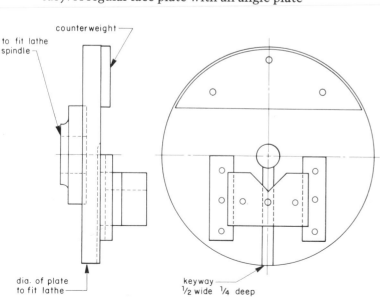

FACE PLATE—GENERAL VIEW

FACE PLATE

99

3

the block in machining an eccentric, I use a dial indicator with a one-inch travel to set the desired offset very accurately.

The drawing shows the general view but without some dimensions which must fit your lathe. Some of the other dimensions are not given. I am sure most model makers are like me in that they have their own ideas and usually make some changes to fit their own needs. The spindle adapter flange must be machined to fit the spindle nose on your lathe. As my lathe will swing 11", with 2¼"-8 thread

on the spindle nose, I made the large plate 9" in diameter. To turn this large plate on a lathe with only a 6" four-jaw chuck was a challenge. There are two ways that this can be done without too much trouble. One way is to tack-weld a piece on the plate of a size that the chuck can clamp. The other way is to drill and tap holes in the plate so that it can be clamped with cap screws to a face plate.

I made my plate from a piece ¾" thick. The first side is machined to fit the flange of the spindle adapter. The second side is machined after the adapter and plate are bolted together with 5-16 socket head cap screws.

One thing I could not do was to machine the keyslot in the plate, so I had to hire this done. If you do the same, make sure they understand that this keyslot must be centered with the plate. Mine was about ¹⁄₃₂" off, and this meant that I had to remachine my V-slot to center it again.

I have shown the dimensions of the movable block as it has proved to be very satisfactory for me. I used ⁵⁄₁₆" threaded rods as studs, which I found more versatile than cap screws. A piece of keystock is fastened in the slot in back of the block as a guide key.

The counterbalance is made from ½" plate cut with an oxy-acetylene torch and ground on the edges. It was just a guess, but it is very close to the right amount of weight. The counter balance could be made so that weight could be added or subtracted as necessary, but mine has worked so well that I have not changed it. The angle plate mentioned earlier is a 3" length of ½" x 3" x 4" angle, carefully machined square (Photo 3). It is drilled to be exactly even with the flat end of the block when bolted in place.

For safety, I drilled and tapped for a small cap screw, to prevent the block from flying out just in case I forgot to tighten the clamping screws before I turned the lathe. I have been pleasantly surprised to find that clamping a piece in the V can be held with two 5-16 studs and not move

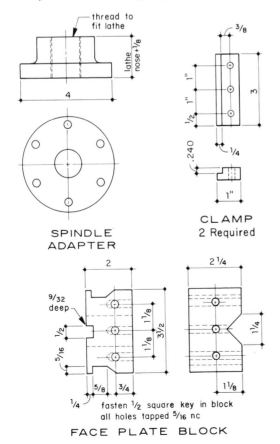

SPINDLE
ADAPTER

CLAMP
2 Required

fasten ½ square key in block
all holes tapped ⁵⁄₁₆ nc

FACE PLATE BLOCK

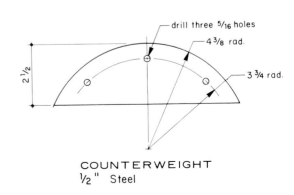

COUNTERWEIGHT
½" Steel

except under extraordinary circumstances. It is now fun to machine eccentrics, as I clamp a piece of shafting in the V of the block, turn the outside to size, carefully move the block the correct distance, finish the bore and hub and part off the finished part.

When I machine the valve face on a cylinder, I clamp the cylinder on end on the flat end of the movable block, after boring and facing the usual way, by using a stud through the bore (Figure 4, Photo 5).

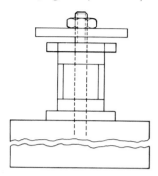

Figure 4

5

In machining the bore on small pillow blocks I use in my models, I clamp them as shown below.

By setting the block the proper distance from center (Figure 6), any number of pieces can be faced and bored at exactly the same height. The

7

above clamping holds if you are careful not to exert too much pressure when drilling.

However, I sometimes bolt small stops behind the bearing after I set up the first piece. Then it is very quick to set up the subsequent pieces (Photo 7).

I have machined the crank pin holes in a set of locomotive drivers on this setup by clamping a shaft in the V, then machining it so it fit the bore of the wheels with the end threaded with a NF thread to clamp the wheel. By offsetting the block the proper amount and using studs through the spokes to keep the wheel from turning, the crank pin holes can be machined very accurately (Figure 8).

Machining eccentrics is fun with this setup. I clamp a short piece of shafting in the V with enough projecting past the block to make one or two eccentrics and turn the outside of the eccentrics to size. I then carefully move the block (shaft and all) the proper distance. Then I can turn the hub, bore and part off my

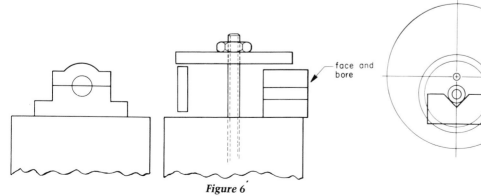

face and bore

Figure 6

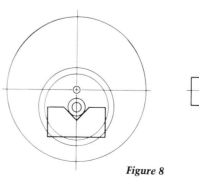

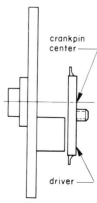

crankpin center

driver

Figure 8

block offset to bore crankpin hole

101

completed eccentric (Figure 9). As the shaft has not moved clamped in the V, eccentrics are quick and easy to machine.

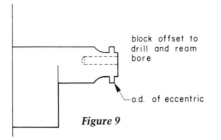

block offset to drill and ream bore

o.d. of eccentric

Figure 9

I am interested in stationary steam engines and now have built over thirty-five different replica models showing the development of the

stationary steam engines from 1629. Over half my models were made from illustrations in old books or from photos. I am now working on a Westinghouse, a triple expansion, a scotch yoke and others. I enjoy taking a picture, drawing it to proportion, making the patterns, making my own brass and aluminum castings, machining it, and then watching it run.

I am sure those who take time to make this attachment will find it most useful, for the more I used it the more use I found for it. This face plate has made many awkward jobs easy and I do not know how I would do without it now.

Spindle Stop for a 10-K

by N. H. Bennett

Photos by Author

When making a production run, a stop for work placed in the chuck will save a lot of time. The bushing (Photo 1) is made from 1″ diameter aluminum 1½″ long turned down to .860″ diameter × ⅝″ long. A ⅜″ hole is drilled and reamed through the center. The stop is placed in the spindle and the location for the bushing set screw is scribed. A ¼-20 hole is drilled and tapped here and ½″ from the rear end to lock the rod. A ¼-20 setscrew is beveled 45° on the socket end and cut off ¼″ long.

The bushing (Photo 2) is then placed in the spindle and the beveled setscrew is backed out to lock the bushing in place. A ¼″ flat is milled or draw filed on a ⅜″ rod 16″ long. The setscrew that locks the rod is flattened on the end to prevent marring.

Note: The hole in the spindle is an existing hole. The gear cover will need a small notch to clear the hex wrench.

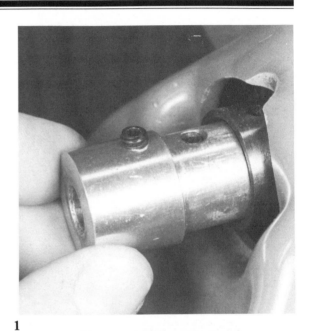

1

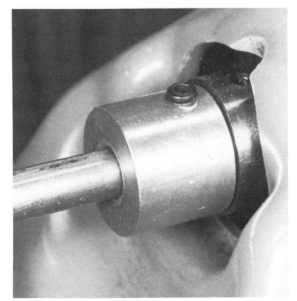

2

DRILL PRESS
ACCESSORIES

1 *The tapping attachment in use on the author's drill press.*

A Drill Press Tapping Tool

by Harold Mason

Photos by Author

One day, I'm tapping a ½" diameter deep hole in a block of steel and using a square to check that the tap stays vertical. It's looking great and I pat myself on the back as I remove the job from the vise to check the side view. GULP! Turning the workpiece through 90° I see the tap leaning drunkenly to one side...Know the feeling?

Now, if you're not like me – a relative beginner in machinist's work – or you don't make mistakes anyway, I'd turn to another article or go out and weed the garden at this point.

The tool shown in use in Photo 1 is intended to make the tapping of holes square with surfaces as easy as pie. I put only basic dimensions on the drawing (Figure 2) because machinists will want to make changes, improvements or just customize their tapper

to suit their drill press and themselves. Photo 3 shows the tapper's component parts (with a tap and suitable hexagon wrench for scale).

Apart from guaranteeing squareness, this idea has two other major advantages: it provides a positive drive with extra leverage to spin big taps deep into the workpiece, and it uses an existing machine so you don't have to build a tapping column.

Why don't I put the tap right into the drill chuck and use a C-wrench on the chuck key holes? The cutting forces on large taps are pretty heavy and taps are hardened and ground to a high finish. To prevent the tap from slipping under load I'd risk damaging the chuck by over-tightening, and you can bet there'd still be some slipping.

Using the tapper goes like this:
1) Remove the spindle drive belt from the drill press.
2) With all the other parts assembled – except for one grub screw – push the tap shank into the body till you see the square in the empty screw hole.
3) Position the flats, put in the grub screw and tighten, "feeling" with the hex wrench till the tips are bearing on the flats.
4) Fully tighten the grub screws and offer the tapper up to the drill chuck.
5) Tighten the chuck with the chuck key.
6) Bringing the tap down with the feed handle, locate in the workpiece and turn until the tap bites.
7) Carry on tapping; the feed handle will return on its own on withdrawal. (If you're nervous, hold onto it.)

Dead easy! Agreed? And you don't have to worry about your verticals any more. The grub screws I used are high tensile steel, but all other parts are CRS. I modified the "W" points so that they'd be kinder to the flats on my taps.

When ruminating on this idea it seemed to me there were three vital points to watch: 1) The fit between the body and collar (so the collar doesn't slop around); 2) tap the socket concentric with the shank (so the tap is in line with the spindle axis); and 3) the shank should be dead parallel (so the body doesn't wobble in the drill chuck). The way to achieve this without going crazy is simple. If you can't rely on the accuracy of your three-jaw SC chuck, shim the jaws, or use a four-jaw independent, but in both cases use a dial test indicator to set the work running true. Don't just drill the ¾" hole in the collar – bore or ream it to a good

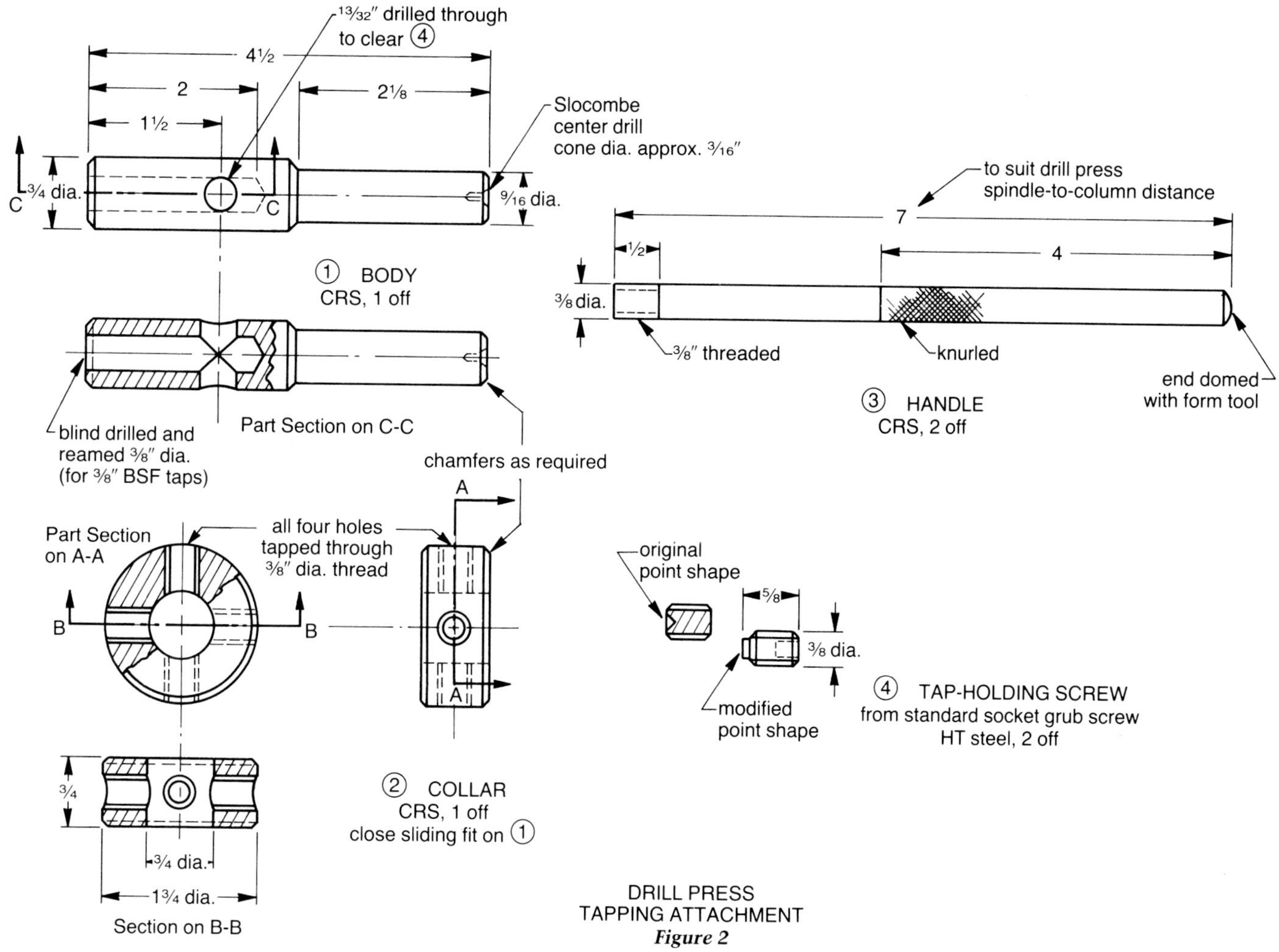
13⁄32″ drilled through to clear ④
4½
2
2⅛
1½
Slocombe center drill cone dia. approx. 3⁄16″
¾ dia.
9⁄16 dia.
C
C
① BODY
CRS, 1 off
blind drilled and reamed ⅜″ dia. (for ⅜″ BSF taps)
Part Section on C-C
chamfers as required
to suit drill press spindle-to-column distance
7
½
4
⅜ dia.
⅜″ threaded
knurled
end domed with form tool
③ HANDLE
CRS, 2 off
Part Section on A-A
all four holes tapped through ⅜″ dia. thread
A
A
B
B
original point shape
⅝
⅜ dia.
modified point shape
④ TAP-HOLDING SCREW
from standard socket grub screw
HT steel, 2 off
¾
¾ dia.
1¾ dia.
Section on B-B
② COLLAR
CRS, 1 off
close sliding fit on ①

DRILL PRESS
TAPPING ATTACHMENT
Figure 2

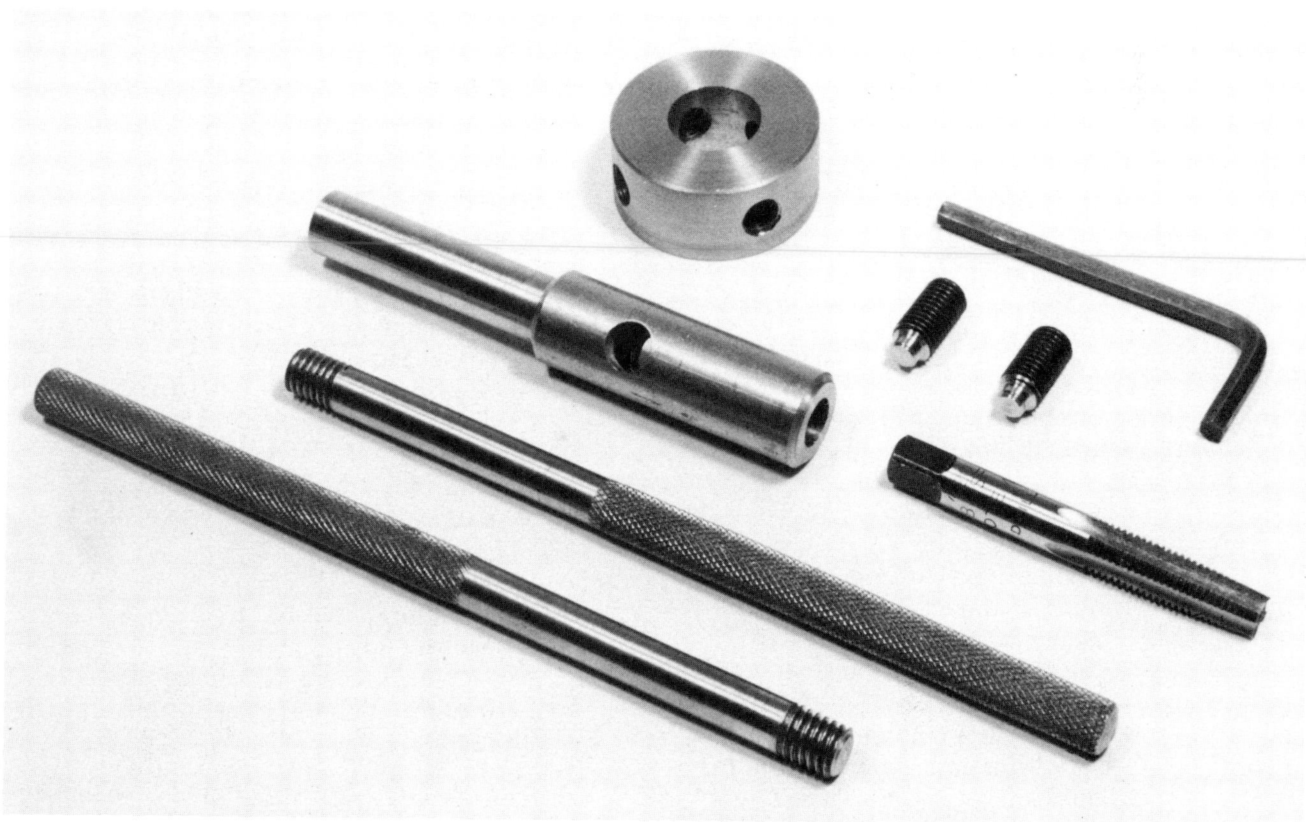

3 ***The components ready for assembly.***

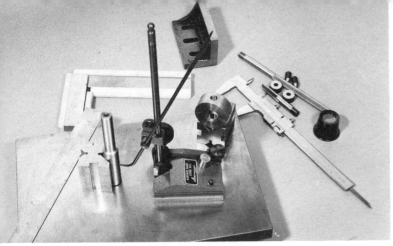

4 *Marking out the body for cross drilling using a vee block and surface gauge.*

sliding fit on the body. If you want to be really picky with the body, chuck a 6½" length of the ¾" CRS, set it true as above, and carry out all operations (except chamfer on the shank end) at one setting.

This is the sequence of machining operations I used:

1. Body
- Chuck a length of ¾" CRS in the three-jaw SC.
- Face and center drill to the drawing.
- Support on the tailstock center and turn the ⁹/₁₆" diameter shank 2⅛" long.
- Chamfer the end and shoulder.
- Reverse in the chuck and center drill.
- Drill ³/₁₆" to 2" depth.
- Open up with ²³/₆₄" or 9mm drill and finish out with a sharp ⅜" drill or ⅜" reamer.
- Chamfer the outside corner.
- Remove to the surface plate and scribe a line 1½" from the socket end (Photo 4).
- Set up in the machine vise and drill through at ¹³/₃₂" diameter (see notes on cross drilling).
- Deburr inside and out, taking care not to damage the bore.

2. Collar
(Mine was made from a ⅞" length of 1¾" diameter CRS, but you could part one off the end of a bar.)
- Set up in the three-jaw SC chuck, face off and center drill.
- Start drilling with ³/₁₆" diameter and work up in three or four stages to ⁴⁷/₆₄" or 18.5mm drill.
- Finish out with a ¾" reamer or bore out to a close sliding fit on 1.
- Remove from the chuck, tap onto a tight ¾" stub arbor. Chuck on the arbor shank.
- Skim the outer diameter to finish; chamfer the outside corners.

106

- Strip from the arbor and set upright on a vee block as in Photo 5.
- Scribe the center lines at right angles as in the notes on cross drilling.
- Lay the collar flat on the surface plate and scribe the center lines around the outside diameter. If you use Frank McLean's method you don't need to center-pop.

5 *Marking out the collar for drilling using a square and surface gauge.*

- Set up and cross drill two pairs of tapping size holes as in Figure 2.
- Remove from the drill vise and tap the holes ⅜" BSF or similar.
- Deburr inside and out. Go easy with the files and *don't* check the ¾" bore with your fingers!

3. Handle
Two pieces ⅜" diameter CRS, 7⅛" long (or to suit *your* drill press).
- Figure 2 is mainly self-explanatory. Each machinist will have his own favorite handle shape.
- Thread one end for ½" length (Photo 6). (Make sure it clears the bore when screwed in tightly.)
- Knurl the other end for 4" length.
- Dome the knurled end with a form tool (Photo 7).

4. Tap Holding Screws
- 2 off HT steel.
- Suitable hexagon socket grub screws with points modified as in Figure 2 and Photo 3.

You do need to take care with the cross drilling because the screws must engage the tap without binding in the body clearance holes. In

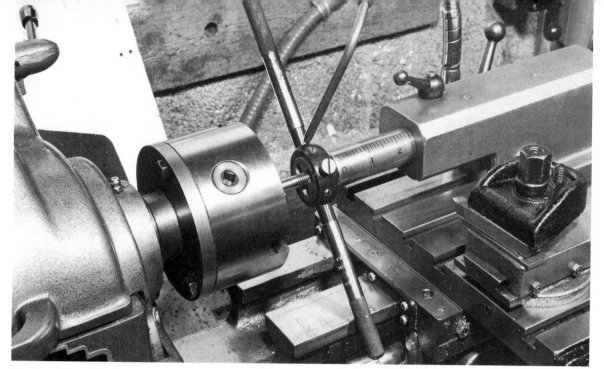

6 *Threading the end of the handle using a dieholder supported by the tailstock barrel with the center removed. (Note the form tool in the toolpost to right.)*

July/August 1983 *HSM* (page 60) Frank McLean's article on cross drilling procedures tells you all you need to know, including neat marking-out methods.

On a bigger lathe, perhaps a traveling dieholder would be better than a loose diestock, but my lathe's a 7″ swing and I'm not risking scoring the no. 2 Morse taper socket, thank you! I use the form tool shown in Photos 6 and 7, also, for rounding the ends of holding-down studs for the miller and drill. I make these from lengths of 10mm studding. They look smart and don't snag the fingers.

Readers will have noticed the main limitation of this design – that it's made for one tap shank size only. I've found, in practice, that it will take several taps with similar shank diameters, but I know you people out there will come up with good ideas for boring out the socket and making sleeves to suit other taps or making a range of bodies, each bored for a separate tap size. A set of these would look fine in a polished block of hardwood.

For those of you who would prefer slots milled down the length of the socket instead of clearance holes – to increase the range of shank lengths you could use – remember, you'll need a clamping screw through the collar onto the body. The grub screws only bear onto the tap square, *not* onto the body (see Figure 2).

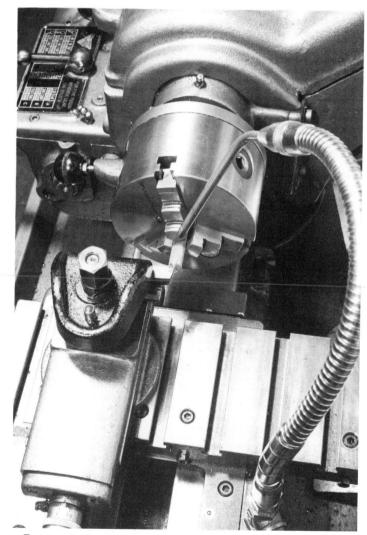

7 *Turning the domed end on the handle using a form tool ground from an HSS toolbit.*

Column Storage Box for a Drill Press

by W. B. Vaughan

Photos by Author

Put the waste space under your drill press table to use with this column storage box. The spill-proof drawer holds drills and accessories while the top provides a shelf for tools or a handy place to put a catch pan for chips and cutting oil.

The top and bottom are identical pieces of 1" x 12" pine shelving. Cut the outside pattern with a sabre or band saw. With the pieces clamped in alignment, drill a ¹⁄₁₆" pilot hole through both at one time to locate the centers of the holes for the drill press column. It's

important that the holes in the two pieces be aligned accurately. The holes for the column itself can be cut with a hole saw mounted in the drill press, or with a sabre saw and scroll blade.

Rout the rabbets in the side pieces with a router, dado head, or with a router bit chucked in the drill press. Use the maximum drill press speed for routing.

After cutting the rear filler piece, assemble the case with glue and #6-1½" flat head wood screws or box nails. The drawer panels are 1" x 4" pine, planed or ripped to ⅜" thickness. Drill pilot holes and counter sink the side panels for #4-⅝" screws which will hold the side guide rails after assembly. Rout again in each piece for the ¼" plywood bottom, as shown, and rabbets on the two side pieces for assembly to the front and end pieces. Assemble the drawer panels with glue and brads. Attach the drawer front, a 1" x 6" x 12" piece, to the drawer box with #8-1" wood screws, and attach the side guide rails.

A piece of plastic laminate or aluminum sheet glued to the top of the case makes an oil-proof cover for the storage box. The rest of the box

Materials List:
2 pcs 6 × 12 pine ① ②
2 pcs. 11¼ × 17" pine ③ ④
1 pc. ¾ × ¾ × 10½ pine ⑤
1 pc. 3¾ × 10½ pine ⑥
2 – ¼-20 bolts 5½"
2 – ¼-20 wing nuts
4 – ¼ washers

DRAWER
2 pcs. 11⅛ × 3½ × ⅜
2 pcs. 10¼ × 3½ × ⅜
2 pcs. 11⅛ × ¹¹⁄₁₆ × ⅜
1 pc. ¼" ply. 10⅝ × 11½
1 pc. 1 × 6 × 12
¼" tee nut
¼" x 1½" flat head screw

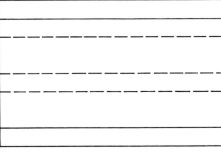

NOTE 1 — diameter to suit — typ. 2¾

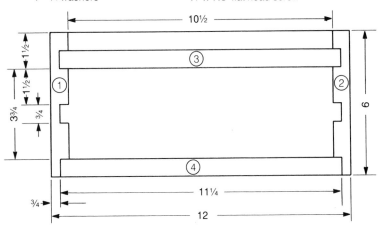

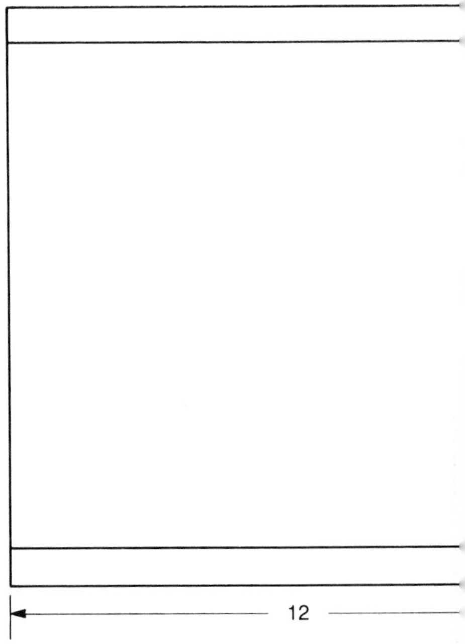

can easily be finished with two coats of linseed oil or penetrating resin finish.

Drill a 1/4" hole in the top as shown and counter sink for a 1/4-20, 1½" long flathead machine screw. This screw attaches to the drawer stop, which is made from a 3/4" length of 3/4" diameter hardwood dowel. Drill a 5/16" hole through the center of the dowel and hammer a 1/4-20 Tee nut into one end. With the drawer inserted part-way, screw the drawer stop into the flathead machine screw inserted through the top of the box.

The drill press head and table will have to be removed to install the box on the column of the drill press. The head is heavy and awkward, so get help in removing it.

Mount the box at a level below the lowest point you usually use for your drill press table. If the full depth of the column is needed for a big job, the storage box can be swung behind the drill press column in the same manner as the drill press table.

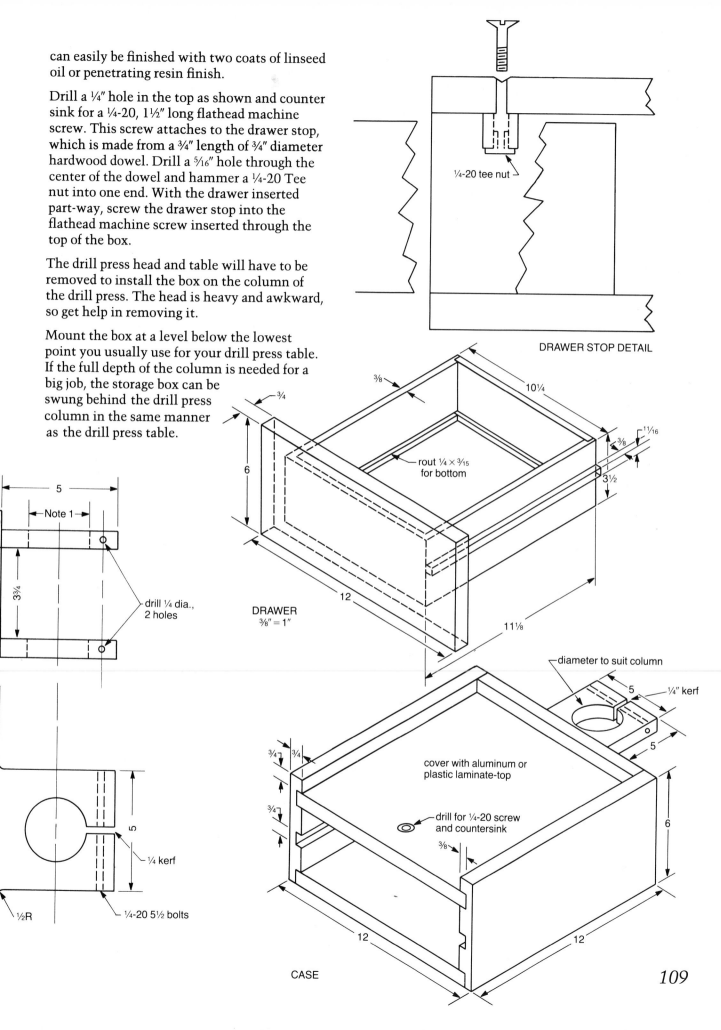

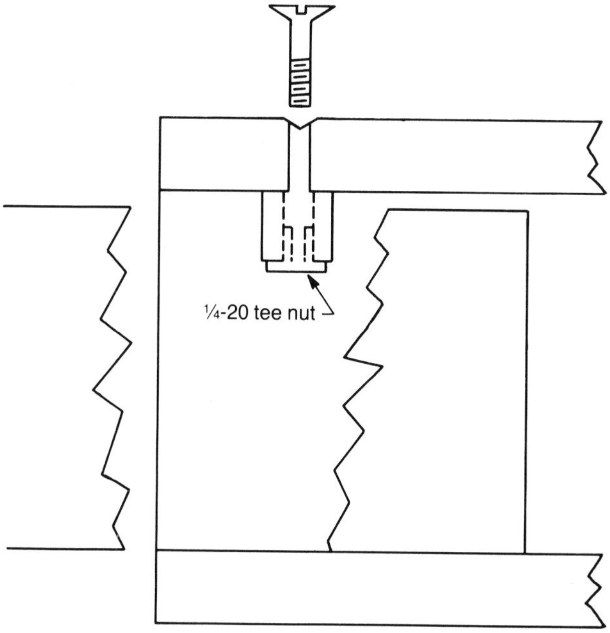
1/4-20 tee nut

DRAWER STOP DETAIL

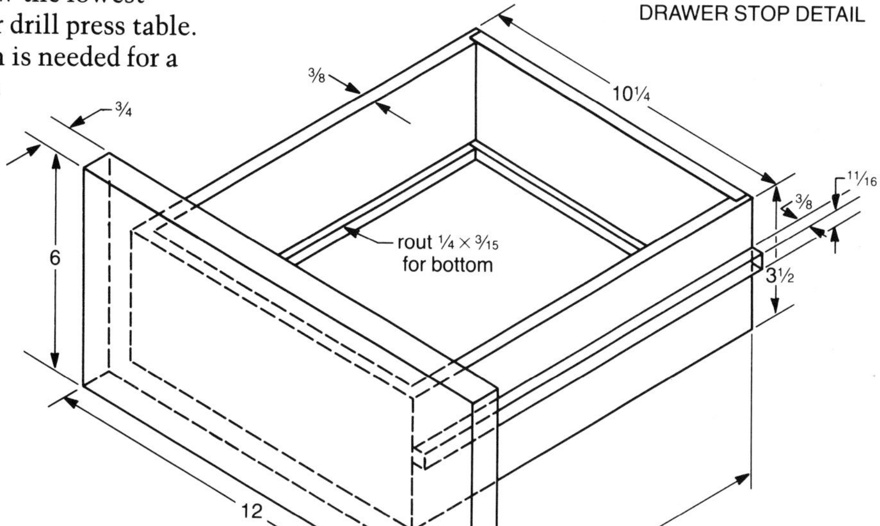
3/8
3/4
10¼
11/16
3/8
rout 1/4 × 3/15
for bottom
6
3½
12
11⅛

DRAWER
3/8" = 1"

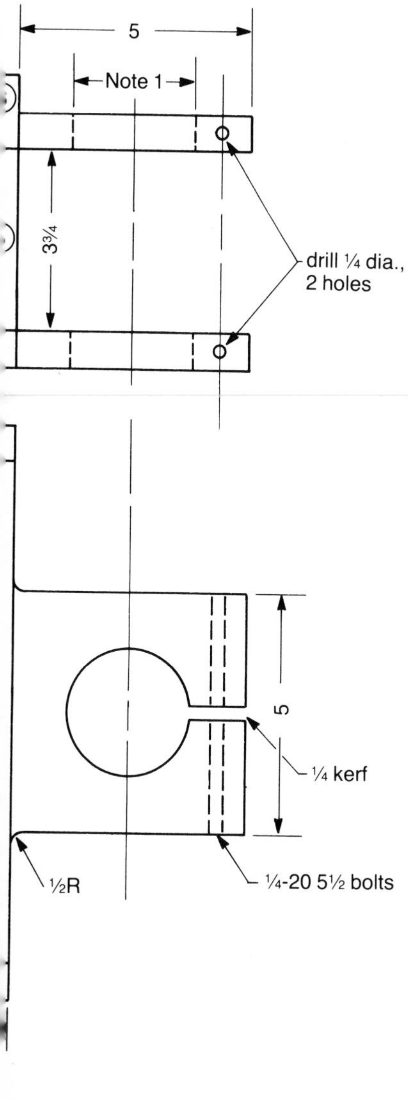
5
Note 1
3¾
drill 1/4 dia.,
2 holes
5
1/4 kerf
½R
1/4-20 5½ bolts

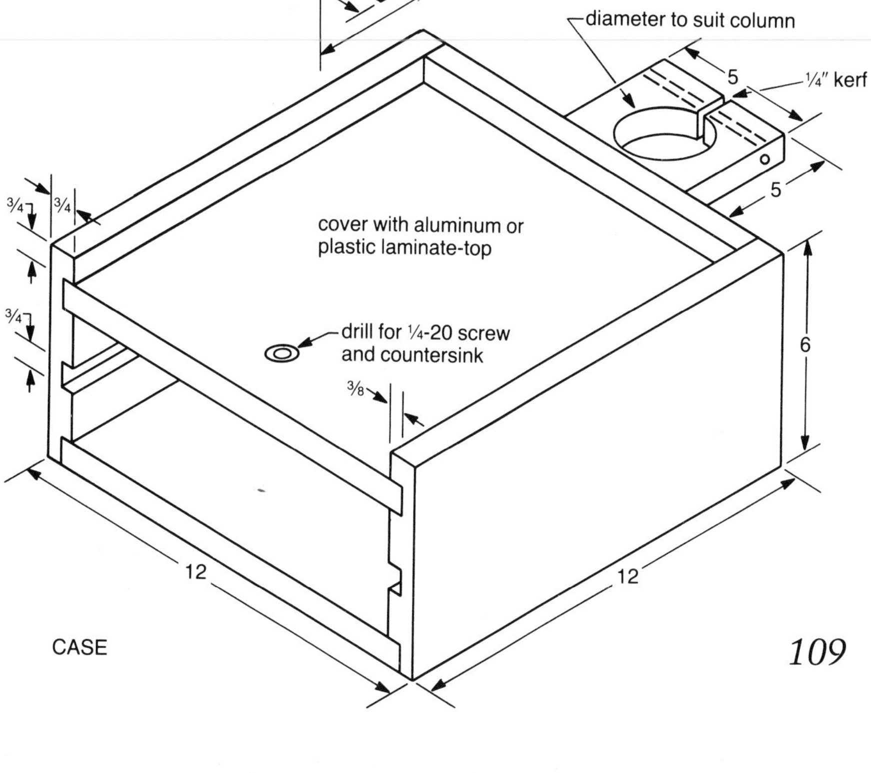
diameter to suit column
5
1/4" kerf
5
3/4
3/4
3/4
cover with aluminum or
plastic laminate-top
drill for 1/4-20 screw
and countersink
3/8
6
12
12

CASE

Five-layer "Lazy Susan" Drill Index

by John Gascoyne

Photos by Author

This "Lazy Susan" Drill Index (Figure 1 and Photographs 2 and 3) has proven itself as a reliable alternative to other drill storage systems for sixteen years. It offers several advantages over other systems and, from a practical standpoint, requires little precious shop space.

During the past sixteen years, this Drill Index has protected 113 drills (all of the number drills, from 1-60; all of the letter drills, from A-Z, with the exception of E and Y; and all of the decimal drills, from ³⁄₆₄" through ½"). Drill E was omitted because it is the same size as the ¼" drill. A Y drill was omitted by accident, but has never been missed.

The drills are stored in a sequential size manner rather than by whether they are number, letter, or decimal size. The smaller drills begin at the top, with number 60 (.040"), and go round-and-round until the last and largest one (½") is reached on the last of the five layers. Vertical storage of the drills makes them easy to remove and to replace. It gives an added bonus in that light tends to reflect from their business ends. Dull drills are more easily spotted. Drill identification is marked in front (outboard) of each hole, on the shelf in which the drill sits.

I constructed the five-layer, rotating Drill Index during 1968 and installed it upon a bench top. It has been rotated an untold number of times, and is in almost daily use as a central drill source for the shop. Early in 1984, my shop acquired an additional lathe. I decided that the most suitable location for the new lathe would require moving the Drill Index from its bench-top location. However, no other bench top seemed appropriate to locations of the various drill presses, so the Drill Index was given its own stand. The stand (a base with one post and a smaller inside telescoping post) was obtained from a local retail electronics (chain) store. It is stocked by them for use as a microphone stand. The inner, telescoping post was removed because it is unnecessary for this project.

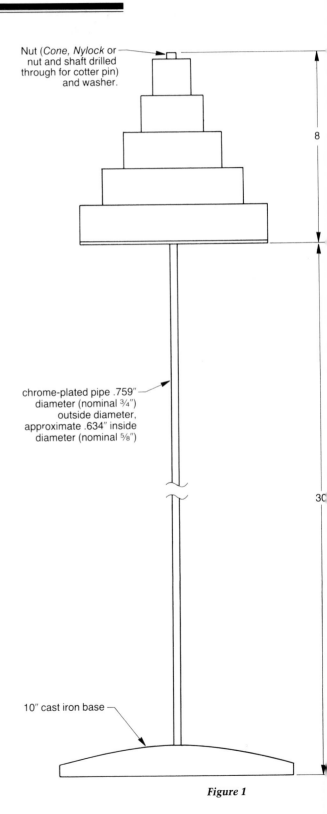

Nut (*Cone, Nylock* or nut and shaft drilled through for cotter pin) and washer.

8

chrome-plated pipe .759" diameter (nominal ¾") outside diameter, approximate .634" inside diameter (nominal ⅝")

30

10" cast iron base

Figure 1

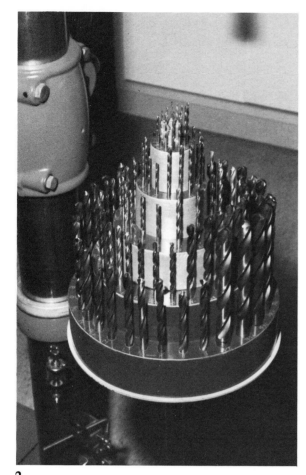

2

ELEMENTS OF CONSTRUCTION (Figure 4)
The Layers

The five round "layers" of the Drill Index were made from a two-by-ten. Clear Douglas fir is nice! Since lumber sizes are "nominal" (i.e., less), the so-called 10″ allowed for the required 8″ bottom layer. The so-called 2″ provided all layers with a thickness approximating 1½″.

The whole five-layer "cake" sits on a ⅛″ thick by 8″ diameter steel plate. Other thicknesses could be used (e.g., ³⁄₁₆″, ¼″). Aluminum or brass could be substituted for steel. Each of the five layers had a plastic laminate applied (a nicety, but not required). A central clearance hole was drilled through each of the five layers and the final steel plate in order to allow acceptance of a long rod threaded ⅜-16. The rod holds the five layers and the plate together. They are not otherwise joined by gluing or other means, and this permits rotation of individual layers during the assembly stage. Beginning and terminal size on each layer can be logically placed with those of the layers above and below.

Drill Storage Hole Size and Spacing

Each layer is drilled for the sizes and quantity of drills it is intended to store in its "shelf"

3

area (Figure 4). Since the drills should be easy to remove and replace, but not lean, each hole should be drilled a size or two over the size of the drill it will store.

Hole spacing is an important consideration for appearance, ease of grasping a drill for removal and replacing it in its hole, and providing the necessary holes without running out of space. Toward this end, a uniform space may be tentatively selected for each layer. For example, roughly ³⁄₁₆″ for the smaller drills on the top layer, ⅜″-⁷⁄₁₆″ for the No. 2 layer from the top, ⅝″ for No. 3 and No. 4 layers, and perhaps ⅝″-1¹⁄₁₆″ for the bottom layer. Once this tentative spacing is selected, the actual center of the proposed hole is located either by reference to the center of a previous hole plus

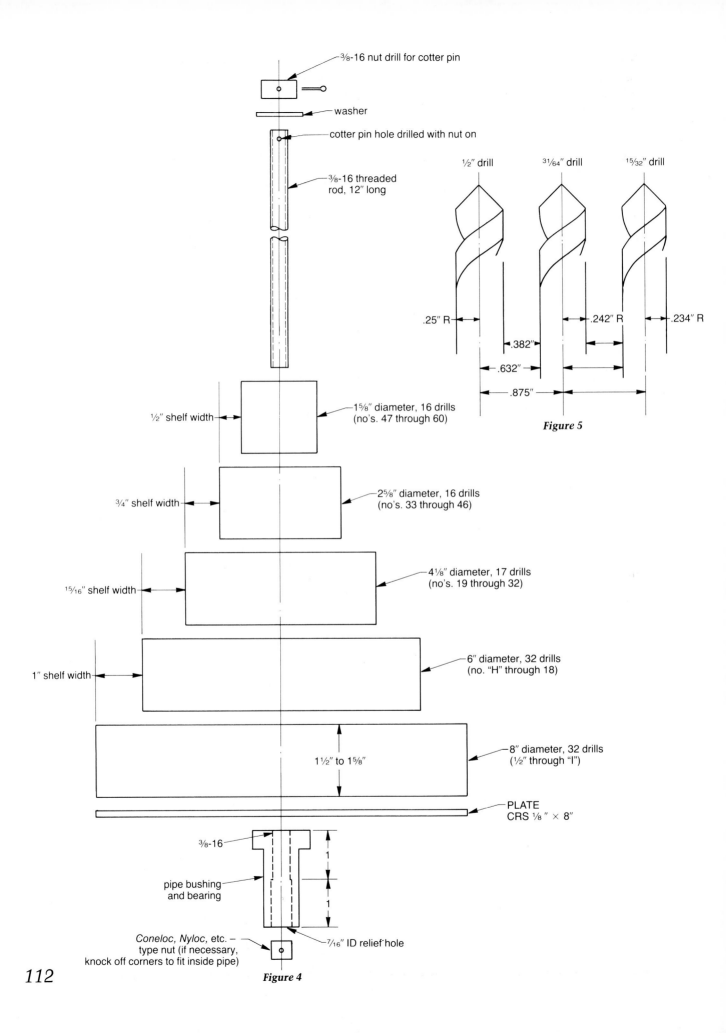

⅜-16 nut drill for cotter pin

washer

cotter pin hole drilled with nut on

⅜-16 threaded rod, 12″ long

½″ shelf width

1⅝″ diameter, 16 drills (no's. 47 through 60)

¾″ shelf width

2⅝″ diameter, 16 drills (no's. 33 through 46)

15/16″ shelf width

4⅛″ diameter, 17 drills (no's. 19 through 32)

1″ shelf width

6″ diameter, 32 drills (no. "H" through 18)

1½″ to 1⅝″

8″ diameter, 32 drills (½″ through "I")

PLATE
CRS ⅛″ × 8″

⅜-16

pipe bushing and bearing

1

1

Coneloc, Nyloc, etc. – type nut (if necessary, knock off corners to fit inside pipe)

7/16″ ID relief hole

½″ drill

31/64″ drill

15/32″ drill

.25″ R

.242″ R

.234″ R

.382″

.632″

.875″

Figure 5

112

Figure 4

an addition of the nominal radius of the drill going in that previous hole, or by addition of the radii of both drills to the tentatively selected spacing. I prefer the first method (Figure 5). The alternative method using two radii is more precise but of dubious necessity. In any event, it is recommended that the holes be "laid out" before any actual drilling is attempted.

Starting from the selected center of the ½" diameter drill, the next center for the 31⁄64" drill would be obtained by adding the ¼" radius of the ½" drill to the arbitrarily selected ⅝". The sum of these distances equals ⅞" (.875"). The center for the 15⁄32" drill would be similarly located by taking the selected ⅝" and adding to it the radius of the 31⁄64" drill, if we wish. However, since the radius of a 31⁄64" drill is so close to ¼", we could use this as the additive. The centers are similarly located by using a nominal radius until it appears appropriate to reduce. Should precision be desired, of course, the actual radii can be used along with the arbitrarily selected distance.

Hole Depth

Holes should be drilled somewhat less in depth than the length of each drill shank. For example, the shank of the standard ½" diameter jobber's drill that I used had a length of 1⅝" (Figure 6). For storage of this ½" drill, a hole 1¼" deep would be sufficient. If the storage holes are drilled to a depth greater than their shank lengths, removal becomes awkward, especially for the smaller drills.

Bench Mounted Drill Index

Figure 7 shows one means of bench mounting the Index. Other methods can be used, such as mounting a ball-bearing "Lazy Susan" on top of a plywood base. The upper element of the "Lazy Susan" would be fastened to the bottom plate of the Drill Index. The whole unit could then be moved around to various locations, as necessary.

Stand Mounted Drill Index

Figure 4 shows one method of mounting the Drill Index on a stand. While a number of other arrangements are possible, the one shown uses a simple and quickly made (on the lathe) bushing. The bushing is threaded internally ⅜-16. The outside diameter of the bushing is made to closely fit the inside of the stand-pipe – tight enough to resist tilt, but loose enough to permit rotation of the entire Drill Index. A collar, which is an integral part of the bushing, sits on top of the pipe. The bushing screws onto the ⅜-16 rod and pulls the plate and the five layers together. It is then "locked" by a nut. The ⅜-16 nut is of a type that resists unscrewing. The whole unit sits on top of the pipe, with the shank of the bushing inside the pipe.

Cover for the Drill Index

Figure 8 outlines a style of plastic trash cans sold in bath accessory, dime, department, drug, and hardware stores. One with an 8³⁄16" diameter mouth and 10¼" tall was found some years ago, and it still fits nicely over the Drill Index.

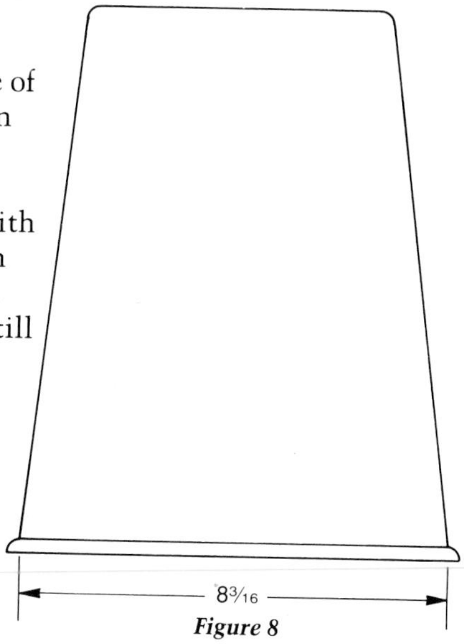
8³⁄16
Figure 8

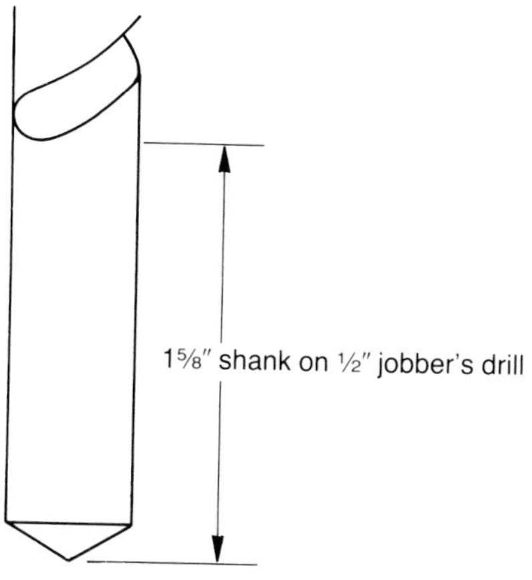
1⅝" shank on ½" jobber's drill
Figure 6

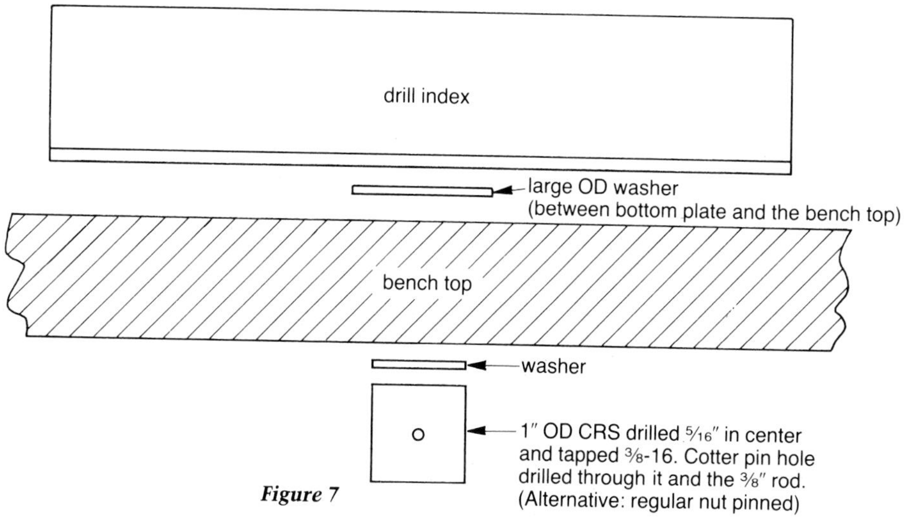
drill index
large OD washer
(between bottom plate and the bench top)
bench top
washer
1" OD CRS drilled ⁵⁄16" in center
and tapped ⅜-16. Cotter pin hole
drilled through it and the ⅜" rod.
(Alternative: regular nut pinned)
Figure 7

Spacing Drill Guide Makes It Easy

by John Dean

Photos by Author

Sometimes a plate with an intricately contoured outline is needed. The shape, thickness and material may make it difficult to cut from stock material by using cutting methods. A common way is to drill a row of closely spaced holes just outside the outline, and the non-skid edge ground and filed to the line.

An outline of the desired plate is scribed on the stock, and another line on the outside, connecting the centers of the holes to be drilled. It gets a little sticky measuring and center-punching the outside line for all the holes needed to shape and part the work from the stock. A little scrap iron spacing guide can make it as quick and easy as placing a row of empty fencepost holes to make a ditch.

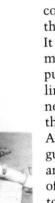

The outside dimensions of the guide are immaterial; the one in the photo just happened to be ½" wide, 1½" long and ⅜" thick, the locator pin and drill guide hole being ³⁄₁₆". A 10-32 machine screw was tapped through at about ⁵⁄₁₆" from one end, screwed into place until the threads were tight, and then the protruding threaded end cut off and dressed flush. The head of the screw was cut off, leaving a portion of the unthreaded body to serve as the locator guide pin.

The drill guide hole is drilled smack against the side of the machine screw. The end of the block is ground off to within about ¹⁄₃₂" from the side of the guide hole, and an index mark filed on the center. An unfinished guide for a ⁵⁄₁₆" drill is shown at the right in the photo.

To use, centerpunch and drill the first hole, place the locator pin in it and, with the drill in the guide hole, move the work right or left until the index mark on the end is on the guide line and drill the hole. As each hole is drilled, it becomes the guide hole for the next one.

V-Blocks Quickly Made

by John Dean

Photos by Author

When welding pipe or shafting together at various angles, or for other work, it is often hard to hold the pieces precisely in place. Suitably sized V-blocks may be hard to come by, but can be made almost suddenly of any size and length needed, by using scrap pieces of angle iron and steel bedrail.

Select a satisfactory size of angle iron for the work, cut four pieces of equal length, to the desired length of the finished fixture, and assemble back-to-back, (pictured above). The pieces are placed together and the ends welded. If preferred, the pieces may be riveted together, using countersunk rivets.

The finished fixture pictured below is a veteran of 40 years of frequent use in my shop.

MILLING
ACCESSORIES

Rotary Milling Table

by S. F. Kadron

Photos by Author

The addition of a rotary milling table to my shop inventory always seemed to be just beyond my hobby budget or, at least, repeatedly delayed by the purchase of something else. The most recent addition, a welder, provided the spark for this project.

A milling table must have a rigid, stable base if accurate machining is expected, so a weldment assembly was selected as the method of construction. The project also provided some functional testing of my welding skills. Luckily, the performance of the table frame is not dependent on weld bead appearance. I would also suggest that a carefully pinned and screwed assembly would do the job just as well if sufficient ¼" pins and cap screws were used.

The completed rotary table in action.

The machine tools needed for this project are a lathe – 9" swing minimum, unless you are scaling the rotary table down to fit smaller needs – and a small milling machine. I have a 10" Atlas lathe and an Atlas horizontal milling machine. A drill press and a metal-cutting band saw are handy but not absolutely necessary. Some source of heat is needed to bend, harden and temper a drill-rod tool, but even a propane torch will do this if you are patient.

The material for the milling table is a mixture of steel, aluminum and brass, and some of these were chosen primarily because they were on hand. The steel for the frame was 1020 and was reclaimed from some scrap fixtures (note the extra holes in some of the photographs). Steel can be substituted for any of the 6061-T6 aluminum parts, but don't go in the opposite direction. The brass dial on the worm shaft knob adds a little color but could be any material, including some plastics.

The frame is assembled and welded in steps to provide the opportunity to correct any misalignment that may occur during welding. I found that tightly clamping each part and leaving the clamps in place until all welding on that phase of assembly was completed kept all parts in their proper place.

Referring to the frame weldment drawing, the two sides (Item B) were positioned, clamped and welded to the face (Item C) and a light trueing cut was taken to assure that the bottom edge of the assembled three pieces was square to the face. Next, the bottom and top (Items A & E) were clamped and welded to the assembly. The bottom surface will be squared after machining the face. The clamping tabs (Item D) are not added until most of the machining operations are completed.

Clamp the welded assembly, face out, in a four-jaw lathe chuck using a dial indicator to position the center of the face on the lathe axis and the face running true. Absolute accuracy is not necessary here, but fuss with it until it is within a couple of thousandths. Use the top edge and the two side edges of the face to establish axial alignment, or you can center punch the face and align using that. I spent a little extra time getting the face to run true just to minimize the amount of metal removed on this cut as well as the later operation which establishes the back parallel to the front. Take a light cut from the entire face using a very slow feed to obtain a good finish as this is one of the bearing surfaces for the table. Bore the center hole and turn the counterbore to the dimensions shown. Fabricate a hook tool (Photo 1) from ¼" drill rod to spotface the rear surface. This provides the parallelism I felt was necessary to have smooth table rotation. Again, provide a smooth finish on the

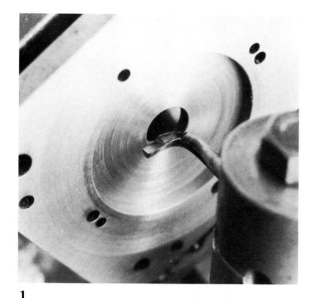

1

2

counterbore diameter and the rear spotface, as these are also bearing surfaces.

Remove the assembly from the lathe and square the bottom to the face on the milling machine (Photo 2). Now the clamping tabs (Item D) can be welded to the assembly and the back can be milled or turned to be parallel to the front. I elected to turn the part on the lathe

(Photo 3), and, with my 6″ four-jaw chuck, there was sufficient face available on the chuck side to use a dial indicator on the four corners of the assembly to obtain the correct position. The holes for the worm axis shaft will be drilled just prior to assembly in case any adjustment must be made for position of the worm.

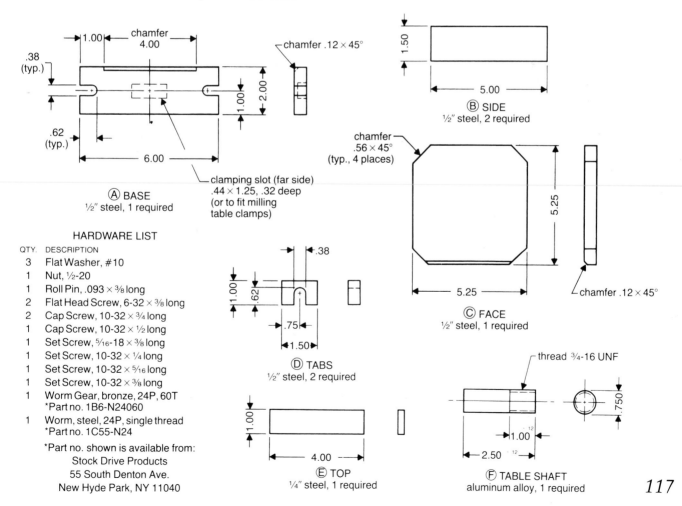

chamfer .12 × 45°

1.50

5.00

Ⓑ SIDE
½″ steel, 2 required

1.00

chamfer
4.00

.38
(typ.)

2.00

1.00

6.00

.62
(typ.)

Ⓐ BASE
½″ steel, 1 required

clamping slot (far side)
.44 × 1.25, .32 deep
(or to fit milling
table clamps)

chamfer
.56 × 45°
(typ., 4 places)

5.25

5.25

chamfer .12 × 45°

Ⓒ FACE
½″ steel, 1 required

HARDWARE LIST

QTY.	DESCRIPTION
3	Flat Washer, #10
1	Nut, ½-20
1	Roll Pin, .093 × ⅜ long
2	Flat Head Screw, 6-32 × ⅜ long
2	Cap Screw, 10-32 × ¾ long
1	Cap Screw, 10-32 × ½ long
1	Set Screw, ⁵⁄₁₆-18 × ⅜ long
1	Set Screw, 10-32 × ¼ long
1	Set Screw, 10-32 × ⁵⁄₁₆ long
1	Set Screw, 10-32 × ⅜ long
1	Worm Gear, bronze, 24P, 60T
	*Part no. 1B6-N24060
1	Worm, steel, 24P, single thread
	*Part no. 1C55-N24

*Part no. shown is available from:
Stock Drive Products
55 South Denton Ave.
New Hyde Park, NY 11040

.38

1.00

.62

.75

1.50

Ⓓ TABS
½″ steel, 2 required

1.00

4.00

Ⓔ TOP
¼″ steel, 1 required

thread ¾-16 UNF

.750

1.00

2.50

Ⓕ TABLE SHAFT
aluminum alloy, 1 required

117

3

4

Chip the slag and splatter from the weld beads and do any grinding or machining necessary to improve appearance (as in my case) or clear mounting slots and bolt head spaces (also in my case). The frame can be painted at this point but do not paint the mounting surfaces (back and bottom) or the bearing surfaces (front and spotface). Also mask the mounting surfaces for items G and L.

Turn the table shaft (Item F) next as it will be needed for assembly before the table can be removed from the lathe. The ¾-16 thread can be cut with a die or turned on the lathe.

The table is next and must remain in the chuck until all operations have been completed. The major objective here is to machine the back parallel to the front and end up with the table shaft axial with the table. Rough cut a 6" disk of 1" aluminum and securely mount it in the four-jaw chuck so that at least ¹¹⁄₁₆" of the thickness extends beyond the end of the chuck jaws. Referring to the Table Detail drawing, turn the boss, back surface and the edge up to and including the 5.35" diameter (Photo 4). Use feed techniques

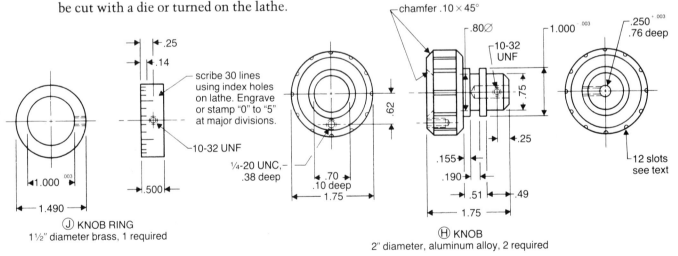

Ⓙ KNOB RING
1½" diameter brass, 1 required

scribe 30 lines using index holes on lathe. Engrave or stamp "0" to "5" at major divisions.

10-32 UNF

¼-20 UNC,
.10 deep

Ⓗ KNOB
2" diameter, aluminum alloy, 2 required

chamfer .10 × 45°

10-32 UNF

12 slots
see text

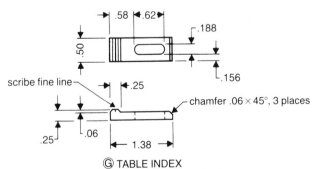

Ⓖ TABLE INDEX
¼" × ½" aluminum alloy, 1 required

scribe fine line

chamfer .06 × 45°, 3 places

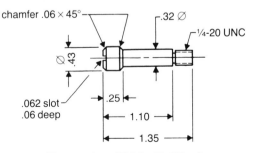

chamfer .06 × 45°

¼-20 UNC

.062 slot
.06 deep

File smooth and finish with 600 grit paper.

Ⓚ KNOB STEM
stainless steel, 1 required

118

5

6

that will provide a smooth surface on all these cuts as they are either bearing surfaces or, in the case of the edge turning, will provide the two reference surfaces for dial indicator alignment of the piece when it is reversed in the chuck to turn the front. The diameter of the boss is turned for a sliding fit in the frame counterbore. A sliding fit is described as a fit that will turn freely but has no perceptible play. In fact, it will probably bind if any significant temperature difference exists between the two parts. It is recommended, then, to allow the part to cool after each cut as you test the fit in the frame counterbore.

Using the indexing mechanism on the lathe, scribe the 60 lines on the circumference of the table. Use a 60° threading tool turned on its side (Photo 5) set to take a cut about .006″ deep. Once the cutting depth is set, don't change it; simply advance the indexing hole and move the carriage up and back once and go to the next index hole.

Now bore the center hole .690″ diameter and .82″ deep and thread ¾-16, .62″ deep for a snug fit on the table shaft (Item F). Clean the threaded hole and the table shaft thread with lacquer thinner and, with the table still on the lathe, coat the shaft threads with *Loctite** 416 and screw full depth into the table, turning the shaft with pliers (Photo 6).

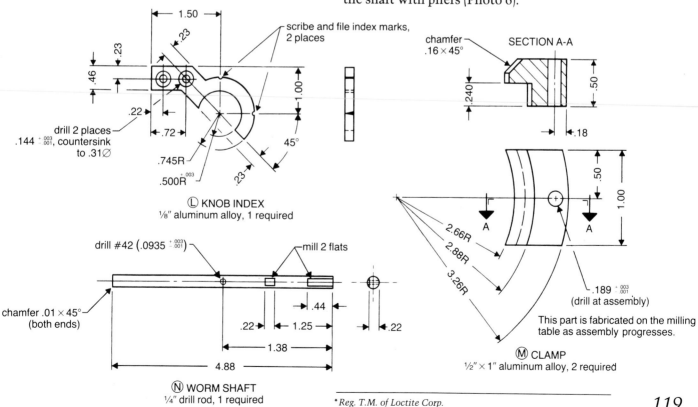

scribe and file index marks, 2 places

Ⓛ KNOB INDEX
⅛″ aluminum alloy, 1 required

drill 2 places .144 $^{+.003}_{-.001}$, countersink to .31∅

Ⓝ WORM SHAFT
¼″ drill rod, 1 required

drill #42 (.0935 $^{+.003}_{-.001}$)

mill 2 flats

chamfer .01 × 45° (both ends)

SECTION A-A

chamfer .16 × 45°

.189 $^{+.003}_{-.001}$ (drill at assembly)

This part is fabricated on the milling table as assembly progresses.

Ⓜ CLAMP
½″ × 1″ aluminum alloy, 2 required

* *Reg. T.M. of Loctite Corp.*

7

8

I had full threads on the shaft and used jam nuts as shown. Wait a few minutes for the *Loctite* to set and then face the shaft to a length of 1.38″ and bore a 60° countersink center hole. Support the shaft end with a center mounted in the tailstock and turn the full length of the shaft to .500″ diameter and then cut the ½-20 thread to within .20″ of the table surface. This completes the rear of the table but check that all operations are finished before removing the part from the lathe.

Reverse the part in the four-jaw chuck and, using soft copper scraps or tape to protect the part, clamp on the 5.75″ diameter. Now use a dial indicator on the 5.35″ diameter to indicate when the part is running true. A test indicator is used on the edge of the 5.75″ diameter to show when the face runout is at zero. If a test indicator is not available, get the part as close to true as possible and rough cut the 35° angle on the edge of the table. This will allow the use of a dial indicator on the edge of the 5.75″

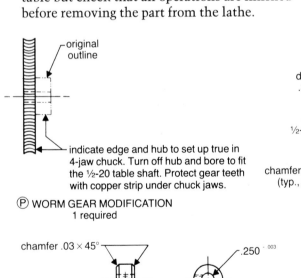

original outline

indicate edge and hub to set up true in 4-jaw chuck. Turn off hub and bore to fit the ½-20 table shaft. Protect gear teeth with copper strip under chuck jaws.

℗ WORM GEAR MODIFICATION
1 required

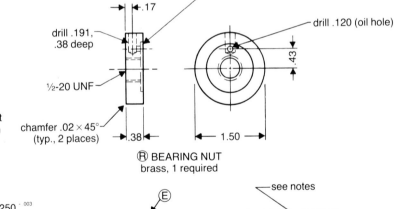

counterbore 1.00 dia., .03 deep

drill .191, .38 deep

.17

drill .120 (oil hole)

.43

½-20 UNF

chamfer .02 × 45° (typ., 2 places)

.38

1.50

Ⓡ BEARING NUT
brass, 1 required

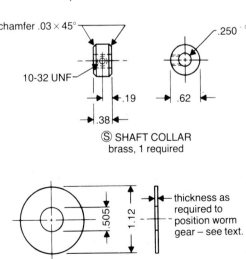

chamfer .03 × 45°

.250 ⁻·⁰⁰³

10-32 UNF

.19

.62

.38

Ⓢ SHAFT COLLAR
brass, 1 required

thickness as required to position worm gear – see text.

.505

1.12

Ⓣ GEAR SPACER
aluminum alloy, 1 required

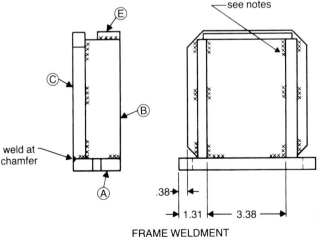

Ⓔ

see notes

Ⓒ

Ⓑ

weld at chamfer

Ⓐ

.38

1.31

3.38

FRAME WELDMENT

NOTES:
1) Clamp parts tightly, filet weld all joints with 1″ long bead spaced 1″ apart.
2) Do not attach tabs, item Ⓓ at this time.

9

10

diameter to establish the face runout. Be in a good mood when you start this and stick with it until the runouts are at zero. Tighten the chuck jaws and check the runouts again.

Now finish turning the edge detail and face the front using a slow feed for a good finish. Touch the center of the table with a center drill to provide a small depression about .03″ deep which can be used with calipers to center work on the table. Now cut a series of concentric rings on the face starting at .400″ from the center and at .400″ intervals out to the edge (Photo 7). Use a 60° threading tool and cut to about .015″ deep, which will give a line width of about .020″. These also help to center parts on the milling table. Again, check that all operations have been completed before removing the part from the lathe.

Assemble the table in the frame and, with a temporary reference mark (arrow in Photo 8) scribed on the bottom edge, locate, drill and tap the 5/16-18 holes on the milling machine or

the drill press. The holes are located on the .400″ spaced rings and at the angular positions shown on the Table Detail drawing. Use clamps as shown in Photo 8 to secure the part while drilling these holes.

The worm gear (Item P) is a modification of a commercial part available from Stock Drive Products as stated in the hardware list. Care must be used to assure zero runout on both the diameter and face of the gear or the rotational accuracy of the table will be affected. Mount the part in the four-jaw chuck using a soft copper strip to protect the teeth, and use the hub diameter and the finished edge of the gear diameter to align the part (Photo 9). Turn off the hub until it equals the face dimension and bore the part for a close fit on the ½-20 table shaft. I would like to refer to the article in *HSM*, July/August 1983, by Theodore M. Clarke, and call attention to his method of cutting a worm gear. For those that have the necessary tools, this may be an alternative to purchasing the gear and worm.

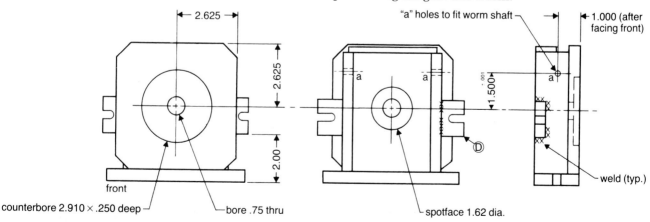

← 2.625 →   "a" holes to fit worm shaft →   ← 1.000 (after facing front)

2.625

2.00

1.500

front

counterbore 2.910 × .250 deep

bore .75 thru

spotface 1.62 dia.

weld (typ.)

FRAME DETAIL

1) Indicate face to set up true in 4-jaw chuck.
2) Face front, bore hole and counterbore. Use hook tool to spotface back before removing from chuck.
3) Square bottom to face on milling machine.
4) Weld on tabs Item D.
5) Mill or turn back parallel to front.

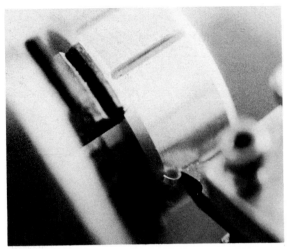

11

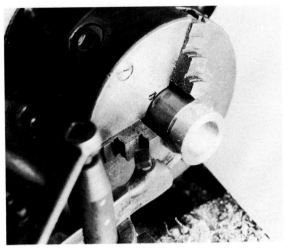

12

Chuck a 2″ long piece of 2″ diameter aluminum in the three-jaw chuck with 1¼″ extending out of the chuck jaws. Referring to the knob drawing (Item H), turn and bore the small diameter end and complete up to and including the .10″ × 45° chamfer on the 1.75″ diameter. Reverse the part, clamping on the 1.000″ diameter (Photo 10), and complete the turning of the part according to the drawing. Don't forget the .10″ deep recess in the end of the knob – it looks neat. Flute the large diameter with 12 equally spaced slots using the indexing holes on the lathe and a round-nosed tool set on its side. Take successive light cuts until the slots are .030″ deep (Photo 11). Remove the part from the lathe and drill and tap the remaining two holes.

Turn the knob ring (Item J) and, using the index holes, scribe the calibration marks to the different lengths by using a carriage stop set to limit the tool travel (Photo 12). Engrave or stamp the numerals "0" to "5" in the direction shown on the drawing and drill and tap the setscrew hole.

The bearing nut (Item R) is turned from brass and is straightforward except for the oil passage holes and the shallow counterbore. Tap the center hole carefully in the lathe to maintain good axial alignment.

The worm shaft (Item N), shaft collar (S), top index (G) and knob stem (K) can be fabricated from the drawings and require no special instructions.

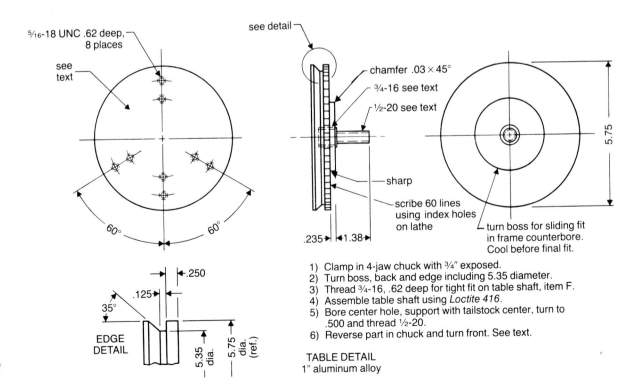

5⁄₁₆-18 UNC .62 deep, 8 places

see text

60° 60°

EDGE DETAIL

.250
.125
35°
5.35 dia.
5.75 dia. (ref.)

see detail

chamfer .03 × 45°
¾-16 see text
½-20 see text

sharp

scribe 60 lines using index holes on lathe

.235 1.38

5.75

turn boss for sliding fit in frame counterbore. Cool before final fit.

1) Clamp in 4-jaw chuck with ¾″ exposed.
2) Turn boss, back and edge including 5.35 diameter.
3) Thread ¾-16, .62 deep for tight fit on table shaft, item F.
4) Assemble table shaft using *Loctite 416*.
5) Bore center hole, support with tailstock center, turn to .500 and thread ½-20.
6) Reverse part in chuck and turn front. See text.

TABLE DETAIL
1″ aluminum alloy

13

14

The knob index (Item L) is made from ⅛"
5052 aluminum and is laid out per the
drawing. Before cutting the outline, mount the
piece in the lathe and center on the small
diameter punch mark. Bore the .500" radius.
Remove the part and cut and file to size. The
mounting holes can be drilled at assembly as
the part must be centered on the worm shaft
axis (Photo 13). The index marks are located
90° from each other and are scribed and then
filed to a triangular shape (Photo 14). The index
and calibration marks and the numberals
throughout the project are eventually filled
with black enamel for good visibility.

The gear spacer (Item T) will be fabricated
during the assembly of the milling table and
the clamps (Item M) will be made on the table
after assembly has progressed to that capability.
The next operation is the most critical in the
entire project. The object is to position the
bearing holes for the worm shaft exactly 1.500"
from the axis of the table. This is the spacing
that precisely locates the worm on the worm
gear without backlash and without binding.
The other locating dimension – 1.000" from the
face – needs adjustment only if the thickness
of the face or the bearing nut are significantly
changed. To determine the correct dimension,
measure the thickness of the face and the
thickness of the bearing nut and add these to
your spacer thickness (I used .032") and half the
thickness of the worm gear at its center. Use a
height gage to lay out both of these dimensions
and your best techniques to drill the holes at
these locations. Don't despair if you think you
can't do it, or if you try and miss by a few
thousandths, because there is an alternative
which will be covered a little later.

The parts line-up is shown in Photo 15 and
assembly of the row is accomplished next.

Lightly coat the back of the table and the
spotface with 20W oil and, referring to the table
axis assembly drawing, put things together.
Select or machine the spacer thickness to align
the worm gear to the axis of the worm shaft
holes. Tighten the ½-20 nut securely using a
piece of ³⁄₁₆" steel rod inserted
in the oil hole in the
bearing nut (arrow
in Photo 16).

The adjustment is
similar to the gib
adjustments on your
lathe or milling
machine that is,
it should move
without the
feeling of strain but
have no perceptible
play. Start out by setting
the table so you

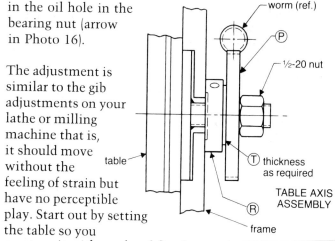

TABLE AXIS
ASSEMBLY

can turn it with one hand firmly grasping the
table. The proper setting will become obvious
after a few parts are milled. I had a tendency to
start out with the table too loose. The 24-pitch
worm and gear have sufficient muscle to turn
even a very firm table.

Attach the table index as shown in Photo 17
by drilling and tapping the top edge of the frame
for a 10-32 screw. Position the tapped hole so
that, when the screw is centered in the slot,
the index line is at the vertical table center.
This allows adjustment of the line to a starting
reference no matter where the work is located
on the table. The table index should bear lightly
against the table when tightened.

The worm axis assembly drawing and Photo 18
show the next assembly area. Start by partially
threading the worm shaft hole farthest from the

123

15

17

16

knob. Use a ⁵⁄₁₆-18 plug tap and tap just enough to allow the ³⁄₈″ long set screw extend ³⁄₁₆″ into the hole just as it starts to bind on the imperfect thread. This set screw will be adjusted to take the end play out of the worm shaft. Now assemble the shaft and other parts according to the drawing. It will be necessary to screw the worm into the worm gear. Add a light coating of 20W oil on the bearing surfaces and the gear pair. Secure the worm to the shaft with a 2-56 screw temporarily. The roll pin will be used after you are sure everything is satisfactory and disassembly is unlikely. Don't be alarmed if you have some gear backlash at this point because the end play in the shaft and screw securing the worm will both allow some free play.

Check the alignment of the worm gear to make sure that its center is on the worm axis. The gear has a ¼″ face (measure, to be sure), so a straight edge laid on the side of the gear should just touch the ¼″ shaft. If more than .010″ clearance or interference is found, alter the table axis spacer thickness to compensate.

If everything works okay, add the roll pin and adjust the ⁵⁄₁₆-18 set screw for zero end play. Do not drive the roll pin home without backing up the shaft as it may bend. Fabricate a small block that just fits between the worm shoulder and the frame, drill a no. 31 hole through it to keep the roll pin from bottoming, and use this as an anvil.

Now you can measure your gear backlash by measuring the free play on the knob. The minor graduations are spaced 12 minutes apart and, if you find more than three divisions of free play (36 minutes), I would recommend using the alternate method of bushing the worm shaft. Proceed to the end of this article, do not pass GO and do not collect $200.

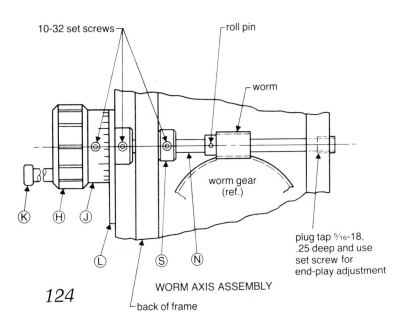

WORM AXIS ASSEMBLY

18

19 *Table milling its own clamps.*

The knob index is mounted next, and its position (Photo 13) is determined by using the 1.000 diameter on the knob to locate the part for drilling. Remove the knob ring to expose the diameter needed on the knob. Drill through the part and the frame with a no. 36 drill, and tap the frame 6-32, ⅜" deep. Open up the part holes to .144" and countersink to .31" diameter. If you use the eccentric bushing approach on the worm shaft, eliminate the countersink and use binderhead screws to allow the positional freedom necessary to follow the shaft.

Now you can use your milling table for the first time and fabricate the table clamps (Item M). Photo 19 shows the first clamp about to be parted off. Don't cut all the way through or you will mess up your table. Deburr the part and add the 45° chamfer. This could be a straight cut, but I clamped the part over the edge of the table with one clamp (Photo 20), took light cuts on one end, moved a clamp to the other end and finished the chamfer. A small piece of doublefaced tape under the part will help hold it in place.

Mount the clamps diagonally on the face of the frame as shown in Photo 21 by drilling through the clamp and the frame with a tap drill and then tapping the frame 10-32, ⁵⁄₁₆" deep. Open the clamp hole to .189" and secure, using the ¾" cap screws with flat washers. Photo 22 shows the slightly angled position the clamp assumes and, if any change is made to the table flange thickness, the clamp dimensions should be changed accordingly.

Now mill the angled flat at each 30° position on the table (Photo 22). I used a ⁵⁄₁₆" end mill at an angle of approximately 20° and, with the table clamped to the milling machine (Photo 21), cut the flats as shown. Use the table clamps

20

at each cut. Stamp or engrave the legend in each of the flats, starting at "0" and continuing for each 30° increment. I use a three-pointed carbide tip in my Dremel tool to engrave and follow up with a sharp scribe to clean up the line work. You can be sure that Photo 17 shows my best set of numbers. The size of the flat can be changed to any size needed to meet your numbering capability.

Photo 23 shows some radial slots being cut in a piece of tubing to make some small clamps. Those finished clamps are being used in Photo 24 to hold a disk being cut with spokes and, in Photo 25, to hold a part to drill a pattern of six cover holes on the drill press. These are just a few examples of the type of work that can be performed on the rotary milling table.

Keep the table lubricated with 20W oil by occasionally filling the oil hole in the bearing nut just before using. After filling, use a plug to retain the oil. I used a piece of the material found in the ubiquitous Gits oil cups, although any sort of soft material will probably do as long as it is impervious to the oil. Keep the bare,

21

24 *Cutting spokes.*

22

23 *Milling radial slots.*

unpainted mounting surfaces covered with a light coat of oil, a good coat of paste wax or whatever method of protection is prevalent in your shop. Oil the worm shaft bearings and the worm and gear as needed.

Don't feel constrained to use the exact design presented here – in fact, it's more of an accomplishment to make changes necessary to fit your needs. I hope some of the ideas presented here will help add the rotary milling table to your tool list.

APPENDIX

ALTERNATE WORM AXIS – Using what is called an adjustable adapter bushing will provide the ability to set the worm at the precise center-to-center distance needed for zero backlash. The drawing shows the bushing detail, the modifications needed on the frame, and the assembly.

Modify both sides of the frame according to the drawing. Keep the two .438" holes on the same axis. Counterbore as shown.

Fabricate the bushings by chucking a 2½" long piece of turned .562" diameter brass in the three-jaw chuck with a .015" thick spacer between the work and jaw number 1. This provides a .010" eccentric for the shaft hole. Extend 1½" of the material beyond the chuck jaws. Find the high spot opposite jaw number 1 and, with a sharp-vee tool laid on its side, cut a full length .03" deep notch exactly on the high spot. Use the carriage in the same manner used to cut the calibration lines on other parts. This vee will remain on the flange of the bushing and will provide positional information during

25 *Pattern of 6 holes on drill press.*

adjustment. Drill and ream the .250″ hole for the worm shaft to a depth of 1¼″. Remove the spacer and complete the two parts according to the drawing. Turn the diameter for a sliding fit in the frame holes if you prefer to fit parts like I do.

Now assemble according to the drawing and rotate the bushings for zero backlash at the knob. Alter the thickness of the table shaft

spacer to maintain alignment. Do not deflect the shaft by overloading as this may cause excessive gear wear. Keep the reference marks on the two bushings at the same position. When all seems satisfactory, secure the bushings with the 6-32 screws.

The most difficult part of this operation for some may be the counterbore in the frame and, if tools are not available, could be omitted and the bushing flange allowed to rest on the surface of the frame. This approach will require small U-shaped washers to support the 6-32 screw heads and a shortening of the knob set screw boss to allow clearance. The bushing length at the knob end will require lengthening by the thickness of the flange.

HOOK TOOL FABRICATION – Heat a piece of ¼″ drill rod until it is bright red and bend one end to about 100°. Allow to cool slowly and cut or file a flat as shown on the drawing. Reheat the end to bright red and quench in water. Polish the working end with 400 grit paper and heat again until the oxide on the tip just turns orange (some call it straw-color), remove from the flame and allow the part to cool in air. Grind the cutting edge and use in a boring bar holder to execute the spotface.

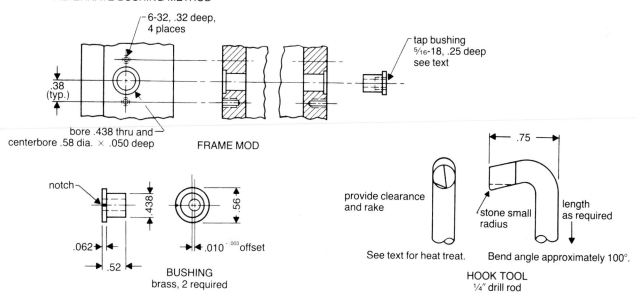

Milling Machine Chip Shield

by James Berger

The milling machine chip shield I built and use in my shop is the complement to the lathe chip shield described in an earlier article (March/April '84).

The method of bending the *Plexiglas* or *Lexan* is the same as described previously – clamp the material between two boards and play a very soft propane torch flame along the bend line on the top and bottom until the material softens. Avoid direct contact between the flame and the material so bubbles don't form in the surface.

The mounting plate was designed to allow the shield to tilt at various angles, since position of the work on the table could cause the belt guard on the spindle head to rub against the

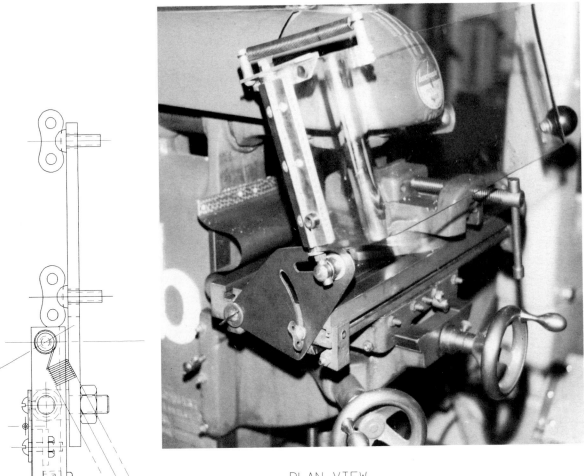

PLAN VIEW

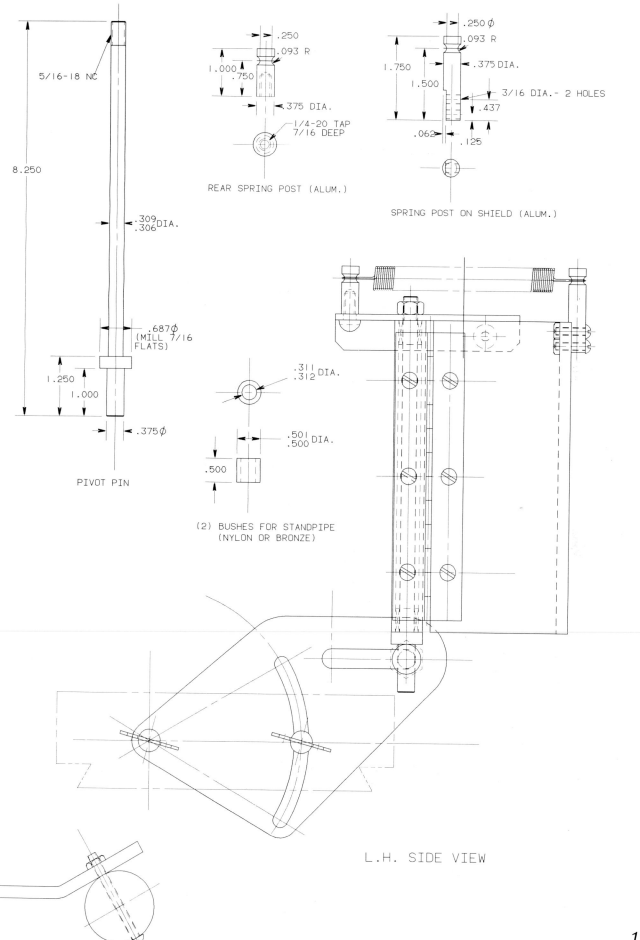

5/16-18 NC

8.250

.309
.306 DIA.

.687 φ
(MILL 7/16 FLATS)

1.250

1.000

.375 φ

PIVOT PIN

.250

.093 R

1.000

.750

.375 DIA.

1/4-20 TAP
7/16 DEEP

REAR SPRING POST (ALUM.)

.250 φ

.093 R

1.750

.375 DIA.

1.500

3/16 DIA.- 2 HOLES

.437

.062

.125

SPRING POST ON SHIELD (ALUM.)

.311
.312 DIA.

.501
.500 DIA.

.500

(2) BUSHES FOR STANDPIPE
(NYLON OR BRONZE)

L.H. SIDE VIEW

129

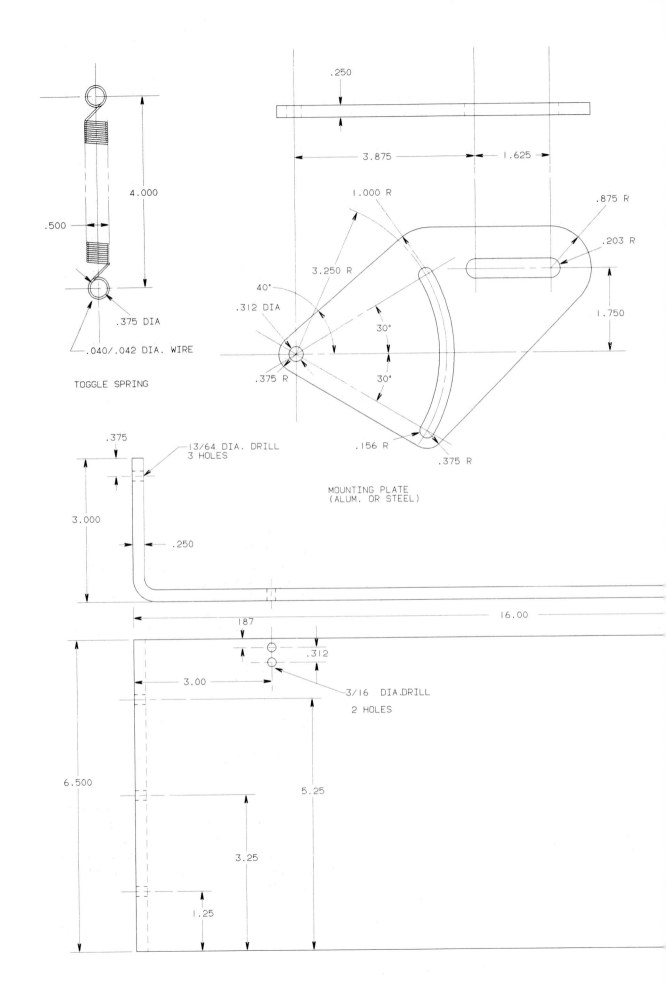

.250

3.875

1.625

1.000 R

.875 R

3.250 R

.203 R

40°

.312 DIA

30°

1.750

.375 R

30°

.156 R

.375 R

MOUNTING PLATE
(ALUM. OR STEEL)

4.000

.500

.375 DIA

.040/.042 DIA. WIRE

TOGGLE SPRING

.375

13/64 DIA. DRILL
3 HOLES

3.000

.250

187

16.00

.312

3.00

3/16 DIA.DRILL

2 HOLES

6.500

5.25

3.25

1.25

130

SHIELD (PLEXIGLAS)

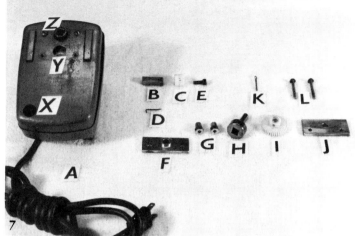

6 7

shaft, so two adapters would work at all three points of table feed. Because the motor I used had no reverse, I must move the motor from one end of the table to the other in order to feed the table in the oppositie direction when required.

To solve item 5. The motor unit must now be attached to the mill table. Naturally, the motor must move with the table as it feeds. I drilled and tapped a 5/16″-18 hole in each end of the table and inserted a 5/16″ all thread to extend 6″. This is locked to the table with a 5/16″ nut. Then on the far end is another 5/16″ hex nut that is secured by jamming the thread. See Photo 5. A hole approximately 5/8″ OD (it must clear the 5/16″ hex nut) is now cut in the corner of the motor housing. This hole is shown at X on Photo 7. In use, the motor simply hangs on this 5/16″ all thread by hooking hole X over the 5/16″ hex nut. This loose motor mounting allows the motor to be easily moved. A similar 5/16″ all thread in the other end of the table permits the motor to hang on either end and feed the table in either direction.

My rotisserie motor included a switch. If yours doesn't have one, I suggest you install a switch at the motor. I also put an outlet in the wiring box on the mill and plug the feed motor into it. Therefore, the feed can't work unless the mill is turned on. This is important because if the mill were shut off as a cutter is working, you don't want the feed to continue.

The automatic feed I made has been working well for almost two years. I'm sure that the rotisserie motor has sufficient power and the construction outlined is satisfactory, even with the plastic (probably nylon) gears.

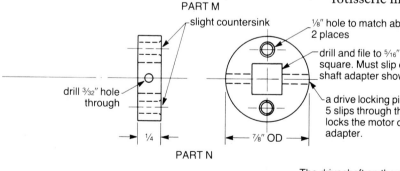

3/32″ hole
1/4″ dia.
slight countersink this side of hole
5/8
drill 1/8″, 2 places
1 1/16
1/8
7/8″ OD

PART M

slight countersink
1/8″ hole to match above, 2 places
drill and file to 5/16″ square. Must slip easy over the shaft adapter shown on Figure 4.
drill 3/32″ hole through
a drive locking pin shown on Photo 5 slips through this hole. This locks the motor drive to the shaft adapter.
1/4
7/8″ OD

PART N

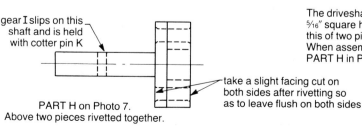

gear I slips on this shaft and is held with cotter pin K

The driveshaft on the motor has a 5/16″ square hole. I made this of two pieces, PART M and N. When assembled they make PART H in Photo 7.

take a slight facing cut on both sides after rivetting so as to leave flush on both sides

PART H on Photo 7. Above two pieces rivetted together.

Figure 8

Clamping Work to the Mill Table

by Harold Timm

Shown here is a drawing of a pair of fixtures I have found to be most useful in clamping work to the mill table. Of course, the hole sizes, slot sizes and spacings are to be made according to the mil used.

The two main pieces are finished ¾"x 2"x10" aluminum. I cast a couple of bars to make mine. After squaring the ¾" sides, the two pieces were clamped to the table. Facing was accomplished with a flycutter, after which the slots were milled. While still in place, centerdrill the 8-32 holes as well as the clearance holes for the tee bolts. It goes without saying that this will accurately locate these holes.

In the meantime, make the locating pieces (size according to your mill) and then drill and tap the 8-32 holes. Drill the holes for the tee

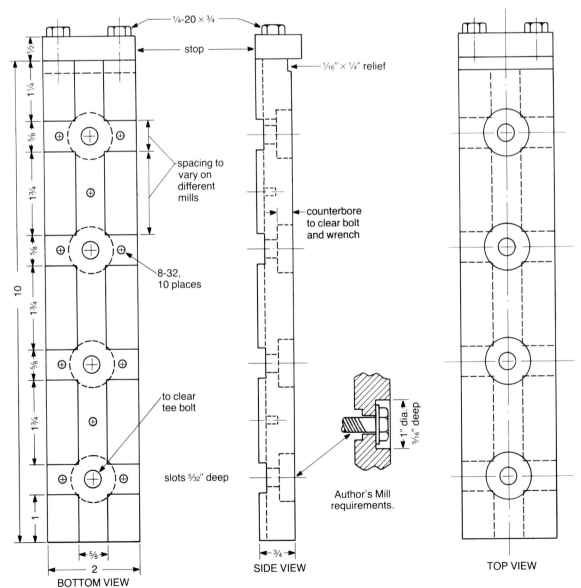

SQUARING FIXTURE FOR MILLS
aluminum, 2 required

bolts, now, about ¹⁄₃₂″ oversize. Turn it over and counterbore these holes to clear a hex head bolt and wrench.

The end stops are ½″x1″x2″ aluminum bolted to the ends as shown.

My mill was an old used machine. Someone had really damaged the table by pulling two tee nuts through the slots in the table. I now use

only tee nuts made of aluminum. Too much torque and the threads strip instead of damaging the table.

The two fixtures with their locating pieces in place are bolted side by side on the table with 1″ long bolts. Mark them *right* and *left*.

Now, face off the top surfaces with the flycutter. With an endmill, face off the inner surface of the stops. Any work project pressed against these faces will then be at right angles and/or parallel to the table. Machine a little relief at the intersection. I also use a piece of ½″x½″x15″ long wedge against these stops on the occasion the fixtures are separated.

These fixtures have been most useful in squaring up work and, with work elevated above the table, you are not likely to mill slots in the table inadvertently.

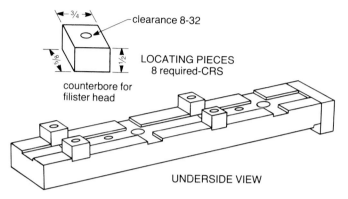

LOCATING PIECES
8 required-CRS

clearance 8-32

counterbore for
filister head

UNDERSIDE VIEW

SHOP TOOLS & IMPROVEMENTS

Conversion of a Gear-driven Shaper to Hydraulic Drive

by Theodore M. Clarke

Photos by Author

Crank-driven horizontal shapers, usually those with broken or worn out drive mechanisms, can be obtained at very low cost. The objective of the article is to describe how, at low or moderate cost, the home machinist can convert a horizontal shaper to hydraulic drive using standard hydraulic components. A key feature is built-in overload protection which can be set just above the cutting force. Another key feature is the ability to readily and precisely position the ram and manually control the stroke reversal (Photo 1).

The horizontal shaper can be a very useful tool for the home machinist who already has the more basic machine tools such as the lathe and drill press. The ability to generate planar surfaces with high metal removal rates using single point tools is a major attribute of the shaper for the home machinist who usually cannot properly sharpen multi-toothed milling cutters which can make milling more efficient than shaping. Another advantage of the shaper is that it can do slotting jobs not possible on a milling machine without a costly slotting attachment.

The condition of the slides and ram ways is of major importance in a decision to acquire a shaper and convert it to hydraulic drive. Accurate machining requires accurate slides. Since most of the gear-driven horizontal shapers were built in the late 1800s and early 1900s, the ways are usually badly worn. It is quite feasible for the home machinist to correct the worn slides if he is willing to learn the skill of hand scraping, a skill which is still of great importance and which made possible the mass production of accurate machine tools needed for the Industrial Revolution.

I learned about the existence of the hand scraping process from a good friend trained as a machinist in Denmark before World War II. However, I had to acquire the skill by practicing on my own what I had learned from a very unique book on the subject. This book is available in many public libraries: *Machine Tool Reconditioning and Applications of Handscraping*, Edward F. Connelly, 1955, Machine Tool Publications, St. Paul, MN 55101 U.S.A

A basic requirement for hand scraping is an accurate surface plate. I was able to obtain a worn cast iron surface plate at a cost of $20.00. My first scraping project was to rescrape this plate using an accurate granite surface plate as a master and homemade scrapers. If I had three iron plates of the same size, I could have generated three plates of even greater accuracy by the basic three-plate method without resorting to use of a reference flat. I also made an angle straight edge and a base for a very sensitive bubble level vial, .0003"/12" scale divisions. The straight edge, long narrow flat, is needed to mark the high spots with Prussian blue on way surfaces which cannot be spotted with a wide surface plate. The master level is used to detect twist when the ways are longer than the maximum dimension of the surface plate.

I located a 15" light-duty shaper which was very old and worn, but the price was reasonable: $75. The cast iron bull gear had partially broken teeth. I purchased the shaper because I could rescrape the ways and had the concept for replacing the drive with a hydraulic drive fabricated from standard components. These components included: 3.7 gpm at 2000 rpm hydraulic pump directly driven by a ¾ hp 1100 rpm motor, a 1" bore double-acting cylinder with hydraulic cushions, a flow control valve with a built-in adjustable relief valve, a four-way open center control valve, two limit switches, two a-c solenoids, and a variable voltage transformer.

Photo 2 shows the layout of the drive control, which is mounted vertically with the axis of the four-way valve spool in line with adjustable

1 2

3

roller stops on guide rods, which are also attached in line with opposed solenoids. An involute cam attached to an oscillating shaft contacts the roller stops, causing the spool valve to switch toward neutral position which causes the ram to nearly stop. Adjustable trips are set to energize the appropriate solenoid to carry the spool valve past neutral and accomplish a reversal of the ram motion (Photo 3). A two-bar linkage, attached to the ram, drives the oscillating shaft for the cam and also powers the cross feed. The limit switch trips are easily set by letting the spool valve be shifted by the cam to neutral with power to the solenoids switched off, then setting the flow control valve to zero flow, energizing the solenoid circuit and, finally, adjusting the trips so the solenoids are activated just before the involute cam brings the spool to neutral.

Since I found it most convenient to mount the spool valve vertically, it was necessary to counterweight the assembly. The centering spring and handle were removed from the four-way control valve for this application. A variable transformer is used to adjust the solenoid voltage so the spool does not bounce during the stroke reversal. Rubber O-rings on

the ends of the spool also cushion the end of the spool travel.

The design parameters for the hydraulic drive depend upon the rigidity of the particular shaper. The motor size used in the mechanical drive can serve as a guide for the motor size for the hydraulic system. A limitation from the use of a standard four-way valve, rather than a much more costly pilot actuated valve, is that acceleration and deceleration are greater. The reversal forces can be limited by relief valves, shown in Photo 2, which shunt fluid between the cylinder ends forming a "cross-over" relief

141

system. The linkage on my 15″ shaper results in a spool valve velocity, when actuated by the cam, of about half the ram velocity. Vibration upon reversal becomes noticeable, at the end of the rapid return stroke, when the cutting speed exceeds 20 feet per minute (33 feet per minute return speed). The cutting speed can be greatly increased for long strokes by letting the hydraulic cushion in the end of the hydraulic cylinder handle the deceleration at the end of the rapid return stroke.

The relief pressure on my system is set at 500 psi which corresponds to a maximum power requirement of about .6 hp at a maximum cutting speed of 50 feet per minute. For quiet operation with short strokes, I usually cut at 20 feet per minute which means that half of the hydraulic power is wasted by being throttled through the flow control valve. The cross-over relief system, set at 575 psi, allows cutting at 50 feet per minute when I am in a hurry and have to put up with the noise.

Most home machinists would probably decide that the cost of a cross-over relief system does not justify the higher cutting speeds obtainable. In this case, the spool valve velocity should be kept below about 20 feet per minute if a common four-way valve without feathering notches is used. A compromise has to be made between reducing the cam velocity and maintaining short stroke capability. The cam could be eliminated by relying solely on the limit switches and the solenoids and using a dash pot to control the spool velocity.

Since the shaper represents a significant investment in time or money, it should have a cover to keep chips off the cross slide. This cover can be made of sheet metal and attached to the vertical ways (Photo 4). Felt wipers on the ends of a the saddle and on the front ends of the ram ways will help to retard wear, particularly when much gray iron will be shaped. If the saddle is not equipped with grease reservoirs, these can be added at the ends of the saddle along with felt wipers, as shown in Photo 5. A clamp-type adjustable stop on the tool slide is a very helpful addition for shaping vertical surfaces or dovetails. A slotting attachment can be readily made with a lathe and adds a very important capability to the shaper. Photo 6 shows a slotting attachment mounted in the clapper box which has the needed locking screws. Photo 7 shows the component parts of the slotting attachment. A rotary dovetail and a four-hole indexing pattern are used so that the cutting edge can be quickly indexed by 90° increments. This permits the shaping of square

4

holes without the use of a rotary table normally found on a slotter (vertical shaper).

A dial indicator stop clamped to a shaft hung from the bottom of the cross slide can assist in accurate machining (see Photo 5). A limit switch clamped to the same shaft and wired in series with the solenoid circuit shuts the automatic feed off before the slide travel becomes excessive. A lathe-type toolholder is a poor choice for heavy cuts with a shaper because the cutting edge moves deeper into the cut as the toolholder deflects under load. Thus, after a heavy roughing cut, there may unexpectedly be no stock for a finishing cut. A properly designed goose neck holder will provide much more stable cutting conditions because the edge moves out of the cut as the holder deflects under load. The slotting attachment permitted me to make the goose neck holder shown in Photo 1. I have also made left-hand and right-hand goose neck holders of similar design. It is important that the square hole for the tool bit be properly located so that the cutting edge will always be ahead of the clapper box pivot axis.

Cutting Unimat size tee slots in a lathe faceplate, which had been previously hardened to about RC 30, was a very demanding job for the shaper which made good use of its special features. Photo 8 shows this job process. The tool is held in a goose neck holder. A planer gauge is used to set the tool height. Photo 9 shows the cutting tool as it exits the cut. Note in this photograph the unusual shape of the tool which permits it to be readily ground from ³⁄₈″ square blank. The clapper box must be locked so that the tool won't pivot and jam in the bottom of the tee. Lack of a pivot to move the tool away from the cut on the reverse stroke

5

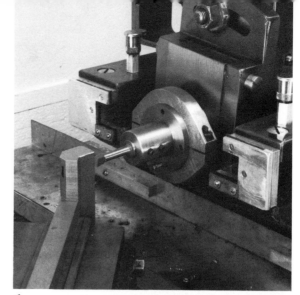

6

7

8

creates serious problems. Swarf caught between the work and the cutting edge can chip the cutting edge on the reverse stroke because the small clearance angle on the tool causes a large wedging force relative to the smaller cutting force. The hardness of the steel necessitated a depth of cut of less than .002″. The dial indicator stop on the cross slide and manual control of the stroke reversals permit the tool to be manually backed away slightly from the cut before reversal and aid in manually advancing the table for a .001″ depth of cut before the forward stroke is manually initiated.

Hopefully this article will help give new life to many of these very versatile machine tools which would otherwise be sold as scrap metal. It is also hoped that this article will encourage some people to want to learn the hand scraping skill.

9

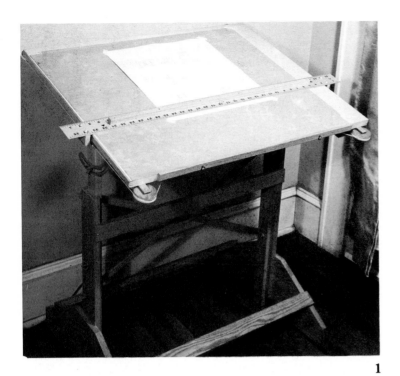

1

FOR THE DRAWING BOARD

An Automatic Parallel

by Rudy Kouhoupt

Photos and Drawings by Author

My drawing board is a commercially built unit that I bought several years ago. It is one of the smaller sized boards with a top surface of 23 x 31 inches. Despite its small size, it is very well built with solid oak framing and a genuine butcher block top which has metal-bound sides. While boards of such quality were not prohibitively expensive at the time I bought it, drafting machines and automatic parallels were. Having invested my money (wisely) in a sturdy, new board, I proceeded to draw with a conventional "T" square. It worked, of course, but a "T" square leaves much to be desired. Very little time passed before.my mind was made up to make some sort of automatic parallel to use on it.

The automatic parallel described in this article is the result of that decision. All of the materials used in its construction are readily available and inexpensive. A check of local hardware stores at the time of writing this article indicates that my original automatic

parallel, which can be seen clearly in Photo 1, can be duplicated today for less than $7.00. Not bad for these inflated times! By comparison, the local drafting supply shop prices a 30" automatic parallel at a figure that wipes out a fifty dollar bill.

The heart of the automatic parallel is the straight edge used for drawing the lines. Many hardware and discount stores have a display of aluminum straight edges made by a company in Milwaukee, Wisconsin, under the Johnson trademark. These are marked with inch marks, numbers, and fractions of inches in addition to other marks for use by the building trades. They range in size from 12" up to five or six feet. The one selected for my use was the 36" model which is designated J36. This particular straight edge is 2" wide and .075" thick.

As you would imagine, with these proportions, it was quite flexible from end to end. Therefore, I added a half-inch square maple stiffening strip to the top surface. The stiffener is 27" long. It is attached centrally to the straight edge by six No. 2-56 flathead machine screws which are spaced at 5" intervals. I match-drilled the stiffener and straight edge to get the holes in the right places. Then I countersunk from the underside of the straight edge to set the heads of the screws just below the surface. The top of the stiffener is counterbored to accept the nuts. I used screws of ½" length to insure that they do not stick up through the top of the stiffener. In use, the stiffener provides a good finger grip for moving the parallel besides making a convenient pencil ledge. While the maple strip was available and convenient for me to use, there is no reason that some other material would not prove just as serviceable. Even a piece of aluminum angle of a small size would be worth considering.

The pulleys (Part 1) were turned for my parallel from a tight, hard grade of furniture plywood that was salvaged from some long-forgotten TV cabinet. I cut them from the piece of plywood using a circle cutter on a drill press. Then I put each of them in the three-jaw chuck on a lathe to true the central hole and turn the groove where the string runs. Lengths of brass tubing serve for the bearings (Part 3) in the pulleys. They are a press fit in the central hole of the pulleys, but they could have been made looser and secured with epoxy or other suitable adhesive. The journals (Part 4) were made at the same time as the bearings. The journals are a free-running fit in the bearings and are about .06" longer than the bearings to give clearance for a washer between the pulley and the pulley mount (Part 2).

Cut the pulley mounts from steel flat stock. Mark out the hole locations, as shown in the drawings. Refer to Photo 2 for a close-up view of the pulley on the pulley mount. Note that a No. 8-32 machine screw passes through a close-fitting washer, then through the journal which is inside the bearing in the pulley. A larger, flat washer is between the pulley and the pulley mount for clearance, as noted above. The larger washer has a central hole big enough to fit over the journal. Note that two No. 6 x ¾" wood screws attach each pulley mount to the lower surface of the drawing board.

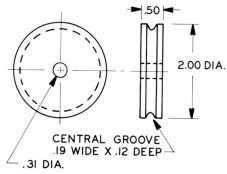

CENTRAL GROOVE
.19 WIDE X .12 DEEP
.31 DIA.
.50
2.00 DIA.

① PULLEY: FURN. PLYWOOD—4 REQ.

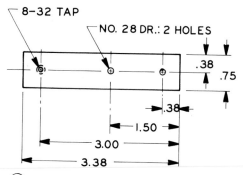

8-32 TAP
NO. 28 DR.: 2 HOLES
.38
.75
.38
1.50
3.00
3.38

② PULLEY MOUNT: .12 THK. STEEL
4 REQ.

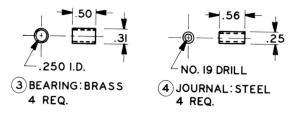

.50
.31
.250 I.D.
③ BEARING: BRASS
4 REQ.

.56
.25
NO. 19 DRILL
④ JOURNAL: STEEL
4 REQ.

At this point, you will have to determine where to place the pulley mounts. Refer to Photo 3 to get the general idea. Pay particular attention to the crossed pattern made by the strings at the back of the board. It is necessary to place the pulley mounts in a position where the strings can run parallel to the outsides of the reinforcing cleats under the board and still get around the

2

3

ends of the cleats to pass diagonally across the center of the board. Obviously, the string has to be clear of the cleats at all points without rubbing, and the pulleys must not contact the cleats. When you are determining the positions for attaching the pulley mounts, hold them in place with small clamps. Then you will be able to stretch a string across the pulleys to be sure that the pulleys are located in a way to provide the necessary clearances. Once you are satisfied with the arrangement, you can put in the wood screws to hold them permanently.

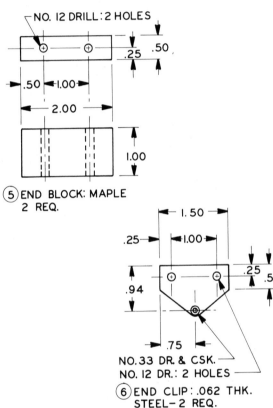

⑤ END BLOCK: MAPLE
2 REQ.

⑥ END CLIP: .062 THK.
STEEL- 2 REQ.

Now is the time to make the end bocks (Part 5) and the end clips (Part 6). The No. 12 drilled holes in these parts are clearance size for the No. 10-24 bolts that secure the parts to the straight edge as shown in Photo 3 and in the close-up view in Photo 4. The end blocks on my parallel were made from maple, as called out on the drawing. There is no reason that aluminum could not be used for this part. Use the end block and end clip assembly to locate the positions for drilling the clearance holes in the straight edge. Once again, clamp these parts in place to find the correct position. The parts detailed in the drawings are exactly to the dimensions I used. When the parts are all assembled, there is .25" clearance on each side of the board between the end block and the side of the board. Also, there is .25" clearance between the end clip and the bottom of the

board. The clearances are needed to permit moving the automatic parallel over the board freely and to give it a little "lift" to clear the papers, triangles, and other thin materials used in drafting. Note that the strings run parallel to the other sides of the cleats as shown in Photo 4.

The No. 33 drilled and countersunk hole in the end clip is for a No. 4-40 flathead screw. The countersink places the head flush and prevents it from digging into the lower side of the board. Cut a short piece of .125 ID brass tubing, about .25" long to fit on each 4-40 screw where it is held by a nut. Its purpose is to prevent the threads of the 4-40 screw from chafing the loops of the strings.

Two separate strings are required to set up the automatic parallel. Notice in Photo 3 that the first string starts out at the 4-40 screw in the end clip on the left. From the screw, it runs up around the top pulley, then diagonally across the board where it runs under the lower pulley and goes up to the 4-40 screw in the opposite end clip. The second string begins at the 4-40 screw in the end clip on the right. From the screw, it runs up over the top pulley and crosses the board on a diagonal to pass under the lower pulley and connect up to the 4-40 screw where the first string started. It is the crossed pattern of the strings that makes the automatic parallel stay in its parallel position.

It is important that both strings be of the same length to keep the parallel in a horizontal position. If the strings are of different lengths, the parallel will hold its position on the board, but it will always be at a slant. The twisted nylon twine which I used on my setup is size No. 12, which has a 106 pound test strength. It was manufactured by Wellington Puritan Mills, Inc., Madison, Georgia 30650, and has catalog number 10469 (G5112Z0300). It is sold in many hardware and other types of stores in this area, but the label information is included here for the convenience of anyone who has trouble finding it.

My first thought was that a spring would be needed somewhere in each string. Not so, however. The nylon strings are a bit stretchy which seems to be adequate. To find the exact length for the strings, make one as close as possible to correct length. Then stretch the second one into place and mark its loop-to-loop length. By taking the average of the two loop-to-loop lengths, you will know the exact length needed for a proper pair of strings. Note in the close-up (Photo 4) that I did not tie any knots in the strings. Instead, I formed the loops around a rod and tied them off by wrapping with a tough button thread. When I was sure that I was satisfied with the fit of the strings, I coated each wrapping with epoxy and allowed it to cure for a permanent, tough job.

There is considerable variation between drawing boards with regard to their top dimensions. Also, there is likely to be quite a difference in the sizes and locations of the reinforcing cleats on the back of the boards. Because of the differences, it is not possible to give exact details for an automatic parallel that will fit every board that comes along. Anyone who wants to make an automatic parallel will have to examine the board first and possibly make some slight changes in the dimensions indicated in the drawings to allow for any variations between boards. However, the principles covered in this article are universally applicable, and the automatic parallel is equally useful for either right- or left-handers. It is much more pleasant and accurate to draw with an automatic parallel than a "T" square. In short, it is well worth the small amount of time needed to construct one and assemble it on the drawing board.

4

Grinding Wheel Arbor

by Jeff Bertrand
Drawing by Author

With my limited funds, a commercially manufactured tool to sharpen carbide tool bits is out of my price range. So, I sat down and designed and machined a grinding wheel arbor for my belt disk sander. The arbor will take the place of the disk sander attachment. This arbor is designed to fit over the shaft that the disk sander was once attached to, and is locked in place with a lock screw.

I recommend stainless 303 as a material, which is a free-machining, non-corroding steel. However, almost any steel could be used.

The arbor can use green silicon carbide wheels as well as almost any other wheel to sharpen tools with. The adjustable compound angle table can now be used to accurately set up and grind the proper relief and clearance angles necessary for proper machining.

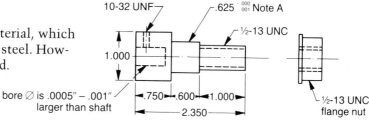

Note A: .625 $^{+.000}_{-.001}$ dimension must be concentric to bore ⌀ to within .001"

Oxy-fuel Cutting Guide Jig

by Orly Phillips

Photos by Author

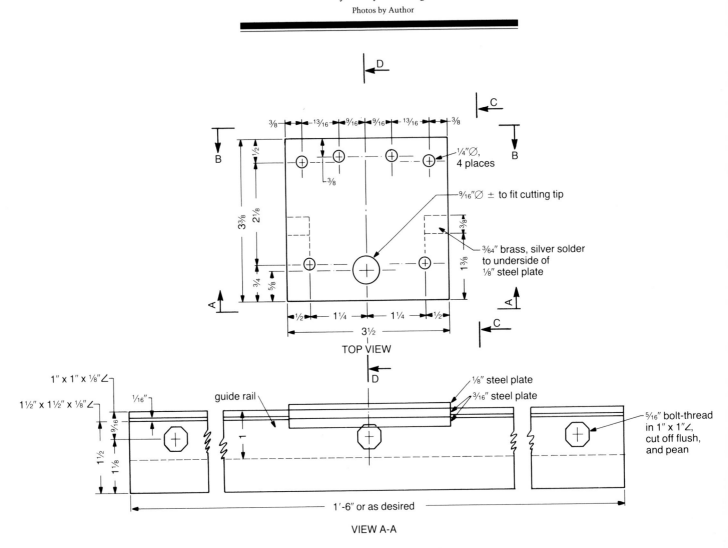

TOP VIEW

¼"⌀, 4 places

⁹⁄₁₆"⌀ ± to fit cutting tip

³⁄₆₄" brass, silver solder to underside of ⅛" steel plate

1" x 1" x ⅛" ∠

1½" x 1½" x ⅛" ∠

guide rail

⅛" steel plate

³⁄₁₆" steel plate

⁵⁄₁₆" bolt-thread in 1" x 1"∠, cut off flush, and pean

1'-6" or as desired

VIEW A-A

For all home shop metal workers, cutting a straight line across a steel plate more than 4" wide with an oxy-fuel cutting torch is impossible unless you are a real expert. The professionals make wide cuts with cutting torches set in jigs running parallel to the proposed cut. Without a jig, a ragged cut results in laborious grinding to achieve a true line. To reduce the grinding to a minimum, I developed a hand-operated jig and guide rail that can be made in the home shop.

Clamp the guide rail to the work at the desired angle parallel to the proposed cut with the centerline of the cutting torch positioned on the cut line. Check the clearance of the torch above the work required for a clean cut. Adjust the height of the torch with cut washer shims. After lighting the torch, pull it to the edge of the work and make the cut at the proper cutting speed.

Although the drawings and the photographs provide all of the information necessary to make the cutting guide jig, a few comments are appropriate and will be helpful. I made my guide rail assembly 18" long. It can be any length desired. For the 3/16" square brazed to the back of the 1" angle, I used 3/16" square key stock. The dimension for the base of the guide rail will depend upon the length of your cutting torch tip. Accuracy in drilling the holes will avoid binding in the operation of the finished jig. The rollers must run free with a minimum

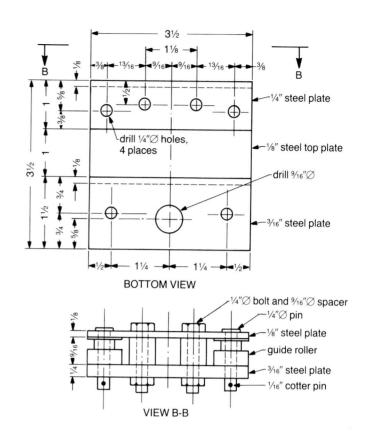

BOTTOM VIEW

VIEW B-B

clearance. The brass strips on either side of the jig provide a smooth bearing for the jig to ride on the top of the 1" angle. The first jig I made with four rollers, two in front and two in back. It did not work well. If the top leg of the 1" angle is rough, work it down with an emery cloth.

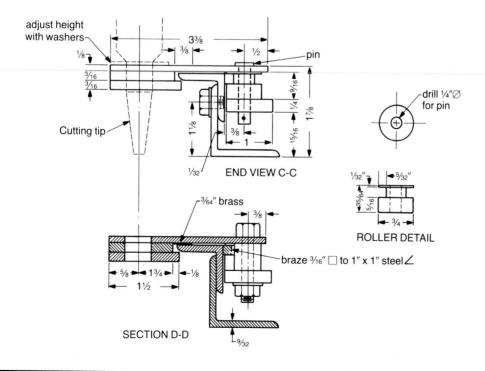

END VIEW C-C

ROLLER DETAIL

SECTION D-D

1

A Temporary Aluminum Furnace

by Philip Duclos

Photos by Author

Many home workshop enthusiasts have probably longed for an easy, inexpensive method of melting aluminum or zinc. All that is needed are six dry bricks (either clay or concrete), two old-fashioned plumber's gasoline blow torches, a small cast iron pot (one pint capacity), an old one-gallon paint can and a small piece of clay brick as a footing to support the cast iron crucible (Photos 1 & 2). Photo 3 illustrates the use of an optional pedestal made from a square, flat piece of steel into which four ⅜" by 1¼" bolts are screwed, thus forming the pedestal. This pedestal is more efficient than the brick one because it allows heat to circulate freely beneath the crucible.

The height of the blowtorches should be adjusted so that the flames are hitting the lower portion of the crucible near its base and at a slight angle so that the flames tend to swirl around the pot.

Cut out the bottom of the paint can with a can opener, and then cut two round holes on opposite sides to allow the torch flames to hit the crucible. Cut down the height of the can so that it's about ½" taller than the crucible (Photo 4).

Don't use regular gasoline in this type of torch; use "white" gasoline or *Coleman*-type fuel used for camp stoves and lanterns. If you don't have torches of this type, you may possibly find them at a swap meet or be able to order them from your local hardware store.

The furnace can be set up outdoors and operated on a *windless* day, or in an open sheltered area. Be sure to fill the crucible with small pieces of scrap aluminum before igniting the torches. After the heat is applied and the aluminum *begins* to melt and settle in the pot, keep adding more aluminum so that the pot is always loaded to the top with unmelted pieces. If your furnace is operating properly, it will take roughly 35 minutes to melt a pot full of aluminum.

Allow the heat to continue for three or four minutes longer to build up to a proper pouring

2

3

4

5

temperature; stir and then skim off any sludge floating on the surface (Photo 5). When ready to pour you can safely lift up the pot with a long-handled offset pair of pliers – use thick leather gloves (Photo 6). I've made many hundreds of castings using cast iron pots, gripped them with pliers and had no accidents. However, if you use a clay or graphite crucible do *not* attempt to lift them with pliers – such crucibles are quite delicate and might break. Always use a crucible tong made especially for your particular size crucible.

For those of you who have not experienced the thrill of pouring your first sand casting, I suggest you read up on the process of sand mold making. There are many excellent booklets available, and a very good source for them is *Lindsay Publications*, P.O. Box 12-PA, Bradley, IL 60915-0012.

6

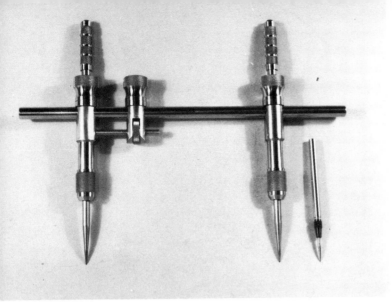

1 *A near copy of the Starrett steel beam tram. The extra point on the right is a Starrett no. 251-H steel point, the actual point of which is interchangeable with pencil lead, so the tram can be used as a compass for drawing large circles. Caliper and other points may also be used to extend the usefulness of this tool.*

A Steel Beam Trammel

by Guy Lautard

Photos and Drawings by Author

Some years ago I saw a beautifully made beam trammel – a copy of a Brown & Sharpe – in the workshop of retired master machinist Bill Fenton. I decided then that someday I would make one like it.

I never did measure Bill's B&S copy, but eventually a Starrett No. 251 Steel Beam Trammel came my way long enough to get a thorough once-over with dial caliper and thread pitch gage. Later, I made a working drawing, then got busy in the shop and made one very similar to the Starrett.

If the sincerest flattery is imitation, there is good reasons for it here: the Starrett Steel Beam Trammel feels exquisitely "right" in one's hands, its proportions ideal. That's not surprising, when one considers they've probably had the best part of a century to refine them! A beam trammel is useful for layout and calipering work involving longer radii than regular dividers and firm joint calipers will span. It can also serve as a compass at the drawing board. The range of accessory points offered by B&S and Starrett are easily made,

and the result is a useful and handsome addition to one's outfit of tools.

I changed the method of attaching the thimbles to the trams and made other minor changes mentioned below. The inside of the chucks will no doubt be similar to the Starrett form but was simply drawn around the tram nose (@ 10x full size) with an eye to how it would be made.

Starrett used 40 threads per inch throughout. Lacking 5/16" and 3/8" taps in the 40 tpi (National Special) series, I used standard NF series threads entirely.

The coarser 24 tpi worked out okay, certainly well enough that one could not justify the cost of sets of 5/16-40 and 3/8-40 taps. The finer 40 tpi would be preferable, because sufficient clamping pressure can be obtained more easily under finger-tightening. If you want to get carried away completely, you could make, flute, and harden a set of 40 tpi taps from 5/16" and 3/8" drill rod – it depends on where you want to put your time. Some machinists like tool making, and some begrudge every minute spent on it. Those in the latter group probably will not make their own taps, nor the beam trammel, for that matter.

In fact, if one puts (or is compelled to put) any reasonable dollar value on one's time, it would be smarter to go out and buy the finished item – but for some of us, that's no fun at all! I hope more experienced readers will not object to the space taken by this description of what is for the most part a relatively straightforward job of turning. Having just completed my own beam trammel, I may be able to offer some helpful advice that will let the less experienced worker proceed more quickly.

I suggest you make the parts in the order described. A comment on the drawings: I do not believe in drawing "the obvious." If a part is round, e.g., the Washer (no. 4), a plan view is usually a waste of ink, and providing *both* side and front views is equally unnecessary. The symbol ∅ means "diameter." All dimensions are in inches, whether marked with the little inch sign (") or not.

It is helpful to have the tapped parts (e.g., Locknut) available as gages against which to work when screw cutting the male threads. As the Chucks will be made after the Trams are done, keep an eye out around the shop for something else already tapped 3/8-24 to use as your gage, or make up a simple gage before proceeding.

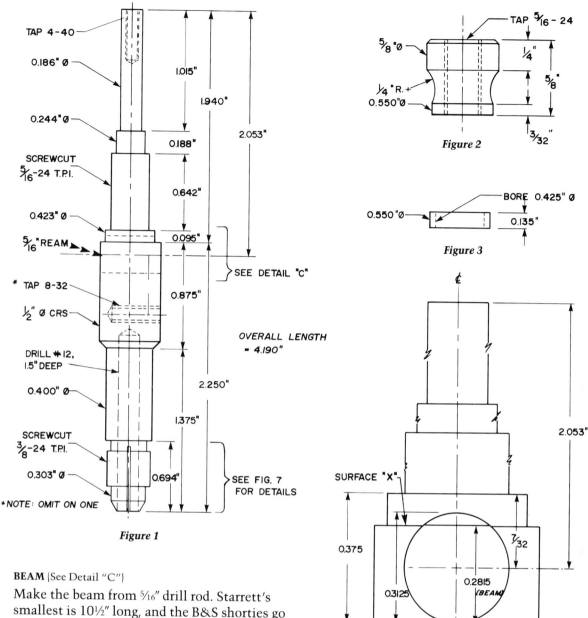

TAP 4-40

0.186" Ø

0.244" Ø

SCREWCUT
5/16-24 T.P.I.

0.423" Ø

5/16" REAM

* TAP 8-32

1/2" Ø CRS

DRILL #12,
1.5" DEEP

0.400" Ø

SCREWCUT
3/8-24 T.P.I.

0.303" Ø

*NOTE: OMIT ON ONE

1.015"

1.940"

2.053"

0.188"

0.642"

0.095"

SEE DETAIL "C"

0.875"

OVERALL LENGTH
= 4.190"

2.250"

1.375"

0.694"

SEE FIG. 7
FOR DETAILS

Figure 1

TAP 5/16 - 24

5/8 Ø

1/4"

5/8"

1/4" R.

0.550" Ø

3/32"

Figure 2

BORE 0.425" Ø

0.550" Ø

0.135"

Figure 3

¢

2.053"

SURFACE "X"

0.375

7/32

0.3125

0.2815
(BEAM)

Detail "C"

BEAM (See Detail "C")

Make the beam from 5/16" drill rod. Starrett's smallest is 10½" long, and the B&S shorties go 5⅛" and 9" for their No. 843 and No. 845 types, respectively. Twenty-inch is the longest one-piece beam offered by either maker. I ended up with three: 6½", 8¼", and 15". It might have been smarter to have made the short one 5" and put the extra 1½" on the next one, making it 9¾" long.

Note: In Detail C the surface "X" is *below* the flat surface of the beam and has been carefully drawn to show this. The dimensions given in Figure 1 and Detail C will give a gap of about 0.012" between the flat of the Beam and surface "X." This is more than enough: some gap is necessary so that the locknut (Figure 2) can clamp the washer (Figure 3) against the beam (Detail C), anchoring the tram (Figure 1) wherever desired.

The flat is best produced by surface grinding. With considerable care, it could be milled, or even filed. If you're going to have to pay for the surface grinding, rough out the flat by whatever means you can devise to minimize the amount of grinding required. Any tool and die shop, and many machine shops, can do the grinding for you. The surface grinder at a technical school or well-equipped high school shop might be available to you through a friend, evening classes, or personal contacts (carefully cultivated, and jealously guarded).

Note: The drill rod, when so flattened on one side, will bow slightly when released from the magnetic chuck of the surface grinder. This will not be detrimental and may be reduced by *careful* pressing by hand while resting the beam, flat side down, on a couple of pieces of

153

½" square CRS or something similar. Mine bowed slightly and remains so.

A SAFETY TIP

Whatever surface grinder you use, its magnetic chuck will require some assistance to get a proper "grip" on the 5/16" drill rod. Have ready to use several pieces of ¼" thick steel (¼" × ½" CRS would be good) to put between, on either side of, and at both ends of each beam to prevent rolling and lengthwise movement.

LOCK NUTS (Figure 2 and Detail "A") 3 off, 5/8"⌀ CRS

Make small end out, and after parting off, reverse on a true running 5/16-24 thread to finish; this will become available automatically: see the section after Main Trams in Part II.

The flaring portion can be cut with a radius tool (see Detail A) made for the purpose, simply roughed in with a file, or any way you care to do it. I made a form tool from 5/16" square drill rod, filing it to shape, filing in the clearance and then hardening and tempering it to a pale straw color (±450°F). Careful stoning after hardening will give a tool that will do a beautiful job (see Photo 3).

Here's a tip or two for making a radius toolbit. Blue the end of the material to be used for the radius tool. Using dividers, or scriber and radius gage, scribe a ¼" radius on the top surface, and grind or file to this profile. Provide a clearance angle of about 7°.

Then stone the cutting edge, making sure your stoning marks all go *with*, rather than *across*, the direction in which the turning workpiece will pass the tool.

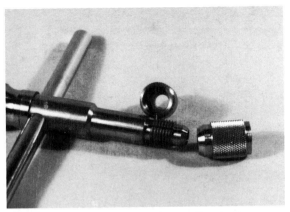

2 *Detail of tram collet nose and two collet chucks, showing interior of one.*

The 0.027" infeed called for in Detail A is made with the cross slide, *not* along the 8° inclination of the toolbit. This 8° inclination is required by the symmetrical layout of the curve on the toolbit and the differing diameters of the workpiece at the ends of the radiussed portion.

To get a good finish with such a broad-edged tool, set the tool up just a hair below center height (or dead on center height, if a thread cutting bit). Make the cut at low speed (say 200 rpm) until near full depth, then drop into slowest back gear, and finish the last 2 or 3 thou of the cut while swabbing on thick brown cutting oil (I use *Procut SC40*). The result should be more than satisfactory. Tailstock support and minimum overhang also help prevent chatter.

3 *Detail of the fine adjust tram. Note the very neat knurling: sloppy knurling on a tool like this ruins the appearance, regardless of how nice the rest of the finish may be.*

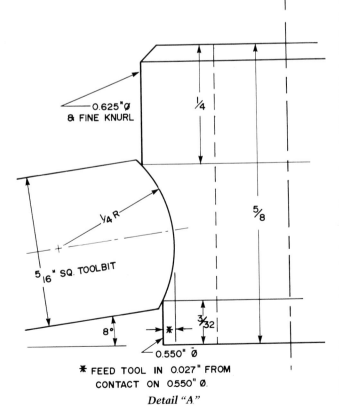

0.625"⌀ & FINE KNURL

¼

5/8

¼ R

5/16" SQ. TOOLBIT

8°

3/32

0.550" ⌀

❋ FEED TOOL IN 0.027" FROM CONTACT ON 0.550" ⌀.

Detail "A"

WASHERS (Figure 3) 3 off, ⅝"∅ CRS

These are steel in the commerical product, and the Starrett unit had a 0.010" thick wave washer in there, too. I planned to make mine of brass, but until I find a piece of brass about the right size, I'll make do with the pair I made in steel. These are made the combined thickness of Starrett's washer plus a spring washer. Brass appeals to me because it will not mar the beam.

THIMBLES (Figure 4 & Detail "B") 2 off, ⁵⁄₁₆"∅ CRS

Plunge cut the ends with a parting tool, cut the radiussed grooves ±0.015" deep[1], knurl, trim the ends of knurling, drill, counterbore the top end per the drawing and part off. Use a ¼"∅ slot drill to do the counterbore. Control the depth thus (if you lack better means of measuring the advance of the tailstock barrel, touch the cutter (a slot drill in the tailstock chuck) to the end of

the work and lock the tailstock movements. Engage the carriage half nuts, and adjust the carriage and compound slide positions so your graduated leadscrew handwheel[2] reads zero and a parting blade in the toolpost just touches the face of the drill chuck Move the carriage (and thus the parting blade) toward the lathe headstock 0.240" via the leadscrew handwheel, then unlock the tailstock barrel and feed the cutter into the work until the drill chuck again contacts the parting tool blade.

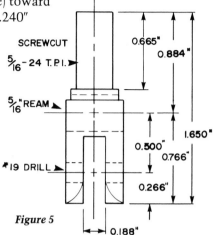

Figure 5

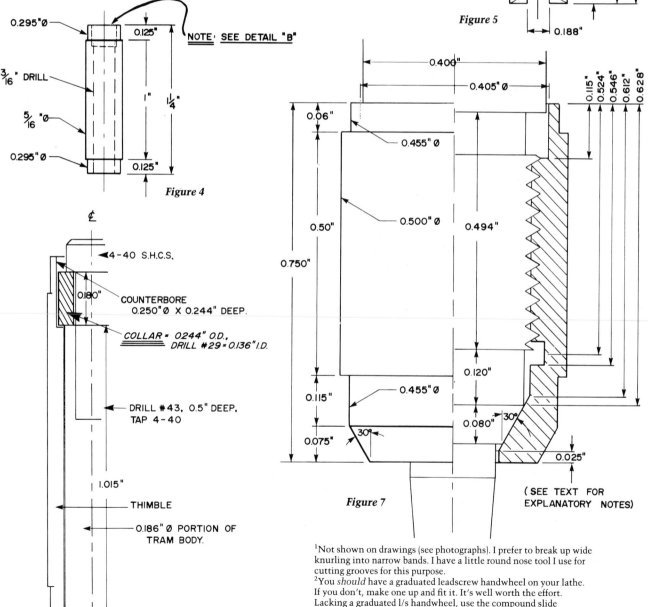

Figure 4

Detail "B"

Figure 7

(SEE TEXT FOR EXPLANATORY NOTES)

---

[1]Not shown on drawings (see photographs). I prefer to break up wide knurling into narrow bands. I have a little round nose tool I use for cutting grooves for this purpose.
[2]You *should* have a graduated leadscrew handwheel on your lathe. If you don't, make one up and fit it. It's well worth the effort. Lacking a graduated l/s handwheel, use the compound slide feedscrew dial for the measurement, the compound slide being set parallel to the lathe bed.

I may have used this trick before, but I don't recall having done so. Having used it here, I made use of it several other times in the course of this job, and will henceforth.

SLEEVE RETAINING COLLARS (Detail "B") 2 off, ¼"∅ CRS

This is a straightforward job. The collar, clamped in place on top of the Tram Body by a 4-40 socket head cap screw, provides a flange which keeps the Thimble in place, yet leaves it free to spin on the tram.

TRAMS (Figures 1, 5, and 7, also Details "B" and "C")

Start making the Fine Adjust Tram (Figure 5) from a straight piece of ½"∅ cold rolled steel (CRS) or brass about 12" long. Chuck it in the three-jaw, and nicely face one end. Dechuck and hop over to the vertical mill.[3] Grip it in the vise with about ¾" sticking out to the right of the vise, and with a parallel of some sort underneath (so it is horizontal), tighten the vise. If the moving jaw lifts, pull the parallel out from under, because you don't want it in there when you start cross drilling. "Pick up" the end of the material, get your spindle centerline zeroed over the end, and then move along 0.266". Stop, lock up, and cross drill no. 19. I'm assuming you've also picked up the fixed jaw and moved it 0.25" inboard, so you can cross drill ½" rod with abandon. Take note of where this useful position is, because you are going to have to lose it for a few minutes when you cut the slot for the Fine Adjust Wheel, and then find it again.

Back to business: drill no. 19, move 0.500" further along the rod, and drill in stages up to 7.8mm (= 0.3071"∅) and ream ⁵⁄₁₆"∅. I am not suggesting for one minute to tool up in metrics. But for reaming, I purchased the drill sizes closest to the nominal reamer sizes I most

4 *Detail showing Lautard's method of retaining the free-spinning thimbles. Starrett's method is perhaps simpler, but less easily duplicated by the home shop machinist.*

often use: ¼" (for this, letter drill D = 0.246"); ⁵⁄₁₆" (7.8mm, = 0.3071"∅, as above); ⅜" (9.4mm = 0.3701"∅); and ½" (12.5mm = 0.4921"∅). These several drills are stored as carefully as the reamers, and are *never* used for any purpose except that final pass through a drilled hole about to be reamed.

Change over to a slitting saw arbor and drop your spindle speed to about 200 rpm or less. (You probably did that before you reamed the ⁵⁄₁₆" hole.) Machine the slot for the fine adjust wheel in three passes: one to take out the middle, then two more to finish to the specified width. Unship from the vise, and move over to the bench vise. Measure from the good end (where you've been doing all the above) about 1¾" and a bit extra, and hacksaw off the fine adjust tram. Cut the remaining piece of ½"∅ CRS in half, and take everything back to the lathe, where you will face all five hacksawed ends. Set the two longer pieces aside, and measure the length of the fine adjust tram as it now is. Subtract from this length 1.650" (= desired length of this part) and face off the excess. Set this part aside for now – there's a good reason for not finishing it yet.

MAIN TRAMS (Figure 1, etc.)

The two pieces of material for the Main Trams are each about 1" over length right now, *and that's just the way we want them.* They're also faced both ends because you just did that. Back to the vertical mill – cross drill and ream ⁵⁄₁₆" each piece 2.053" from one end, just as you did for the fine adjust tram. Before you remove the second one from the vise, move along

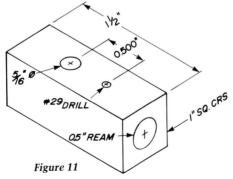

Figure 11

[3]I'm also assuming the use of a vertical mill for all cross drilling and slitting saw operations. If you have a vertical slide for your lathe, you will do it there. If you have neither, a jig (above) could be made up in a 1½" long piece of 1" square CRS, bored ½"∅ full length and with 2 holes (⁵⁄₁₆ and no. 29) put through crossways. Next fit a setscrew (not shown) and the job can be done in the drill press. Such a jig is shown roughly above, and those needing to adopt this method will be able to work out the details for themselves.

0.500", drill no. 29 about ⅜" deep, and tap 8-32. When this is finished, we're done with the mill until we come to splitting the noses of the Tram Bodies.

The rest of the work on the trams is largely straightforward turning and screwcutting. One could use a ½" collet, if available, to hold the ½"∅ CRS material: turn each tram to specified diameters, then set up a threading tool and do all the screwcutting (two off at ⅜-24, three off at 5/16-24) at one go. I used a good, accurate three-jaw and did my screwcutting as I went along. Note: be sure to turn the compound rest back to 30° for screwcutting, after slewing it to 45° for the bevel at the ½"∅/0.400"∅ juncture.

Turn the top end of the tram bodies down per Figure 1 and drill and tap the end 4-40. Move the material outboard in the chuck to make the plunge cut for the ½"∅/0.400"∅ transition on the lower portion of the tram body. Now you know why we wanted the material a little over length!

Dechuck, measure the overall length of the material, and part off the amount necessary to bring each tram body to 4.190"∅ overall length. Turn and screwcut the nose of the trams. Drill the ends for Tram Points. Do not split the Tram Noses yet.

Finally, chuck the unfinished fine adjust tram again, gripping it (carefully) by the cross drilled and slotted end, and turn and screwcut the top end per Figure 5. Then, *leaving this part undisturbed in the chuck*, screw each Lock Nut in turn onto it, and neatly face off the ⅝"∅, (and perhaps imperfect) faces left when the lock nuts were parted off.

FINE ADJUST WHEEL (Figure 6) AND SCREW
(not drawn), one off, each.

Make the wheel a good fit in its slot in the fine adjust tram. You can die the screw, or use a commercial screw – I blew 20¢ on a 2" 8-32 cadmium plated screw and cut off the head. Now I am keeping an eye out for a similar screw in brass. A quick polish with Brasso before installation would make it look quite snazzy. (The Starrett trammel employed a 5-40 thread for this screw.)

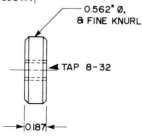

Figure 6

Break the sharp crest of the thread at the exposed end. If it wants to come loose when you screw it in to the side of the tram, put a dab of *Loctite* on it at final assembly.

TRAM CHUCKS (Figure 7) 2 off, ½"∅ CRS

If you are scared off by a part like this, don't be – it's easy to make if you first make a big enough drawing. The smaller the part, the bigger the scale. I like a drawing I can crawl into and walk around in. I can pick off all the necessary dimensions, and then making the actual part is easy. Get the knurl on first, drill no. 5 to ⅞" deep, and then drill or bore tapping size to the specified depth for ⅜-24. Form the internal cone with a no. 4, ⅛" center drill, which has a 5/16"∅ body. Tap (see notes accompanying Figure 7), counterbore, finish OD and part off.

If you don't have a letter Q drill, which is the "correct" tapping drill size for ⅜-24, don't worry. For ⅜-24 tpi, Q (= 0.332"∅) will give you a 75% thread, R (= 0.339"∅) will give a 70% thread and 11/32 (= 0.3438"∅) a 60% thread. So drill 21/64 (= 0.3281"∅), then run a boring tool on center height into the mouth of this hole and feed out (towards you) till you hear it start to kiss the side of the hole. Feed out about 0.003" more, and make a pass into the bottom of the drilled hole and back out again. It'll be fine for size and better for round and straight than a drilled hole.

The little retaining collars, though only the size of a match head, can cause some trouble if one is not careful. As the Collar must be drilled through large enough to clear the fillet on the underside of the socket head cap screw, it can shift off center when the screw is snugged up. If it does so, it may prevent the Thimble from spinning freely. One might suspect burrs to be the culprit – but if there are no burrs, then what? Well, slack the screw, give the thimble a spin, and retighten the screw. This will probably centralize the collar. If not, repeat until it does. The thimbles should rotate freely, and if nicely made will spin for a few seconds when spun smartly. Another fix would be to drill the collar no. 33 right through and enter the no. 29 drill only about 1/32" into the top end. This will make the collar a better fit on the screw.

With the tram bodies, lock nuts and chucks now done, apply a little fine valve grinding compound to each external thread, run on the mating part, and screw them together several times until the feel is smooth. Wash the abrasive grit from all parts: soap, water, a

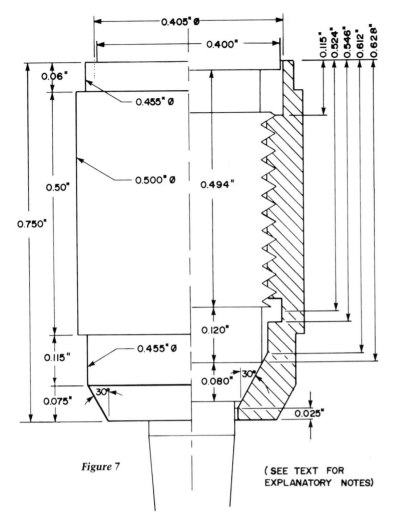

Figure 7

(SEE TEXT FOR EXPLANATORY NOTES)

fingernail brush, and a good high speed squirt of *hot* water from the tap will suffice. Dry the parts.

SPLITTING THE COLLET NOSES

Set up a thin (e.g., 0.025″) slitting saw in the mill, and split the nose of each tram body two ways (to produce four collet "fingers"), carrying the cuts back to about halfway through the thread relief groove behind the thread. Deburr as necessary. I found a good brushing with a brass bristle brush, plus running a round needle file up and down inside the Tram Point Hole, was all that was necessary to get rid of burrs. The points then went into their holes easily, and the chucks screwed on the noses of the tram bodies equally well. And the "collets" that were created worked!

TRAMMEL POINTS (Figure 8) 2 off, ³⁄₁₆″ drill rod

Set your compound at about 4½°, and carefully turn the tapered portion of the point to shape. Finish with a fine cut file, well oiled, and cleaned frequently. Harden the points, temper to pale yellow (430°F), and stone to final sharpness.

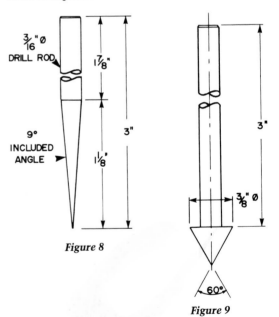

Figure 8

Figure 9

NOTES:

Figure 7 is a partial section of the assembled tram nose and chuck. The tram point is also shown. On the left, the exterior profile of the chuck is shown. On the right is the tram nose, unsectioned, and the chuck in section.

The thread relief groove *in the chuck* is there because I planned to cut same before tapping (not screwcutting) each chuck. When I went to make the chucks, I found that none of my three internal thread relief cutting tools would enter the hole. So I scrapped that idea, and just deepened the hole. That explains the 0.524″ dimension on the right side of Figure 7.

The 0.628″ dimension is the distance *in* to enter the no. 4-⅛″ center drill to form the closing cone in the chuck. To wit, bring the center drill up until the point where its cone and cylindrical sections meet is *just* at the top (= big) end of the chuck, then advance the center drill by 0.638″ more (using the same "parting tool touching the nose of the drill chuck" trick described earlier).

What else can we get off this drawing? Well, I got the ⅜-24 bottoming tap in there pretty good, and I started wondering, "Is it in far enough?" So I looked at the original of Figure 7 (drawn big enough to fill an 8½″ × 11″ piece of paper), which was taped to the fuse box on the wall behind the lathe, and I counted the number of thread crests shown on the right side. There were ten of them. So the tap had better take ten full turns backing out of the chuck. If it doesn't, the chuck might not squeeze the tram collet down on the tram point. Well, it *did* take ten full turns to back the tap out, so I relaxed and finished off the 60° included angle nose taper on the outside of the chuck, and parted it off. Later, when the tram nose was split, thus making it into a collet, sure enough, the whole business worked!

HOLE POINT (Figure 9)

Straightforward. This follows Brown & Sharpe practice, simpler than Starrett form, which could be emulated by annealing a ball bearing about ½″∅, drilling and tapping 10-32, and attaching to a piece of ³⁄₁₆″∅ drill rod so threaded. For the B&S type, tap a short plug of ⅜″ drill rod 10-32, screw onto a piece of ³⁄₁₆″ drill rod, turn to conical form, harden and temper, and there you are. Mount the conical point on a "dummy" 10-32 threaded shank for heat treatment.

In using the conical Hole Point, if you know the size of the hole into which the conical point is to be put, work out the depth to which the point will enter the hole. Then set the opposite point to protrude from its tram about that amount *less*, i.e., far enough to reach the surface to be scribed on *with the beam level*. For a 60° point as shown, simply multiply hole ∅ by 0.8, a close-enough approximation of 0.866 (= cos 30°).

LEAD HOLDER (not drawn)

I bought mine (Starrett no. 251H). Here's how I believe you could make a simple one: Drill no. 48 = 0.076", about 1" deep up the end of a piece of ³⁄₁₆" drill rod. Split four ways – i.e., two cuts at 90° – with your thinnest slitting saw. The regular collet chuck should squeeze it hard enough to make it grip the lead securely. This will hold short pieces of standard pencil leads and will require the use of a shorter point in the other tram body. A standard length point may not go into the point tram far enough to keep the Beam more or less level.

Note: The purchased Starrett no. 251H steel point/lead holder shank miked 0.195"∅. As the tram noses were drilled no. 12 (= 0.189"), it was necessary to turn down the shank of the Starrett part by about 0.008" so it would be usable.

CALIPER POINTS (not drawn) ³⁄₁₆" drill rod

These are similar to trammel points. I didn't make a pair, but if I decided to, I would make them as follows. Turn the taper on ³⁄₁₆" drill rod as for tram points, then heat and bend the ends around a rod of about ¼"∅. Shape the tip of each caliper point to suit (see the Starrett or B&S catalogue), and harden after polishing. Temper to a dark straw/purple color.

COUPLING PIECE (Detail "D") ⅝"∅ CRS

Straightforward. Make the screws from brass, or fit them with copper pads. I have yet to make one. When I do, I intend to drill ⁵⁄₁₆" from both ends, after turning the OD and parting off to length.

B. & S.-TYPE COUPLING

Detail "D"

SCREWS: 10-32 X 0.23" UNDER HEAD. HEAD 0.4"∅ X 0.15" DEEP.

0.625"∅   0.50"∅   0.5"   0.6"   2.5"

MISCELLANEOUS NOTES:

If the beam does not enter the ⁵⁄₁₆" reamed cross holes in the trams, put the reamer through again, then ease the hole with fine abrasive paper wrapped around a drill twirled between thumb and forefinger. Also, wrap the beam with a piece of the same sort of stuff (400 grit wet and dry paper) and smooth it. The trams should then slide along the beam nicely.

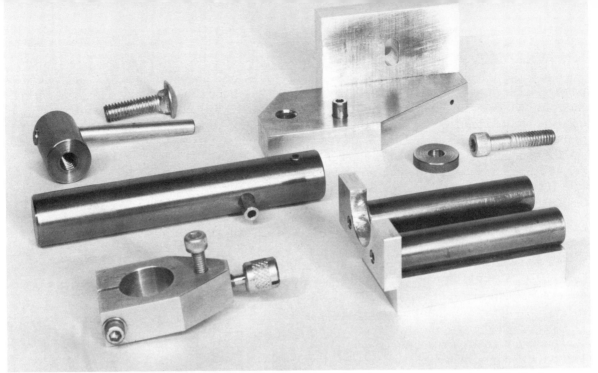

1 *The assembled parts include a knurled knob that was available, although a socket cap screw is specified in the parts list.*

End Mill Sharpening Fixture

by R. S. Hedin

I never could hand sharpen end mills on my tool grinder, so I made a fixture to help me do the job. It fits my grinder at the same location as the work support supplied with the grinder. The primary clearance angle is built into the fixture and the "fishtail" clearance for the center of the cutter can be set so these angles remain the same each time the fixture is attached to the grinder. The only adjustment required is the amount ground off in sharpening. The fixture will fit a Sears Model 397-19390 grinder with 6" wheels and is used on the right-hand side with the fine grit wheel. The finished fixture is such that the center of the arbor is about .37" above the center of the grinding wheel, thereby generating the primary clearance angle. The arbor is made to hold end mills with .375" diameter shanks. It

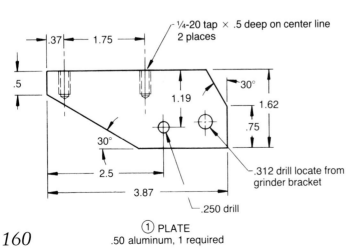

① PLATE
.50 aluminum, 1 required

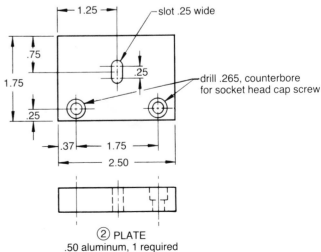

② PLATE
.50 aluminum, 1 required

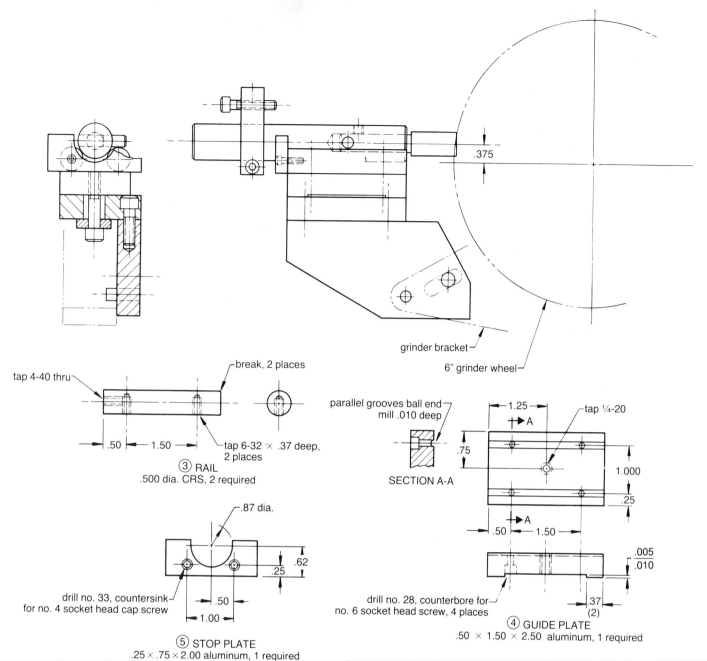

.375

grinder bracket⌐

6″ grinder wheel⌐

tap 4-40 thru⌐

break, 2 places⌐

.50 1.50

tap 6-32 × .37 deep, 2 places

③ RAIL
.500 dia. CRS, 2 required

.87 dia.

.62
.25

drill no. 33, countersink for no. 4 socket head cap screw

.50
1.00

⑤ STOP PLATE
.25 × .75 × 2.00 aluminum, 1 required

parallel grooves ball end mill .010 deep

SECTION A-A

1.25

tap ¼-20

.75

A

1.000

.25

.50 1.50

A

.005
.010

drill no. 28, counterbore for no. 6 socket head screw, 4 places

.37
(2)

④ GUIDE PLATE
.50 × 1.50 × 2.50 aluminum, 1 required

2 *The support on the Sears grinder is filed flat where the fixture is attached.*

can be made to fit .500″ shanks as well. The arbor assembly is laid between the rails with the pin against either rail. The geometry is such that rotating the arbor either way to its extremes moves it 180°.

Fabricating and assembly of the parts are shown clearly in the drawings and photos, so no great explanation is required. However, a few points must be made. To do accurate sharpening the Rails (Part 3) must be parallel on the Guide Plate (Part 4). The grooves milled parallel in the plate will assure this. Also, the tapped ends of the rails must be in line with each other so the Stop Plate (Part 5) will be square with them. Otherwise, the end mill lips will not be the same length after sharpening.

3 *The fixture is attached to the grinder. The .25" diameter pin fits in the hole in the grinder support shown in Photo 2.*

File the mounting surface on the grinder flat, as shown in Photo 2, so the fixture will mount without rocking. Assemble the parts as shown in the photos. Attach the mounting bracket to the grinder using the carriage bolt and handle. The Washer (Part 8) and .25 NC × 1.12" cap screw clamps the arbor guide assembly to the bracket. With an end mill in the arbor, set the guide assembly so the center of the mill is on the corner of the grinding wheel with the "fishtail" set as desired, 2° to 4° is okay. Tighten the clamp screw. This adjustment is now permanent.

To use the fixture, place an end mill in the arbor. Lay the arbor in the fixture with the pin against the rail with the setscrew up. Rotate the mill in the arbor so one lip is horizontal, and tighten the setscrew. Hold the lip against the wheel, slide the stop up to the stop plate so the feed screw is against the plate and tighten the clamping screw. Pull the arbor back and start the grinder. Slide the arbor toward the

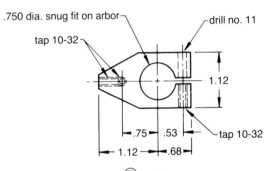

.750 dia. snug fit on arbor

drill no. 11

tap 10-32

1.12

.75 · .53

1.12 · .68

tap 10-32

⑦ STOP
.50 × 1.12 × 1.81 aluminum, 1 required

.250 ream

1.25

.37

ream .3750 dia. × 1.50 deep

tap 10-24 90° to .250 hole

⑥ ARBOR
.750 dia. CRS × 4.5 long, 1 required

⑨ ARBOR PIN
.250 dia. × .50 long steel or brass, 1 required
P.F. or *Loctite* in ⑥

⑩ PIN
P.F. or *Loctite* in ①
.250∅ × .75 long steel or brass, 1 required

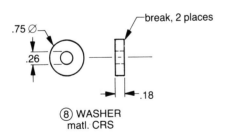

.75 ∅

.26

break, 2 places

.18

⑧ WASHER
matl. CRS

⑫ CARRIAGE BOLT
1.12 long

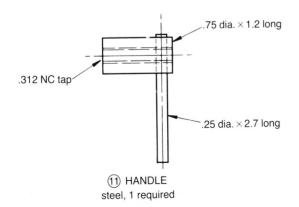

.75 dia. × 1.2 long

.312 NC tap

.25 dia. × 2.7 long

⑪ HANDLE
steel, 1 required

COMMERCIAL PARTS
(1) .25 NC × 1.12 Socket Head Cap Screw
(4) no. 6-32 × .50 Socket Head Machine Screw
(2) no. 4-40 × .37 Socket Head Machine Screw
(2) .25 NC × .62 Socket Head Cap Screw
(1) no. 10-24 NC × .19 Socket Head Set Screw
(2) no. 10-32 × 1.25 Socket Head Cap Screw
(1) no. 10-32 × .37 Socket Head Cap Screw

4 *The fixture is on the grinder and ready to assist in the sharpening of an end mill. Note the position of the pin in the arbor and the stop with the feed screw against the stop plate. The setscrew holding the end mill is on the underside of the arbor.*

wheel with the pin on the rail until the end mill lip contacts the wheel. Grind this lip, pull the arbor back, rotate 180° and grind the other lip. If more grinding is required, back off the feed screw in the stop slightly and repeat the operation on each lip.

Trim the grinding wheel flat with a sharp corner on the right-hand side.

1

Setting Up a Home Foundry

by Dave Gingery

Photos by Author

When the idea of setting up a home shop occurs, the first item of importance is naturally a place to work. Then it is a matter of acquiring equipment and tools with which to perform various operations, and finally we discover just how costly and difficult to find are the materials and supplies we need. For the metalworker it is metal stock, hardware and, above all, castings which are both costly and very difficult to find. It is so simple a matter to establish a basic foundry at home that I am often amazed to learn that few people even consider doing it. I propose to demonstrate here just how easily you can set up shop to produce your own castings, and you may be surprised to learn how low the costs are once you inquire.

Though generally said to be a highly technical craft that requires much exotic equipment, you can see in Photo 1 just how little is really needed for a foundry. Shown here is a complete foundry contained in a space measuring just 8 feet wide and 3½ feet deep. It can actually be much more compact than this; I know of at least one man who carries his entire metal casting outfit in his auto trunk.

On the right in Photo 1 you see the molding bench with its sand bin and a supply of molding sand. On the molding board, which slides on the bin, are a flask and the few simple tools required. All of these can be made at home with little cost or effort. Under the bench are more flasks and a water can of the garden sprinkler type. The riddle, or sifter, leans against the wall. These items are all one needs to prepare green sand molds, into which the molten metal is poured.

On the left is the melting and pouring area with its furnace, crucible and tongs. In my shop this area is a bed of dry sand contained in a simple frame of wood. The sand is graded so that any spill of molten metal will run to the center of the sand bed and not under the wall or onto damp concrete floors. It is so easy to melt metal that many people may fail to realize just how dangerous it can be – you must give serious thought to all aspects of safety from the very first moment you consider it. Molten metal can be spilled by tipping a pot or when a pot breaks, and provision must be made for any possible spills in advance. Naturally if molten metal contact anything combustible, it will be ignited, and you don't want it to run under a wall or through cracks in a floor. If you were to spill it on damp concrete, the resulting steam pressure could cause a very violent explosion. Recognizing potential danger and preparing in advance is the most important consideration in designing your foundry setup. It is just about as easy and safe to melt metal as it is to boil water, but you must realize that boiling water is *a very dangerous operation*.

The melting equipment shown is of commercial manufacture, and it is specifically designed for, and offered to, the home hobby shop or small school shop user. My unit is a model number 4 gas-fired crucible furnace I purchased from Pyramid Products Company, whose ad regularly appears in this magazine. Units are available from a very small number 1 with a capacity of 3 pounds of red brass to a number 16 with a capacity of 53 pounds of red brass. The manufacturer is presently considering larger units, and I understand that a large tilting furnace is under consideration. Available for use with either natural gas or propane, the basic units consist of a furnace body, lid, forced draft burner and a silicon carbide crucible with tongs to fit. Parts, components and supplies are available separately, or you can order sets in the various sizes which include all essentials. Descriptive literature from the company is free upon request. Supplies such as molding sand and parting are offered, and so are crucibles, tongs, pouring shanks, pyrometers and other items of interest to small foundry operators.

You will note in Photo 1 that I have hooked up my unit permanently with rigid pipe, and I have fastened the electrical cord to the pipe and suspended it above the floor to the outlet on the wall. The closer view in Photo 2 shows how I have fastened a metal outlet box to the blower motor with a length of perforated metal strap, and a single pole switch is installed to operate the forced draft blower. Also note the hand valve in the gas line, and the union used to join the rigid pipe to the burner inlet. You can easily imagine the disastrous effect of spilling molten metal on an electrical cord left lying on the floor or sand bed. Even worse would be a spill on flexible hose or tubing that carries fuel gas under pressure. It is a simple matter and a small expense to make a secure installation, and operation will be much easier with a switch and valve installed just where you need them.

The unit itself is a masterpiece of simplicity and very well built. In Photo 3 you can see how the burner port enters the furnace at a tangent. It is a thrill to see the intense blue flame surround the crucible, and impinging the flame on the furnace wall maintains ignition at high velocity and lean mixture, even when the crucible is removed. The blower speed is constant, and air volume is adjusted by moving the air inlet shutter seen in Photo 4. The switch, the valve and the air shutter are the only controls, and you can adjust and maintain a flame of any practical analysis easily.

To light the furnace you need a length of stiff wire, such as a coat hanger, to which you fasten a small piece of rag soaked in kerosene or fuel oil. You simply ignite the rag and hold it near the burner port in the furnace. The blower is turned on with the shutter open a very small amount. Then the gas is turned on slowly until ignition occurs. You slowly increase the size of the flame by opening the gas valve, and air volume is increased by opening the air shutter. In normal operation the crucible is filled loosely with metal and set in the furnace before lighting. Melting can be observed through the vent opening in the lid and with dark protective glasses, and metal can be added to the crucible with tongs as the charge settles during the melt. When the proper pouring temperature has been reached,

2

you simply shut off the gas valve and immediately turn off the blower. The crucible is lifted from the furnace with tongs and set in a ring shank which is used for pouring into the prepared molds. The smaller units, such as my number 4, can quite easily be poured using the lift-out tongs.

3

4

165

Since the melting of the metal is generally considered the main technical obstacle to home casting, it would seem that there is little to stop you now. It is really more accurate to say that melting is quite the least of the technical problems, and a Pyramid Foundry set will put that matter to rest in the easiest possible way at quite a reasonable cost. You can build your own melting equipment, too, either completely or partially, so it is quite within reason to consider adding a melter to any shop budget.

The forced draft gas melting furnace is capable of supplying molten metal to cast lead, tin, type-metal, zinc alloy, aluminum, copper, brass and even iron, and all that is required now is a mold into which to pour the molten metal. There is no reason to feel intimidated by the task of preparing the molds, for there are a number of very clear guidebooks on this simple craft that can be ordered from advertisers in this magazine.

Green sand molding is the practical choice for one-of-a-kind items to be cast in the home shop. This simply involves ramming a pattern into moist, clay-bonded sand in a two-part flask, and then the flask is opened to remove the pattern and re-closed to pour molten metal into the cavity. The result is a duplicate in metal of the pattern. Ordinary skill and common materials are all one requires to produce the patterns, and most shop hands enjoy the activity.

More precise castings can be produced by the investment process, and it is not very difficult to establish variations for several commercial methods to produce very precise castings such as gears, cams and other intricate shapes.

It is entirely fair to say that if you have made mud pies, you can make a green sand mold, and if you have boiled water, you can melt metal. In my mail the most common statement I get from those who have added a foundry to their shop is, "It opens a whole new world of shop activity!" In my own experience I can say that I would not have been able to complete my projects without castings, and I would let all of the rest of my shop go before I would give up my foundry.

A HANDY

Metal Forming Brake Attachment

FOR YOUR HYDRAULIC PRESS

by J. O. Barbour, Jr.

The *Home Shop Machinist* has presented plans for small hydraulic presses in the 10- to 20-ton range, using standard inexpensive hydraulic jacks. All of the various designs have been simple, quite easy to build, and capable of performing many everyday shop tasks.

I consider my 12-ton press, built years ago, one of the most valuable pieces of equipment in my shop and believe every home shop should have one. With it, you can press in and out all kinds of bushings, bearings, and seals, broach keyways, straighten shafts (including small engine crankshafts), and, last but not least, you can build a brake attachment for it, and extend its capabilities tenfold.

To build one, obtain the following (approximate cost, $25). One $\frac{5}{16}'' \times \frac{5}{16}''$ socket head setscrew; one piece of $\frac{3}{4}'' \times 4'' \times 14''$ HR flat steel; one piece of $\frac{3}{4}'' \times 4'' \times 16''$ HR flat steel; three pieces of $1\frac{1}{4}'' \times 1\frac{1}{4}'' \times \frac{1}{4}'' \times 16''$ steel angle; one piece of 1'' square key stock $\times$ 16'' long; one piece of $1\frac{1}{2}''$ schedule 80 pipe $\times$ $4\frac{1}{2}''$ long. These dimensions were right for my press, but can be adjusted to suit yours.

The Bed Plate is assembled (Figure 1) by placing the "V" of the 16'' center angle on the center line of the $\frac{3}{4}'' \times 4'' \times 16''$ flat bar. Then place the other two angles "V" up, flat down on their two legs, and nest them up firmly to support both sides of the center inverted angle, which will become the lower forming die.

Check carefully to assure the "V" of the center angle is bearing firmly against the entire length of the base plate, and the two outside angles are nested to properly support it. Clamp securely and tack weld.

Continuous welds along the entire length of the base plate, and angles, are not necessary. Interrupted welds are adequate and, if you alternate the direction of the welds, distortion will be reduced. Should minor distortion occur, the completed assembly can be straightened in your press.

Since my press is often used to form $\frac{1}{16}''$ and $\frac{1}{8}''$ sheet brass, I elected to use standard angle, with its existing radius in the bottom of the "V" for the bed plate die. This radius, with a conforming radius on the ram plate die, will eliminate fractures that might occur in too sharp a bend. Photo 1 does show extra dies for forming sharp 90° bends in stainless steel and other ductile metals, and an adjustable die with attachments for creating radius and circular bends.

1 *The metal forming brake is shown in position forming a section of $\frac{1}{16}''$ aluminum for a corner break.*

Now, to machine and fabricate the Ram Plate and Upper Die assembly, clamp the $\frac{3}{4}'' \times 4'' \times 14''$ flat bar in a milling machine or shaper, vise, and cut a 90° "V" slot in the center of the $\frac{3}{4}''$ bar, through its full 14'' length (Figure 1). The finished "V" slot should measure $\frac{9}{16}''$ wide at the top surface of the bar, at which time it will be ready to receive the $1'' \times 16''$ key stock, which will serve as the upper forming die.

Center the $1'' \times 16''$ key stock in the "V" slot in the ram plate, with a 1'' overhang at each end.

7 pieces make the complete press brake assembly.

tap ⁵⁄₁₆" NC

1½" schedule 80 pipe

4½

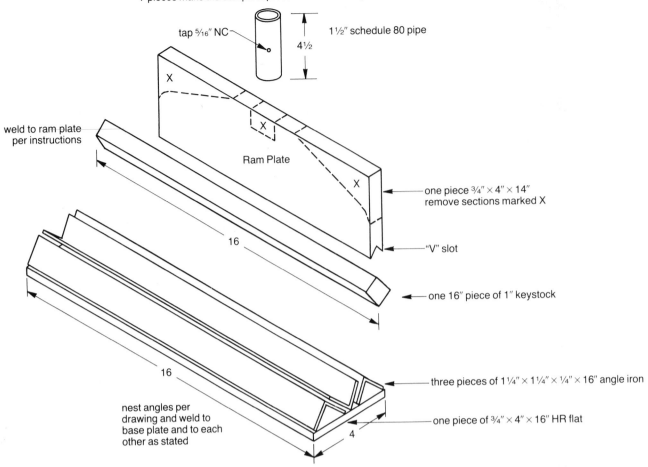

X

weld to ram plate
per instructions

Ram Plate

one piece ¾" × 4" × 14"
remove sections marked X

"V" slot

16

one 16" piece of 1" keystock

16

three pieces of 1¼" × 1¼" × ¼" × 16" angle iron

one piece of ¾" × 4" × 16" HR flat

nest angles per
drawing and weld to
base plate and to each
other as stated

4

Figure 1
METAL FORMING BRAKE ATTACHMENT

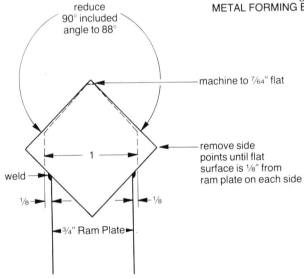

reduce
90° included
angle to 88°

machine to ⁷⁄₆₄" flat

1

remove side
points until flat
surface is ⅛" from
ram plate on each side

weld

⅛

⅛

¾" Ram Plate

Figure 2
METAL FORMING BRAKE ATTACHMENT

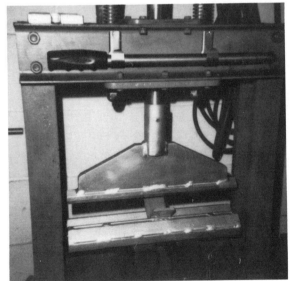

2 *Here, the forming brake is bending a 90° bracket of ¼ × 2" stainless.*

Center the 1" × 16" key stock in the "V" slot in the ram plate, with a 1" overhang at each end. Clamp it securely with several clamps, and electric weld with interrupted welds. Now return the ram plate to the milling machine, or shaper, vise with key stock in the up position for its final machining (Figure 2).

First mill off the top point (apex) of the key stock to a ⁷⁄₆₄" wide flat. The outer edges of this flat should be rounded with a slight radius but this can be done with a flat file. To insure sufficient clearance for other bending opera-

168

3 *The adjustable die is shown in the foreground.*

tions, mill off the two projecting side points until the flat surface is ⅛″ from the ram plate on each side.

The next operation is to reduce the 90° included angle of the die bar (key stock) to 88° to give adequate clearance for making 90° bends. A 45° milling cutter and thin shim at the top and bottom of the vise, on opposite sides, will make this easy in any horizontal mill.

You will notice, from the photo, the upper corners of the ram plate have been tapered to reduce weight and improve its appearance and utility. The slot in the top center of the ram plate allows the ram bushing to be mounted lower to provide greater clearance (daylight) when attached to the press. If you do not have access to a cutting torch, both the tapering and the slot can be accomplished by sawing or drilling a series of connecting holes, removing the unwanted section and grinding smooth.

Whatever your method, it is now time to machine the final item – the Ram Bushing – to fit your press ram. The ram diameter on my hydraulic press is 1½″, so a 4½″ section of 1½″ schedule 80 pipe was used to make the bushing. Machine a suitable bushing to a sliding fit for your ram, and drill and tap for a ⁵⁄₁₆″ × ⁵⁄₁₆″ socket head set screw. Slide the finished bushing on the hydraulic press ram, assemble all components of the brake attachment in proper position and alignment, with the ram plate die resting in the bed plate die, and apply light pressure with the press to hold them in position. Check alignment from all angles, tack weld, and remove the ram plate assembly for final welding, sanding and painting.

The complete unit is small, easy to store, and can be set up or removed by adjusting one set

4 *The adjustable die is being used to make a ⅜″ U-bolt.*

5 *The complete unit is shown with the adjustable die and other attachments.*

screw. It is great for making small tanks, machinery covers, "U" bolts, and all manner of brackets and supports, including 90° brackets of ¼″ by 2″ stainless steel.

The adjustable lower die was a natural development after using the brake a bit, and greatly extended its range and versatility. Its construction is simple and quite obvious from the photos.

"Slow Poke" Small Keyway Broach

by Philip Duclos

Photos by Author

Aset of small keyway broaches costs about $85-$90, which is probably fair enough – but if you only have one or two keyways to cut, this price will cause you to stop and think. So, after a period of cogitation, I came up with the "Slow Poke" keyway broach. As things turned out, it was such a fun project I ended up making *three* different size broaches.

Shown in Photo 1 are the three parts that constitute a "Slow Poke" – the guide, the cutter, and the wedge. Operation is simple; the bushing and wedge allow only an upward or downward movement to the cutter. Each pass of the cutter through the workpiece takes off about .002" of metal. The cutter and wedge are then repositioned and the process repeated until the proper keyway depth is reached.

as a regular broach. An ordinary drill press can safely be used as an arbor press (Photo 2). Furthermore, *all* of the broach parts are made from cold rolled steel. Of course the cutter's tooth must be casehardened, but this is a very simple process. *Kasenit* hardening compound is easily obtainable. The "Slow Poke" performs beautifully.

Three cutters, 1/8", 3/32", and 1/16", are shown in Photo 3, together with three bushings, sizes 1/2", 3/8", and 5/16". A single wedge is used with all three setups.

2

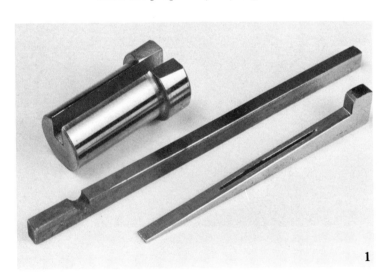

1

Calling this broach a "Slow Poke" is quite appropriate. A standard small keyway broach, which has perhaps 18 cutting teeth, needs only one or two passes through the workpiece to complete the job. Since our broach has only *one* cutting tooth, it's necessary to push it approximately 30 times through the hole to make a 1/8" keyway. Of course *fewer* passes are required for smaller keyways. This slowness is offset by the fact that the "Slow Poke" requires only about 1/5 the force to make a cut

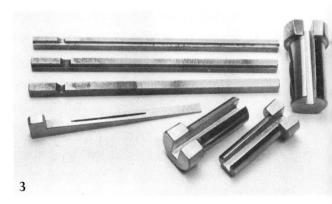

3

Begin by machining the guide bushing. Turn out the bushing and head to size, but leave it attached to the stock piece. At this point two milling operations must be performed. The workpiece is supported on a 5° angle block in a mill vise as shown in Photos 4 and 5. If you don't have a standard 5° angle block, one is easily made from a piece of steel about 3" or 4" long by ¼" thick and ½" wide; merely mill a 5° taper along the ¼" width of the piece. In any event it's important that the 5° angled slot milled in the guide bushing is *exactly* the same angle as that machined on the *wedge* piece — therefore use the *same* angle block for support when making each piece. Mill a flat on the bushing collar down to a point flush with the smaller diameter of the body (Photo 4). There's a dual purpose for this flat; first, a ⅛" end mill will be used to cut a slot the entire length of the bushing. Since standard ⅛" mills are rather short, it would be difficult to reach the required depth without the flat (Photo 5). Second, the flat affords good visibility during the broaching process. The depth of the slot at the *lower* end of the bushing should be about ¹³⁄₆₄". After reaching this depth, move the end mill .002" to one side and widen the slot to .127". Now proceed to finish the bushing by parting it from the stock piece either with a hacksaw or with a cutoff tool in the lathe.

Make the wedge next. Photo 6 illustrates one way to position the steel blank for machining.

4

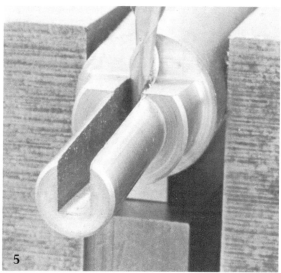

5

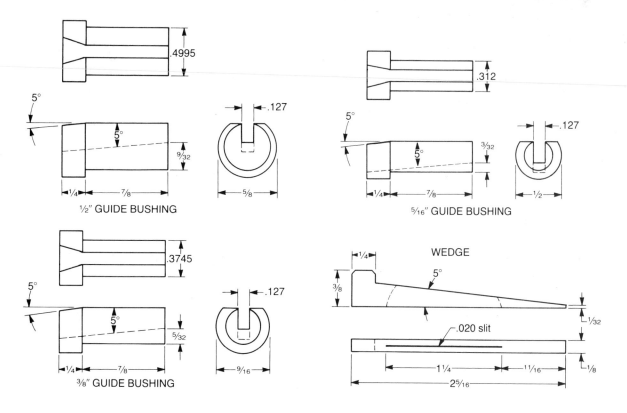

½" GUIDE BUSHING

⁵⁄₁₆" GUIDE BUSHING

⅜" GUIDE BUSHING

WEDGE

Use the same 5° angle block you used with the bushing. Naturally, the line to mill down to is slightly above the vise jaws. Now make a "sacrifice" parallel from a piece of cold rolled steel ⅛" thick, ½" wide, and about 2⅛" long. This will be used to clamp the workpiece securely in the vise jaws as in Photo 7. Now mill the taper on the wedge blank (Photo 8).

A thin slot about 1¼" long is cut through the center of the wedge (Photo 9). After slitting, force a small screwdriver blade into the slot to spread it apart slightly – just enough to make the wedge fit snugly in the bushing. This will prevent the wedge from slipping during the broaching operation.

Fly cutting is the easiest method of forming the cutting tooth on the broach as shown in Photo 10; use an ordinary tool bit and grind it to the correct shape. Mount the broach blank in a mill vise at an angle of 10°-15° from the vertical. I prefer the 15° because it seems to ease the force required to broach. Fly cut the notch.

If you are making a 3/32" or 1/16" broach, it's necessary to mill down the ⅛" width of the broach body as in Photo 11.

In order for the broach to cut properly, it's essential to machine a slight top relief angle to the cutting edge. Mount the broach in the vise at a 1° angle; mill off *just* enough so the angle forms a sharp edge on the cutting tooth (Photo 12). Reposition the broach on a straight parallel in the vise. Now, in order to raise the height of the tooth about .002" or .0025" above the rest of the broach, it's necessary to remove that amount from both in front and behind the cutting edge. Start first on the longer section of the broach and carefully bring the end mill down so that it barely scratches the surface; machine a small area. Remove the broach from the vise, mike the machined section and compare this with a reading taken over the cutting tooth. It's likely that the tooth is still too low, so carefully reposition the broach in the vise; then lower the end mill the required

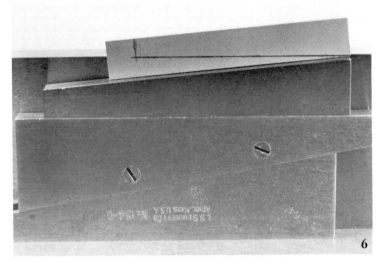

6

7

8

9

172

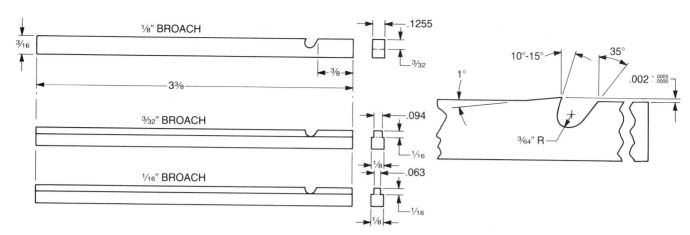

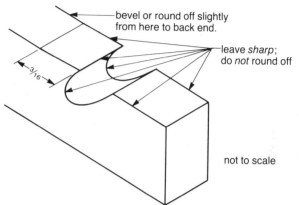

distance to obtain a .002″ or .0025″ figure. Mill the broach shaft, stopping at an area about ³⁄₁₆″ *behind* the cutting tooth, at which point your end mill should intercept the 1° angle you've already cut behind the tooth. Now finish off the short section in front of the tooth. After machining, *carefully* scrape away any burrs that have formed on or around the cutting edge of the tooth. The sides of the tooth as well as the top cutting edge should be *sharp* and clean.

Only the cutter end of the broach shaft is case hardened, a length of about ¾″. Don't be in a hurry to complete the process. Heat the first inch of the tool to a bright red (using an ordinary propane torch) then dip it in the *Kasenit* compound; immediately return it to the flame, keeping the broach end as hot as the torch allows, about 1600°. After 30-40 seconds again dip the piece in the *Kasenit* and then back to the flame. Repeat this several times. When it's ready to harden, plunge the broach straight up and down in plain water. *Don't* stir the piece around in the water – use

bevel or round off slightly from here to back end.

leave *sharp*; do *not* round off

not to scale

11

10

12

13

14

only an up and down motion; this will minimize warpage.

To broach a hole, insert the guide bushing first; then follow with the wedge into the bushing slot, but only about ¾″ of its length. Now the broach is pushed into the slot until its cutting tooth is about ¹⁄₁₆″ above the hole to be broached (Photo 13). Using a finger or thumb, firmly push down on the wedge – this will force the pilot portion of the broach solidly against the wall of the hole. If you use your drill press for the broaching operation, be sure to center the work over a slot or hole in the table – no point in broaching the table too. You can use your *closed* drill chuck to do the pushing. Begin the broaching operation, but stop pushing *before* your drill chuck hits the wedge piece. After the first stroke, reach under the drill press table and pull out the broach. You'll discover that this first cut has produced only two little grooves in the hole. Reposition the broach in its guide bushing for the second cut, making certain that the two corners on the leading edge of the broach enter the grooves you have just formed in the workpiece. Again locate the cutting tooth just above the hole, firmly press the wedge into place and push the broach through the hole. If you are broaching steel, the addition of a few drops of cutting oil into the hole will help, but *don't* use cutting oil if the workpiece is cast iron or brass. Continue repeating the entire process until the keyway groove approaches the proper depth. You'll notice that the wedge piece is now quite low in the bushing (Photo 14). If you are broaching a ⅛″ keyway, the depth of the keyway should be about .064″. A fairly accurate way to measure the slot depth is to mike the height of the broach tooth above the guide bushing as in Photo 15. Be sure the wedge remains in the *same* position it was in during the last cut of the broach. Now remove the broach and wedge from the bushing and measure the bushing diameter – with one of the micrometer anvils straddling the slot. The difference between the two readings is the slot depth.

15

Tool Holder Retainer

by H. T. Biddle

For those who have made or are considering making a drill press conversion to milling operations, here is a bit of help. The tapered spindle, while nice for adapting lathe tooling to a drill press, presents a problem in milling. The vibrations and chatter encountered loosen the holder, permitting it to drop out and allowing the cutter to gouge the work.

The illustrated tool holder retainer, which I have successfully made and have been using, solves this problem by holding the tool holder firmly in place.

The cam action of the wedge on a "T" bolt 20° surface tries to lift the tool holder, keeping it in place.

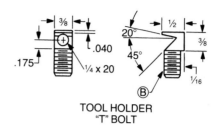

TOOL HOLDER "T" BOLT

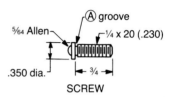

SCREW

TO USE
1) Install "T" bolt in tool holder and back out one half turn.
2) Install tool holder firmly in drill spindle.
3) With wedge on screw, install in "T" bolt thru spindle slot and tighten.

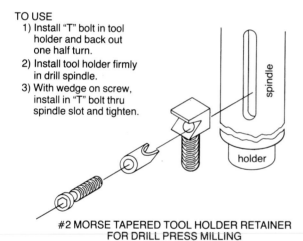

#2 MORSE TAPERED TOOL HOLDER RETAINER FOR DRILL PRESS MILLING

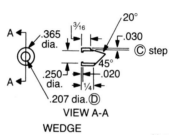

VIEW A-A

WEDGE

Note: all parts heat treated steel.

Ⓐ Make .190 dia. x .030 to fit and retain wedge piece. Grind threads to .230 dia.

Ⓑ ⅜ x 16 or to fit your tool holder.

Ⓒ Not critical, designed to leave maximum material at back of wedge.

Ⓓ Thread ¼ x 20 to clear threads when installing on screw.

A HANDY MATRIX FOR SHOPMADE

Toolmaker's Clamps

by Guy Lautard

Photo and Drawings by Author

Toolmaker's clamps (hereafter referred to simply as clamps, because we aren't going to be talking about any other kind), are useful in many applications around the workshop – for sheet metal work, for clamping parts for marking out, drilling, riveting, soldering, machining, etc.

The accompanying matrix and drawings cover six sizes of toolmaker's clamps from 1⅝" to 5" overall length (OAL). Measurements were taken from several commercial clamps of various makes, and a review was made of working drawings for various sizes of clamps found in numerous textbooks of machine shop practice, and other like sources. The various dimemsions were then tabulated, standardized, and rationalized to form a convenient and logical progression through the normal range of sizes of such clamps. (Obviously, if the available material is of a slightly different size section, e.g. ⅜" × ⁷⁄₁₆" instead of ⅜" square, a clamp can be made to suit the material at hand – the matrix is not written in blood and stone.)

The suggested methods of construction are based on having made about 14 such clamps covering all but the 5" size. The making of one or two clamps is not entirely practical proposition, as the cost of a single clamp is not great, even from famous-name makers, such as Starrett. However, if an extensive set of clamps in several sizes is wanted, the cost begins to add up, and if you make several clamps all of one size at one time, the time per clamp goes down significantly. The notes which follow may be helpful in this respect.

HOW MANY? HOW BIG?

The size of clamps you will want to make and the number of each size will be governed by the type of work on which you will use them. However, as a starting point, two of each of the smallest sizes will be found useful on small work and/or where space is limited, while four each of the 2⅝" and 3⅛" sizes, plus two 4" clamps, would round out a pretty comprehensive assemblage.

Decide at the outset how many clamps of each size you want, and then make all the pieces for a given size at one go, to reduce the time per clamp.

Let's get down to specifics (See Figure 1 for nomenclature):

GENERAL ARRANGEMENT AND NOMENCLATURE
FOR TOOLMAKERS CLAMPS

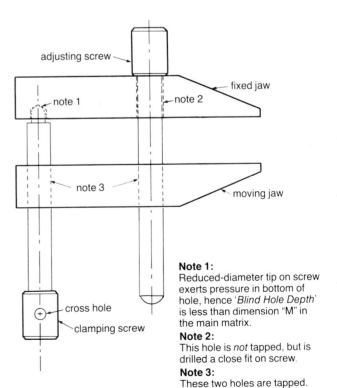

Note 1:
Reduced-diameter tip on screw exerts pressure in bottom of hole, hence '*Blind Hole Depth*' is less than dimension "M" in the main matrix.

Note 2:
This hole is *not* tapped, but is drilled a close fit on screw.

Note 3:
These two holes are tapped.

Figure 1

Materials: I would suggest: For the jaws – Cold rolled steel (CRS); for the screws,..."ready rod" (National Fine series thread), with separate add-on knobs, loctited on. *Note:* For toolmaker's clamps, unlike cabinet makers wooden parallel jaw clamps, both screws are right hand thread full length.

Most knobs will come from the scrap box, I suspect, but if you can get your hands on some, use CRS for them too.

MAKING THE PARTS

JAWS

Cut the pieces for the jaws slightly over the specified OAL; face both ends of each piece, measure and machine to length. Apply marking out ink to all pieces.

Mark out the limit of taper on the top of the jaw (dimensions G&F in the main matrix). A surface gage, surface plate, and an angle plate make short work of this job.

Machine taper in the lathe, mill, or shaper, and deburr with a sharp file.

Do not rely on marking-out and centerpunch marks for locating the four holes per clamp!! I would suggest you do the job on an assembly line basis in the vertical mill, if you have one, or hew as close to that approach as your particular equipment will allow, assuming the milling machine vise has been dialed in parallel to the table movement.

Locate the machine spindle centerline with respect to the left (or right) side of the vise's fixed jaw, and move the table in and left (or right) to locate for the clamp screw holes in the heel of the clamps. Stick a center drill in the spindle. Grab a clamp jaw in the vise on a parallel. Drill the hole, tap it, unship and repeat, 'til half your jaw pieces have that hole done. Do the corresponding (blind) hole in the opposite jaw next, then shift the table with respect to the spindle centerline and do the holes for the adjusting screw.

It goes fairly fast this way. Keep the chips cleaned out of the vise, butt each piece up against the same stop (I use a rule plastered flat against the side of the vise), and don't drill holes in your parallels! Also, lock up your gibs to preclude accidental shifting of the milling machine table. And keep an eye on what you're doing and what you want to do with it ... 'Nuf said.

When the jaw pieces are all drilled and tapped as required, and the noses tapered, the heel of each jaw can be radiused or beveled to suit.

GENERALIZED DETAIL OF PARTS FOR TOOLMAKERS CLAMPS

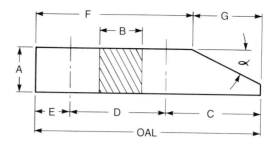

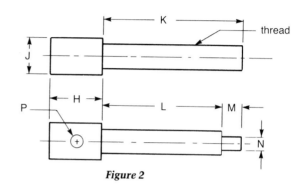

Figure 2

MATRIX A
Refer to Figure 2

Dimension (Letter)	CLAMP SIZE (= OAL)					
	1⅝	2⅛	2⅝	3⅛	4	5
A	5/16	3/8	7/16	1/2	5/8	3/4
B	5/16	3/8	7/16	1/2	5/8	3/4
C	11/16	15/16	1 3/16	1⅜	1 15/16	2¼
D	11/16	15/16	1 3/16	1½	1¾	2¼
E	¼	¼	¼	¼	5/16	½
F	1⅛	1 7/16	1¾	2 3/16	2¾	3¼
G	½	11/16	⅞	15/16	1¼	1¾
∝	25°	22°	22°	23°	22°	19°

Hole Sizes: in fixed jaw						
Through hole	#19	#11 or #10	¼	¼	5/16	7/16
Blind hole ∅	#36 (0.1065)	#29 (0.1360)	#19 (0.1660)	#15 (0.1800)	¼	11/32
Blind hole depth	⅛	3/16	3/16	3/16	¼	¼
In moving jaw, drill both holes	#29	#21	#3	#3	Letter I (0.2720)	25/64
and tap them	8-32	10-32	¼-28	¼-28	5/16-24	7/16-20

Screws Thread	8-32	10-32	¼-28	¼-28	5/16-24	7/16-20
H	3/8	½	½	5/8	¾	1
J	¼	5/16	3/8	7/16	9/16	5/8
K	1⅝	2¼	2¾	3½	4	5
L	1 5/16	1⅞	2¼	3	3½	4½
M	3/16	¼	¼	¼	5/16	3/8
N	.100	.130	.160	.175	.240	.332
P	3/32	⅛	⅛	5/32	3/16	¼

NOTE: All dimensions are in inches.

Here I shall make a confession. My clamps have all square heels. (Confession is said to be good for the soul, but it doesn't seem to have done much good for the heels!) Maybe one of these days I'll radius them, but other things keep pushing that task down the list. In the meantime, they work just as good the way they are.

SCREWS

"Ready rod" can be used in making the screws, plus separate knurled knobs, drilled, tapped, and loctited in place. This considerably reduces the amount of time and material needed to make a clamp. Details and information are given in Figure 3 and Matrix B.

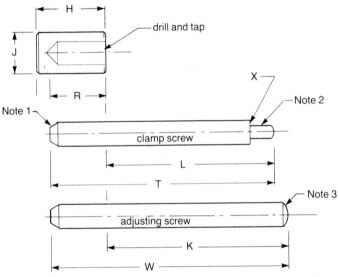

DETAILS RE: SCREWS AND SEPARATE KNOBS
FOR TOOLMAKERS CLAMPS
refer to Matrix B for dimensions

Note 1: Bevel this end with a file to permit it to screw fully into tapped hole in the knurled knob.
Note 2: Turn down to dimensions "M" and "N" in main matrix above. Round tip as shown.
Note 3: Round with file, then blunt sharp edges of thread crests.

Figure 3

MATRIX B
Refer to Figure 3

Dimension (Letter)	CLAMP SIZE (= OAL)					
	1⅝	2⅛	2⅝	3⅛	4	5
H	⅜	½	½	⅝	¾	1
J	¼	5/16	⅜	7/16	9/16	⅝
Drill and	29	21	3	3	I(i)	25/64
Tap	8-32	10-32	¼-28	¼-28	5/16-24	7/16-20
to Depth R	¼	⅜	⅜	½	⅝	¾
T (Clamp Screw)	1¾	2½	2⅞	3¾	4½	5⅝
W (Adjusting Screw)	1⅞	2⅝	3⅛	4	4⅝	5¾
Knurling	Fine	Fine	Fine	Med	Med	Med

NOTE: All dimensions are in inches.

KNURLED KNOBS

Knurling to full depth (i.e. to the point of producing sharp diamonds) is neither necessary nor desirable. In fact, it is a good idea to put a file to the knurled surface to make it a little easier on the thumb and forefinger when using the clamps. If you don't have a knurling tool, or don't want to bother knurling the knobs, leave them plain. In any case, I would highly recommend you cross-drill the knob of the clamping screw for a tommy bar. (Another confession would be too much of a good thing – don't look too closely at the photo accompanying these pearls of wisdom!) As far as I can see, a cross hole in the adjusting screw knob serves no purpose – only the clamping screw needs a hole.

To assemble knobs to screws, when all the parts are ready, degrease with rubbing alcohol, apply a drop or two of *Loctite 601* (or similar) in the knob, run the screw into the knob and back out again to suck the *Loctite* to the bottom of the hole. Then screw fully home, wipe off the excess *Loctite* and leave it to set. Cross drill the knob/screw assembly after this has been done.

FINISHING TOUCHES

Remove toolmarks from the tapered nose of each jaw piece with a well-chalked, sharp, fine-cut file, then with a piece of abrasive cloth backed up with the same file. A quick rub with steel wool or worn emery paper will produce a nice dull finish on clean CRS. Sand blasting or glass bead blasting is quick and will give you a very nice looking finish. The jaws could be blued with one of the proprietary cold touch-up gun blues, if you like. If you've made a whole pile of them, you might even go around to your local gunsmith and see if he'd run them through his bluing tanks next time he's in the mood.

CASE HARDENING THE JAWS

Many factory-made clamps are case hardened and display the attractive mottling of reds, blues, browns etc., associated with "color case hardening." Personally, I very much doubt the need for case hardening clamps for home-workshop use. However, for those who disagree, there are commercial heat treaters who would no doubt do it for a nominal fee. You might, however, be wise to have them do just one clamp first, before you commit your whole output: a friend told me that years ago, during his days as an apprentice, he made a pair of toolmaker's clamps, and case hardened the jaws. The first time he used one, the fixed jaw broke in half at the adjusting screw hole! The case hardening had gone too deep, and had left the thin section on either side of the hole hard right through and brittle. (This, of course, is a case of failure of "technique" rather than "application," and could perhaps have been corrected by annealing the area around the screw holes.)

The same chap also said he'd made one little wee clamp about an inch or so long, using socket head cap screws for the screws. He's had it in his toolbox ever since, and gotten much use out of it where a larger clamp would not fit, but where a little nipper was just the thing.

And here's an idea: How about a fully functional, miniature toolmaker's clamp, nicely polished (and maybe blued), as a lapel pin or tie tack? Why not? You might meet a fellow machinist that way, who'd otherwise never know you had a common interest.

SOME NOTES ON MAKING THE OPTIONAL CLIPS

One feature commonly found on factory-made clamps is not shown in the main drawings and matrix. This is the clip, or retaining fork, on the fixed jaw (see Figure 1 for nomenclature), which engages the head of the adjusting screw. While this clip is convenient, particularly if the clamps are to be in constant use, I have found that clamps made without it work equally well in all other respects. The clip requires additional work to make, and adds little to the utility of the clamp. For those who want to incorporate this feature, an additional drawing and another matrix is provided which should be helpful.

Usually, the clip on commercial clamps is a stamped metal part. Such is quite satisfactory in practice, but forming the bend might be a little tricky without a purpose-built bending jig, different sizes of which would be required for different sized clips. If I were making clips for a run of shop-made clamps, I would make them from black mild steel sheet or bar, thus:

1. Machine the material to the leading dimensions ($E \times F \times B + C$).
2. Mark out and center punch for hole A.
3. Put the material in a four-jaw chuck and indicate the center punch mark true (or clamp it in the vise of a vertical mill and pick up the centerpunch mark with a centerfinder), then drill hole A.
4. Mill the step across the underside.
5. Drill the attaching hole on an assembly line basis as for the holes in the jaws.
6. Cut the piece in half with a hacksaw (thus producing two clips, enough for two clamps).

DETAILS RE: OPTIONAL CLIP FOR TOOLMAKER'S CLAMPS

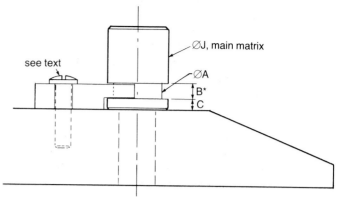

*Note 1:
After knurling the adjusting screw knob, machine groove B slightly oversize to give clip fork a free fit in the groove.

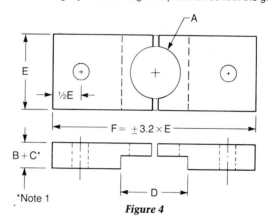

Figure 4

SUBMATRIX "C" FOR OPTIONAL CLIP
Refer to Figure 4

Dimension (Letter)	CLAMP SIZE (= OAL)					
	1⅝"	2⅛"	2⅝"	3⅛"	4"	5"
∅A on knob	0.198	0.245	0.308	0.370	0.433	0.525
"A":drill in clip	¹³⁄₆₄	¼	⁵⁄₁₆	⅜	⁷⁄₁₆	¹⁷⁄₃₂
B	¹⁄₁₆	¹⁄₁₆	¹⁄₁₆	³⁄₃₂	⅛	⅛
C	¹⁄₁₆	¹⁄₁₆	¹⁄₁₆	¹⁄₁₆	⅛	⅛
B + C	⅛	⅛	⅛	⁵⁄₃₂	¼	¼
D	0.270	0.33	0.42	0.47	0.62	0.70
E	¼	⁵⁄₁₆	⅜	⁷⁄₁₆	⁹⁄₁₆	⅝
F (approx)	0.80"	1.0"	1.2"	1.4"	1.8"	2.0"

NOTE: All dimensions are in inches.

7. Clean up that cut, and break all corners and edges with a sharp, fine-cut file.

The use of a screw for attaching the clip to the jaw is probably preferable to a rivet, as it permits easy disassembly at some future date, if desired. Also, if a screw is used, the hole in the clip will be clearing size, and eases (somewhat) the need for accuracy in locating the corresponding hole in the fixed jaw.

Adjustable Parallels

by Philip Duclos

Photos By Author

2

Do you know it's possible to make your own adjustable parallels merely by using standard size end mills? No special dovetail cutter is needed. Briefly put, an end mill is used to make two *outward angled* cuts that originate from a single groove, thus creating a dovetail.

Photo 1 shows the cold rolled steel bars that were employed to make two sizes of parallels. In theory cast iron is best, but I certainly don't have any cast iron bars lying around. The pair of small bars are $5/16'' \times 1/2'' \times 2 1/8''$ long. The other two are $5/16'' \times 5/8'' \times 2 11/16''$.

1

Machining time will be improved by working alternately on both parallels. In mounting your angle vise on the mill, it's *very* important to check the accuracy of the solid jaw with a dial indicator. It should be as parallel as possible to the travel of your table. Also, the bed of the vise should be level to the mill table; if it's off, the use of shims under the supporting parallel will be necessary.

Mount one of the smaller workpieces in the vise (Photo 2). Use a $1/8''$ end mill and cut a groove $5/32''$ deep in the *center* of the bar. The method I used to arrive at the center is to position the end mill close to one side of the bar and, with the cutter turning about 1500 rpm, advance it just enough to barely scratch the side of the workpiece. Set the calibrated dial on the mill table to zero. Since our workpiece is about .312'' thick, we take half of that *plus* half the diameter of the end mill. That's .156'' plus .062'', which comes to .218'' as the amount necessary to move the cutter over to the center of the work – not perfect, but close enough. Begin milling the groove. Unless you have a drawer full of $1/8''$ end mills, be very careful; limit each cut to $1/32''$ in depth.

Consequently, you'll have to make five passes through the bar before reaching the required depth. Now remove the bar from the vise, install one of the larger bars and repeat the milling process.

At this point it's *important* that the workpiece be seated *solidly* on the supporting parallel beneath it. I've found that as soon as the vise jaw is tightened, the workpiece will rise slightly. Use a *lead* hammer and pound it down until it is positioned *snugly* and *evenly* on the support. Unless you have a tilting head on your mill, it's now time to tilt the angle vise up 5° as in Photo 3. Take a light cut – just enough to resurface the top side next to the groove *nearest* the solid jaw of the vise. Now lock the height adjustment of your spindle to maintain the vertical position of the cutter. Loosen the vise jaw and remove the workpiece. With a brush, *carefully* remove any chips that have fallen on the support parallel in the vise.

Reinstall the workpiece, *reversing* it end for end. Again, and *every* time it's reversed in the vise, seat it solidly with a *lead* hammer. Now

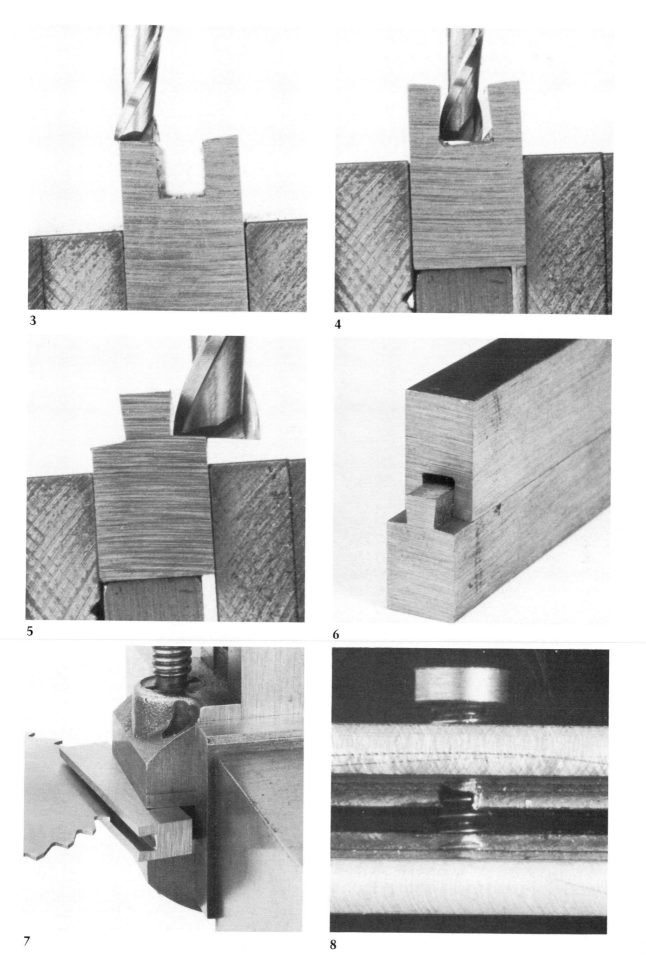

3

4

5

6

7

8

mill the other top surface. Next, lower the end mill (be sure it's a sharp one) and proceed to mill the *side* of the groove nearest the solid jaw of the vise (Photo 4). Mill just enough to resurface the side up to the top edge. Run the cutter back and forth until it stops cutting. Lock the mill table so that the end mill maintains its position. Now remove the workpiece and reverse it end for end; make certain there are no chips underneath it. Mill the other side of the groove, and again run the end mill back and forth until it stops cutting.

Now install the other grooved bar for your second parallel. Repeat the whole process, beginning with Photo 3. When you've finished set these two pieces aside, and install one of the other blank pieces in the vise just as you did the first. When you mill the male dovetail (Photo 5), use a ¼" or ⅜" diameter end mill (more rigidity), but be sure to see that the outer end of the cutter clears the vise. Lower the end mill ⅛" from the top surface of the blank, then lock the height adjustment of your milling machine. Move the cutter into the work about .050" and machine a step along one side.

At this point, don't change the position of the end mill. Now remove the workpiece and reverse it end for end; be careful to reseat it properly in the vise. Mill that side. You now have a roughed-out, oversized dovetail. From now on it's a matter of whittling away at the width of the dovetail until it mates snugly with its counterpart. You can get a rough estimate of how much more material is to be removed by measuring with a rule across the width of the grooved piece down ¹⁄₁₆" from the outer edge and comparing that with the width of the tongue ¹⁄₁₆" up from the bottom of the step you are working on. Remember, every time you remove .001" from one side, you'll also have to remove .001" from the other side by reversing the workpiece in the vise.

While all of this is going on, bear in mind that you can take metal *off*, but you *can't* put it back on. After each cut check to see if the mating part will fit. When it will almost go on, it's time to reduce the cut to perhaps .0005". Face one side and again check for fit. If it still refuses to slide on, then reverse the workpiece again and machine the other side. The ideal fit is one that slides fairly easily but with little or no side play or wobble. Photo 6 illustrates how your parallel will appear at this point.

Photo 7 is the next step, that of milling a slot in the parallel. A cut is made in the grooved section along the entire length of the parallel

9

at a point slightly above what will become the *base* of the parallel. Since the dovetail of the parallel is at an angle to the true base, this angle must be used when cutting the slot – in other words, the slot will be deep on one end and so shallow on the other as to disappear. Height and length of the workpiece determines the angle. Measure from the bottom of the *groove* at one end and down to a point about ¹⁄₃₂" *above* the corner at the other end. The angle to use for our short parallel is 8° and for the long, 6°. Clamp the small parallel, groove side out, at an angle of 8° in a vise. Then position the vise in a larger vise as illustrated. Two alternative holding methods would be to clamp the vise to an angle plate – or, as visible in Photo 9, merely hold the workpiece to a 1-2-3 block in a vise. Use a ¹⁄₃₂" slitting saw to cut a slot along the center line of the dovetail.

Now remove the workpiece and lay out the location for a 4-40 (or 4-36) clamping screw. This screw should be centered lengthwise on the parallel and crosswise at a point where the *tap drill* will just miss breaking through into the bottom area of the dovetail groove – when threaded, it probably will break through. Photo 8 is a view looking into the dovetail of the parallel. The tap hole through the lower half of the parallel has been threaded and the hole through the upper section enlarged to allow the screw to slip through; this hole has been counterbored to accommodate the screw head. I used a Phillips-type filister head screw but found it necessary to shorten the depth of the head to ¹⁄₁₆" – it wouldn't have been wise to counterbore the head into the parallel any deeper than that.

Since there's only one screw in the small parallel, it's necessary to cut a 1″ long slit on the parallel behind the bolt hole (Photo 9). This allows the screw to exert more clamping pressure on the mating part. On larger parallels this slit is eliminated and *two* clamping screws are used.

Now, with the parallel assembled and the clamping screw tightened, place the parallel in your mill vise; support it on parallels so that its *flat* surface is slightly exposed above the vise jaws. Use a large end mill or fly cutter and take a light cut – just enough to clear up that side. Do the same with the other side.

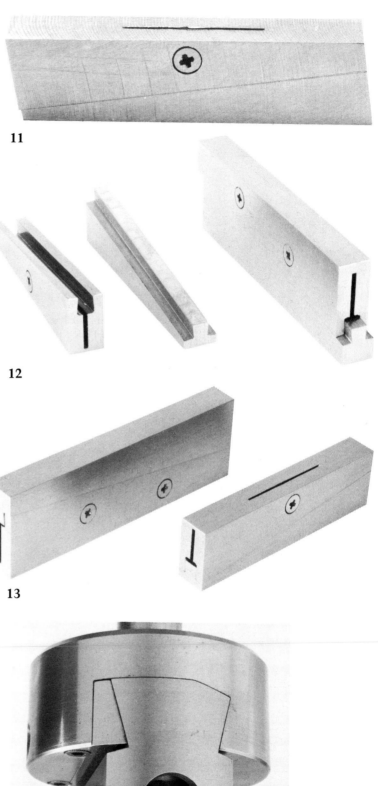

11

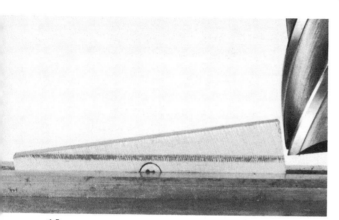

10

12

Now mount the work edgewise in the vise at an angle of 8° (Photo 10). The area above the dark line must be removed, but not all in one swipe as the photo might indicate. Take light cuts until evidence of the 8° angle is gone. Then remove the workpiece and eliminate any burrs that may be present. Return the parallel to the vise; support the *edge* you've *just machined* on an *accurate* parallel. Repeat the machining process as indicated by Photo 10. At this point your workpiece should resemble the one in Photo 11. Again clamp it in the vise, this time in a vertical position, and square off each end.

Well, that's it – you're finished. Of course, if you have access to a surface grinder you can pretty-up the parallels as in Photos 12 and 13.

This method of making dovetails has other applications, too. As an example, Photo 14 illustrates the use of this principle in building my homemade boring head.

13

14

Some Light on the Subject

by Art Crow

Photos By Author

I have created a light fixture that will put some real light on the subject. As my grandson says, "We're talking megalight here." The fixture uses a 500 watt halogen quartz bulb and sheds a lot of light on that close job at the lathe, tune-up of mom's car or work in 100 other places. I have made a number of these lights and sold them to machine shops, paint stores and garages.

A four-legged base can be fabricated, but an old car wheel makes a dandy base. Two pieces of 14-gage square tubing that telescope are used for the riser. I use 1" and 1¼" about 40" long. The other items include one electrical junction "handy box," one ½" NPT hub, one single pole light switch, and a 25-foot three-wire drop cord. The quartz light fixture itself is available at any electrical supply store (I use one made by ITT outdoor lighting of South Haven, MS).

This completes the recipe, except for the thumbscrew assembly and cord brackets you will fabricate. Make the thumbscrew assembly out of a ½-13 × 1" cap screw (slot the head and weld in a 3" piece of 1" flatbar) and a piece of steel ½" × 1¼" × 1½" drilled and threaded ½-13.

Drill a ⅝" hole near the top end of the 1¼" tubing, and weld the thumbscrew assembly over the hole. Weld the bottom cord bracket to the 1¼" riser near the bottom. When that's complete, run the cord through it so if someone trips over the cord, it won't tip the fixture over. Weld the handy box and the top cord bracket to the top of 1" square tubing, slide it into the 1¼" riser and lock with the thumbscrew.

The fixture comes with a ½" NPT threaded end with a locknut to fit a ½" NPT hub. Cut the dropcord 8" from the female end and make up connections for the light, switch, and pigtail inside the junction box. Leave the pigtail with the female end hanging out of the junction box for an extra outlet. Be sure to use proper wire nuts, connectors and grounding techniques.

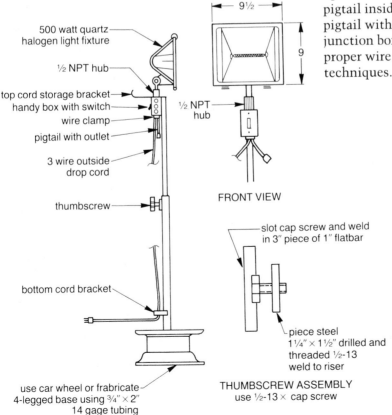

500 watt quartz halogen light fixture

½ NPT hub

top cord storage bracket
handy box with switch
wire clamp
pigtail with outlet

3 wire outside drop cord

thumbscrew

bottom cord bracket

use car wheel or frabricate 4-legged base using ¾" × 2" 14 gage tubing

SIDE VIEW

9½

9

½ NPT hub

FRONT VIEW

slot cap screw and weld in 3" piece of 1" flatbar

piece steel 1¼" × 1½" drilled and threaded ½-13 weld to riser

THUMBSCREW ASSEMBLY
use ½-13 × cap screw

Drawing Up A Bargain

by Guy Lautard
Photos and Drawings by Author

In any sphere of purchasing, it pays to "know the market" before you buy. If you attend an auction, and see something that looks to be in good shape, and you outbid everyone else for it, the frosting is gone from the cake if the next day you phone the dealer and find you paid more than the price of a brand new one. However, you can't always know the new price ahead of time – sometimes you've gotta act, Now! or miss a bargain. In which case it pays to have a general idea of what a certain type of goods costs.

Such was the case for me some time ago when I saw a second-hand Brown & Sharpe #750B* V-block for sale. Had a look at it – no flaws, two or three little burrs that could be stoned off. Missing the clamp.

"How much?"

"$10."

My wallet came out with my thumbnail smokin'! A clamp would be easy enough to make, and the cheapest pair of hardware quality V-blocks has to run the thick end of a 20 dollar bill, never mind what a hardened-and-ground, ±0.0003"-on-all-sides Brown & Sharpe V-block would cost! As you will see from the accompanying photos, the #750-2

---

*My V-block is marked "Cat. No. 750B"; the same item in the most recent B&S catalogue I have is referred to as a 750-2.

B&S is of the type which can be turned on its side with a job clamped in place. Next day I phoned the B&S dealer. How about $160 (Canadian) c/w clamp? A bargain? I guess so.

The next job was to design a clamp. I laid about the neck and ears of my new V-block with a 6" dial caliper, and made a 2X full size drawing of its end profile (reproduced here at half size, so you'll see a full size V-block, half the size I drew it). I quite enjoy drafting, and you can get all the info you'll need from an accurate, scaled up drawing of something you want to make. As few people are likely to be faced with the need to make a clamp for a B&S #750 V-block, I have shown only leading dimensions. So, here's how I went about "drawing up a bargain."

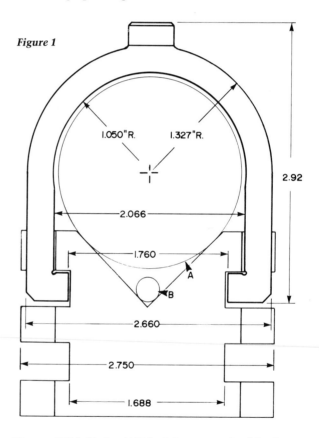

Figure 1

First, a 2X full size (2X f.s.) drawing of V-block. Next a peek in B&S catalog for capacities. "…to 2" diameter (approx.)." The minimum size the block was happy with, influenced by the width of the relief groove in the bottom of the Vee, turned out to be ¼"∅ approximately. This from experiment, as it is not stated in the catalogue.

Next, two circles (A&B) were drawn to scale, representing the maximum and minimum sizes the block would hold, on the vertical centerline of the drawing, and so they just touch the Vee faces. The clamp must clear the biggest one (**A**) so the clamp was drawn in place with its feet hooked onto the top pair of side grooves.

Next, a quick tracing was made of the clamp, and, with this overlaid on the drawing with its feet hooked into the lower grooves, a clamp screw was drawn in long enough to reach the smallest diameter work the block would hold (circle **B**). *The screw is not drawn*, but, for the record, it was made to the following spec: Head: ⅝"∅ × ¾ long, medium knurl; ³⁄₁₆"∅ cross hole in head; Screw: ⁵⁄₁₆-24 tpi × 2" long under the head.

It was made by *Loctite*-ing a knurled knob, drilled and tapped ⁵⁄₁₆ NF one end, onto a piece of ⁵⁄₁₆ NF ready rod. No need for one-piece construction. The ³⁄₁₆"∅ cross hole was drilled after assembly of the knob and screw. Come to think of it, a 2" ⁵⁄₁₆ NF socket head cap screw would make an ideal clamp screw.

The clamp was made from a scrap of ½" black iron plate, long since pulled from the scrap box of a benign steel fabricating shop owner. The material was hacksawed roughly to size, then brought to the specified overall dimensions of the clamp using a flycutter in the vertical mill. A coat of layout ink was applied and the clamp was laid out, hole locations centerpunched, and the job was set up on the lathe for boring the 2.045"∅ hole.

Having done this, the two holes per foot were drilled (see Detail **A**). The ¼" hole removes most of the metal over the hook, and the #56 hole (not to scale on Detail **A**) eases the job of cleaning out the corners. Upend the job, clamp up in the milling machine vise (or rechuck in four-jaw) and locate the spindle centerline over the centerpunch mark for the clamp screw. Drill letter **I** (i) and tap ⁵⁄₁₆-24.

Rounding the outside shoulders of the clamp arch is next. (This could be done on a rotary table. However, I considered that approach before starting the job, and rejected it. The following procedure seemed to me to involve easier setups, because if I milled the outside areas first, the part would be more difficult to grip in the four-jaw afterwards, for boring out the inside of the arch. To continue...)

"If you just want stock removal, use a hacksaw. If you want accuracy, use a machine tool." So runneth a wise dictum of the shop. Grab the hacksaw, and beaver off the excess material over both shoulders. Next, into the vertical mill again, flycutter in place, and mill down to the outside scribed circle, shifting the

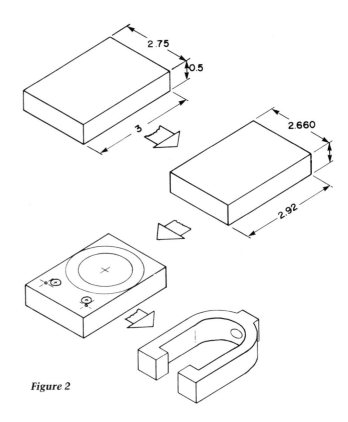

Figure 2

work between times, producing a series of flats all along the desired arc. The flats should be less than ⅛" wide, when done.

The shoulder arcs are then finished by filing: as the curve is nearly to shape, there's not much filing to do, and the milled flats provide a good visual reference to help keep the filed surface square to the sides of the clamp. On jobs such as this, you'll often find you can "feel" departures from the desired profile better than you can see them.

With the arch shoulders brought to final shape, the feet are next. The waste material is hacksawed out and the feet and legs filed to the scribed layout. A little fitting against the V-block is required at this stage, and pretty soon it's all done! Then bevel edges and knock off corners to make the clamp nice to handle.

Here's a detail which I've incorporated into the drawings, but which I overlooked in doping out the clamp I made. See Detail **B**. If the hole forming the interior arch of the clamp is made slightly larger in diameter than the distance between the inner surface of the legs, i.e., 2.100" vs. 2.066", it will be found easier to file the inner face of the legs, because the curve and the straight line are not tangent to each other at the point where they meet. If the job is made as at **B**, the file runs out into thin air as it completes its work on the leg.

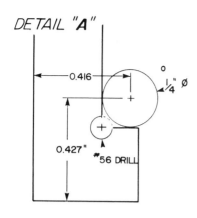

DETAIL "A"

0.416

$\frac{1}{4}$" Ø

0.427"

#56 DRILL

DETAIL "B"

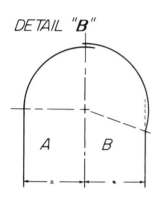

A   B

DETAIL "C"

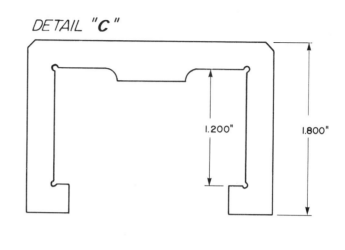

1.200"   1.800"

At Detail **C,** I have drawn another clamp, this one of lower profile, which could be an advantage at times. One of these days I may make one. Again, no point in giving detailed dimensions.

A word about the final finish. Some readers will be quite content to leave all the tool marks visible on such a job. Others, with nobler taste, would·dress it up with one or another degree of polish. But to my way of thinking the nicest finish, once you've worked out the majority of the tool marks with a well chalked fine file, is to *glass bead blast* it. The result is a soft, satiny grey finish, handsome, rust resistant (in my dry basement in this rainy coast climate, at least), and completed in a matter of seconds. Having said that, I have to add that I then proceeded to blue the freshly "beaded" clamp with Brownell's* Dicropan T-4 cold blue. Why? All V-block clamps are black; there are no exceptions!

I'm going to knock off with a nudge at our Editor: How about an article on sand blasting? Brownell's, Inc., sells a portable sandblast outfit for about $90 that needs only an air compressor to get it into action. A sandblast cabinet would improve it. Or, if you can make a good connection with a commercial shop which has a sandblast outfit, betake thyself

and thy creations thither at infrequent intervals, and avail thyself of same. A contribution to the outfit's coffee fund, or a sack of "donuts" or like that once in a while is low cost "rent" for access to a sandblast outfit. Just make sure it's not packin' a 40-grit wallop when you want a 200 grit finish! (Phone ahead, and ask.)

Maybe that's a good note to end on – *another* way to draw up a bargain!!

*Brownell's, Inc., Route 1, Box 2, Montezuma, Iowa 50171.

187

1

2

Sliding Band Saw Vise

by Ed Merrifield

Photos by Author

Several years ago, I acquired an elderly 12-inch Craftsman bandsaw and reduced its speed for metal cutting with an arrangement of multiple pulleys and V-belts. I soon discovered that holding workpieces in my hands while feeding them slowly to the blade produced inaccurate cuts, was often dangerous, and was almost as tedious as hand hacksawing.

The fixture shown is the most useful of several I built to simplify the process. It is merely an old (and rather battered) 3″ drill press vise (Photo 1) attached to a scrap piece of ⅜″ aluminum plate and flathead machine screws, which fit into ¼–20 holes tapped in the underside of the vise. A ⅜″ × ¾″ bar bolted to the bottom of the plate slides in the bandsaw's miter gauge slot. A ¼″ cord with a weight on the other end runs through a pulley and loops around the vise handle, providing a simple but very effective gravity feed (Photo 2).

For weight, I use a small pail filled with one pound lead bars, which can be added or subtracted as needed to vary the feed rate (Photo 3). The pulley, actually a double idler pulley from an old machine, is bolted to a board attached to a convenient joist overhead with a door hinge; it swings up out of the way when not in use. The object at the rear of the miter gauge slot is a woodworking bar clamp; it serves as a stop, preventing the vise from running off the table at the end of a cut.

To make the fixture, machine or file a suitable length of ⅜″ × ¾″ bar until it is a nice sliding fit in the miter gauge slot. Attach the bar to a somewhat oversized piece of steel or aluminum plate with bolts or machine screws, then place the bar in the miter gauge slot, turn on the machine, and push the plate forward to saw off the excess stock. The edge of the vise can then be accurately aligned with the cut you have just made in the plate. Clamp the vise to the plate, lock it upside down in another vise on the drill press, and drill, tap, and countersink for three or four flathead machine screws. When sawing the plate, use a new blade, carefully adjusted for a good straight cut, since the accuracy of the initial cut will determine the accuracy of the fixture.

My fixture makes cuts about as "square" as I can measure, leaving a minimum of subsequent machining. The gravity feed gives a much smoother and more accurate cut than hand-feeding, even when the fixture is used. What I like most, though, is being able to clamp a hefty piece of bar stock in the vise, switch on the machine, and work at the lathe or relax with a cup of coffee and the latest issue of *HSM* while the bandsaw cuts away. Some of the other fixtures I have built along similar principles allow use of the gravity feed for cuts up to 12″ long in steel plate. I have made cuts in steel and cast iron up to 4″ thick, requiring upwards of an hour of sawing time, so these fixtures have already saved enough elbow grease to pay for themselves.

3

1

WELDING

Building a Portable Vise Bench

by Charles K. Hunt

Photos by Author

The value of a shop workbench cannot be overstated. In most shops, it is the center of activity from project layout to final assembly and detailing. Because the workbench is such a utilitarian device, it is often found to be too small, cluttered, or not located close enough to where it's needed. One solution to this dilemma is to add a portable vise bench to one's shop. Portable vise benches can be built in a variety of configurations (Photo 1).

When planning the construction of a portable vise bench, there are several considerations to note. Some of them are its primary function, size of work surface, work height of existing workbenches and equipment and, finally, if economics is a factor, what materials are on hand.

The actual construction of the bench should start at the base. There are a couple of configurations that can be utilized. One uses a large diameter truck split-rim wheel (Photo 2)

and the other uses three legs to form a rigid tripod (Photo 3). If a truck wheel is used, a ¼" or thicker plate will have to be welded to the center hub portion of the wheel prior to installing the pedestal column. If the tripod base is used, the legs should be cut out of ⅜" stock. The layout sketch for the legs and feet is shown in Figure 1.

Photo 4 shows the component parts for the vise bench laid out. Once the legs and feet are flame- or saw-cut, they can be assembled by centering the legs on the feet and tack-welding on diagonal opposite sides of the legs.

When welding the legs to the feet, start at the ends opposite the tacks and weld to the tacks. This will help control the weld-induced distortion and reduce the crater size at the termination of the welds. The legs are now ready to install on the pedestal column.

The pedestal column should be 3" or 4" schedule 40 pipe. To locate the legs, divide the

189

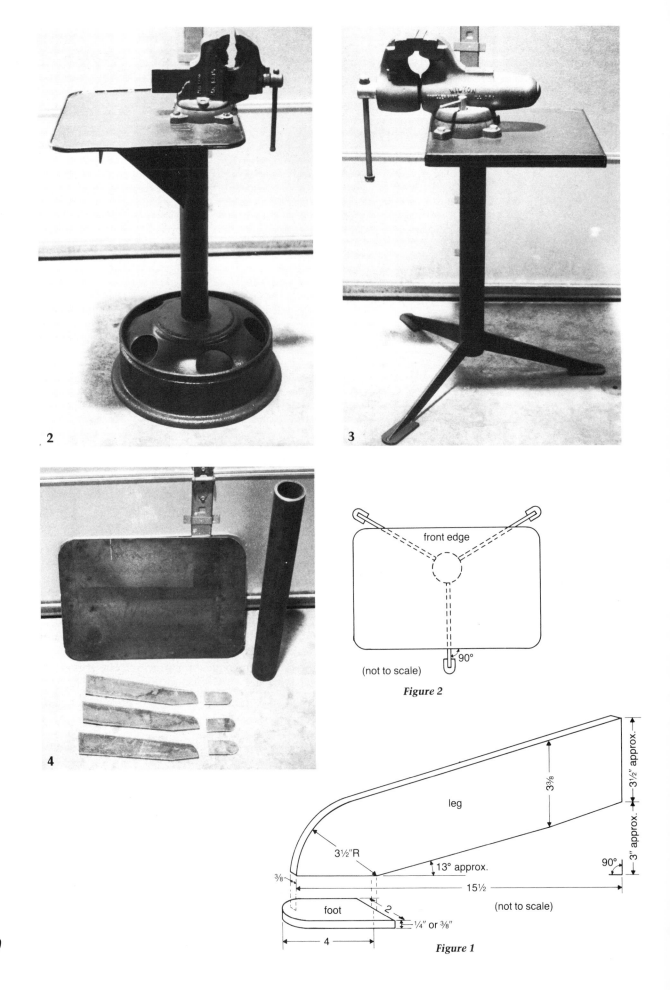

2

3

4

front edge

(not to scale)

Figure 2

leg

$3\frac{3}{8}$

$3\frac{1}{2}$''R

13° approx.

90°

$3\frac{1}{2}$'' approx.

3'' approx.

$\frac{3}{8}$

$15\frac{1}{2}$

(not to scale)

foot

2

$\frac{1}{4}$'' or $\frac{3}{8}$''

4

Figure 1

circumference of the pipe into three equal segments and mark each with a soapstone line. The legs are tacked on one at a time by locating each on the soapstone lines and by placing a framing square against the bottom of the feet and side of the pipe.

After the legs are diagonally tack-welded to the pipe, check their location by measuring between the spread of the legs at outer points prior to finish welding them. The legs are welded in place by starting at the end of the joint opposite the tacks and welding into the tacks.

The bench top work surface should be at least ¼″ thick plate with ⅜″ material being even better. If ¼″ plate is used, gussets should be added to the bottom side of the surface to make it rigid.

When locating the work surface on the pipe, offset the plate to one side so that when the vise is installed, the weight will still be centered. The front edge of the work surface should be placed parallel with the line that goes between the spread of two of the tripod legs. The third tripod leg will extend out perpendicular to the plane that the back edge of the work surface lies in (Figure 2).

Once the location of the pipe column is determined on the bench top, place the bench top face down on a level surface. Place the pedestal pipe upside down on it and check it with a level prior to tack welding. Next, place three tack welds 90° apart and start the finish weld at the fourth 90° point. Reinforcing gussets are suggested. When they are installed, use the skip or alternate welding technique so as not to cause distortion of the work surface (Photo 5).

The vise bench is finished by rounding the corners of the bench top, painting, and installing the vise (Photo 6).

Variations of these designs also work very well as stands for grinders, belt sanders, wire wheels, buffing wheels, drillpresses or stock rollers, as well as welding tables.

Because most hobby craftsmen have an AC buzz box welder, the shielded metal arc process with ⅛″ E6011 or E6013 electrodes at approximately 90-120 amps is the suggested welding process for assembling a vise bench of this type.

5

6

Screwdriver Blade Grinding Jig

by Kim E. Plank

True and parallel screwdriver blades can be ground on a drill press with the use of a simple jig.

OPERATION

The jig pictured in Figure 1 consists of two sheet metal links with a V-block for securing the screwdriver as it pivots into the grinding wheel. The outer link is clamped to the drill press table so that the screwdriver clamped to the V-block pivots through the centerline of the grinding wheel. Move the jig to one side, lower the grinding wheel to the level of the screwdriver and swing the screwdriver blade into the wheel. When the first side has been ground, raise the drill press quill, move the jig to the other side of the grinding wheel, lower the wheel to the level of the screwdriver and swing the blade into the wheel. The tip can be inspected any number of times by swinging the jig clear, and the operator can still return it to the same place on the grinding wheel. By moving the drill press lever up and down, the entire wheel can be used so that it remains square.

CONSTRUCTION

The construction is simple and the dimensions are not critical. The V-block can be made out of wood or metal, but it must be tall enough to allow the handles to clear the pivot bolt. The V-block must hold the screwdriver shaft parallel with the drill press table and in line with the pivot bolt. After the V-groove has been made in the block, drill a half-inch hole in the side of the block low enough so it does not cut through the V-groove. Then square off the top of the hole so it will accept the stationary end of a C-clamp. Next, clamp a long screwdriver or a rod in place on the V-block to act as an alignment guide, and epoxy the block in place on the jig arm so the centerline of the screwdriver passes over the center of the pivot bolt. When the glue is set, bolt the two jig arms together loosely enough so they still can be moved, and the jig is ready to be installed on the drill press table.

MATERIALS

2 each 12" x 2" pieces of sheet metal for jig arms
1 small bolt for pivot
1 small block of hardwood for V-block
2 small C-clamps
1 small grinding wheel (1 to 1½" in diameter is good)
Epoxy glue

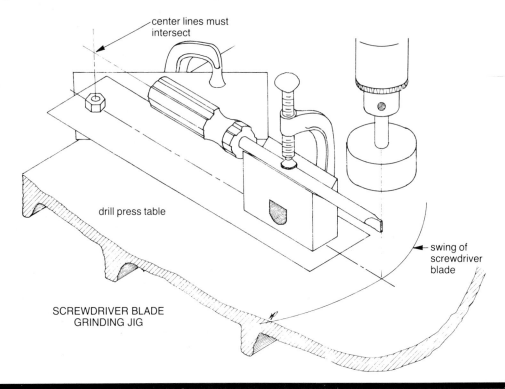

center lines must intersect

drill press table

swing of screwdriver blade

SCREWDRIVER BLADE GRINDING JIG

HOBBY PROJECTS

A Napoleon is displayed at Petersburg National Battlefield Park in Petersburg, VA.

A Firing Model
Napoleon Field Gun

by William F. Green

Photos and Drawings by Author

Widely used in the Civil War, the Napoleon 12-Pounder (M-1857) was a favorite of the artillery. With a charge of 2½ lbs. of black powder, it had a range of approximately 1600 yards and fired a 12-pound projectile. Napoleons were used by both the Union and Confederate Forces. Specimens of these popular cannons can be seen in most of our National Military Parks. The tube of the Napoleon was made from bronze (some

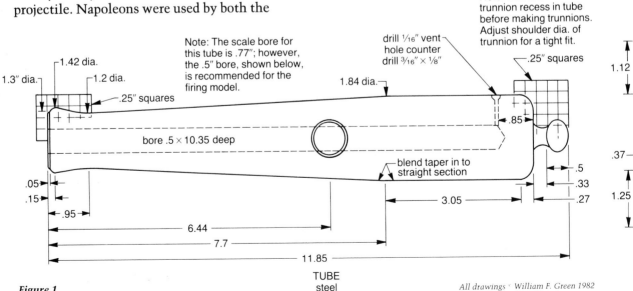

Note: The scale bore for this tube is .77"; however, the .5" bore, shown below, is recommended for the firing model.

Note: Drill and thread trunnion recess in tube before making trunnions. Adjust shoulder dia. of trunnion for a tight fit.

drill ¹⁄₁₆" vent hole counter drill ³⁄₁₆" × ⅛"

1.3" dia.
1.42 dia.
1.2 dia.
.25" squares
1.84 dia.
.25" squares
1.12
.85
bore .5 × 10.35 deep
blend taper in to straight section
.37
.5
.33
.27
.05
.15
.95
6.44
7.7
3.05
1.25
11.85

TUBE
steel

Figure 1

All drawings · William F. Green 1982

Several Napoleons create an authentic atmosphere at Vicksburg National Military Park in Mississippi.

The muzzle details of the Napoleon are more apparent in this close-up (Vicksburg National Military Park).

Details of the breech and some of the hardware may be studied from this angle. This particular Napoleon is exhibited at the Chickamauga National Military Park in Tennessee.

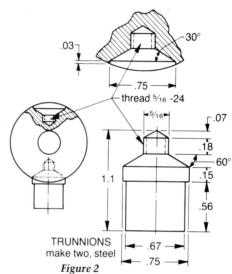

TRUNNIONS
make two, steel

Figure 2

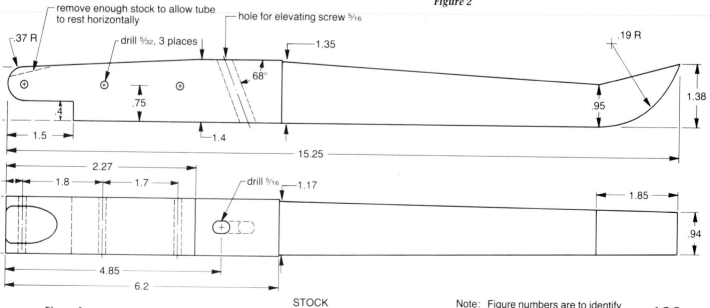

Figure 3

STOCK
make one, wood

Note: Figure numbers are to identify parts in the assembly illustrations.

A model Napoleon gleams after completion.

A quarter-size 6 PDR model provides a background for the firing of a model Napoleon.

Confederate Napoleons were made of iron), and the carriage hardware was made from wrought iron. However, it is recommended that a firing model be made from a good grade of steel.

Caution: The builder and user of firing model cannons should recognize that these are *NOT TOYS*. They should be handled with the proper respect and responsibility due to any firearm.

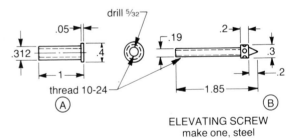

ELEVATING SCREW
make one, steel

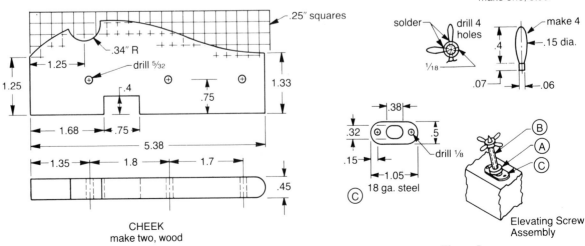

CHEEK
make two, wood

Figure 4

Elevating Screw
Assembly

Figure 5

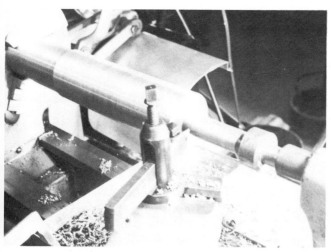

Turn the excess or chucking stock, at the breech end of the tube, to a diameter just a little larger than the knob at the end of the tube.

The recess for the trunnions is made with a drill press. This must be drilled before turning the taper.

The taper can be turned by using the "tailstock offset" method.

A trunnion is turned on the lathe and should be left in the lathe until it is fitted to the tube.

BUILDING THE MODEL

Make the tube first. Referring to Figure 1, select a piece of steel round stock of the proper diameter and about 1½″ longer than the tube. This extra stock is handy for chucking purposes and can be cut off after all operations are completed. Machine the tube to the dimensions and shape shown in Figure 1. The trunnion holes should be drilled before the taper is turned. This can be done on a lathe, drill press, or with a milling machine. The preferred way is to clamp the tube in a vertical milling machine, drill a pilot hole, and then counterbore with an end mill. If a mill is not available, use a drill press at its slowest speed. Remember, when boring the tube, the drill must be cleared frequently, to prevent the chips from binding and breaking the drill.

Turn the trunnions as indicated in Figure 2. Since the trunnion holes in the tube may vary slightly from the specified dimensions, due to drill wear, for example, it is best to alter trunnion dimensions as required to fit the tube. Try them in the tube occasionally, as

A trunnion is "tried for fit" in the tube.

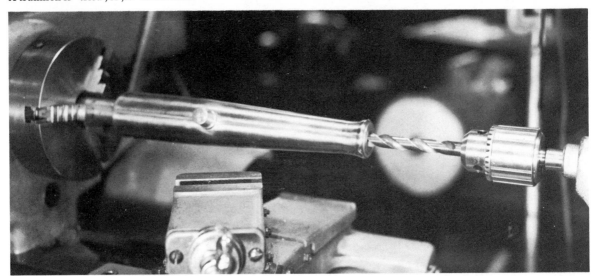

The tube is bored in the lathe.

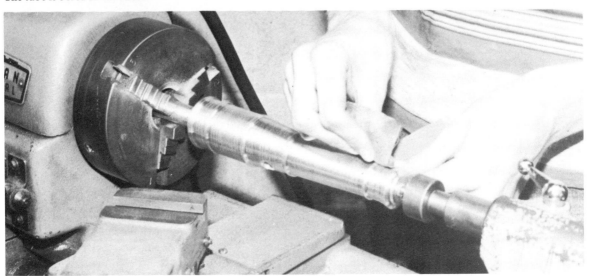

With the lathe turning, use emery paper to put a fine finish on the tube.

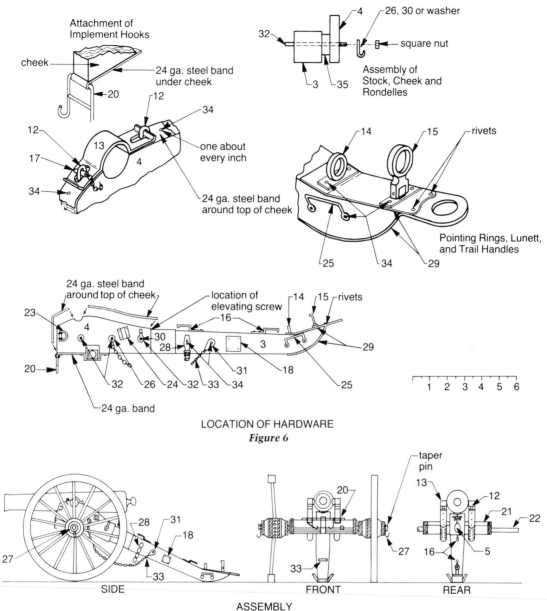

Attachment of
Implement Hooks

cheek

24 ga. steel band
under cheek

one about
every inch

24 ga. steel band
around top of cheek

4 — 26, 30 or washer

square nut

Assembly of
Stock, Cheek and
Rondelles

rivets

Pointing Rings, Lunett,
and Trail Handles

24 ga. steel band
around top of cheek

location of
elevating screw

rivets

24 ga. band

LOCATION OF HARDWARE
Figure 6

taper
pin

SIDE

FRONT

REAR

ASSEMBLY
Figure 7

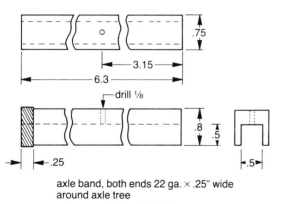

.75

3.15

6.3

drill ⅛

.8

.5

.25

.5

axle band, both ends 22 ga. × .25″ wide
around axle tree

AXLE TREE
make one, wood

Figure 21

they are being turned and before removing the trunnion from the lathe. This procedure will assure a tight fit. When the trunnions are completed, attach them to the tube.

The stock and cheeks are made from wood (I prefer mahogany); see Figures 3 and 4. Lay out the parts on wood and saw them to shape. Where holes must match, the parts should be clamped together and drilled at the same time. Cut the axle tree from wood, as shown in Figure 21.

Since the wheels may be the most difficult parts for most builders, I have devised an easy way to build them. The wheel construction is

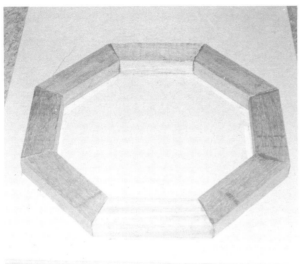

The wheel rim segments (felloes) have been glued to the cardboard and plywood, ready to be cut to shape with the router.

A circle cutting attachment, pivoted on a bolt through the plywood, is secured onto the router to cut the wheel rims. This method is used when the wheels are too big to chuck in the lathe.

The rim is cut with the router and circle cutting attachment.

Spoke locations are transferred from a paper diagram to the wheel rim and hub.

illustrated in greater detail to simplify this task (Figures 8, 9, 10, and 11 and the wheel construction photos). The builder is given some choice in wheel construction as to the spokes and the number of wheel segments (see notes with Figure 9). Once the wheel rim glue-up is completed (Figure 8), assemble the rim hub and spokes by clamping the rim to the plywood jig with C-clamps and bolting the hub with the center pivot bolt. Shim the rim with blocks of wood to produce the correct angle between the rim and the hub for the spokes. Position the spokes through the holes in the rim and then push them into the hub. Add glue just before seating them into final position.

Sand all wood parts to a smooth finish and paint a light gray color. I use a paint mixture of five parts light gray and one part olive drab.

All metal hardware should be constructed as shown in the drawings and photos. In most cases the drawings are self-explanatory. In some instances, such as the trunnion cap squares, you will find it easier to heat the metal for shaping. The slots in the cap squares can be cut with a milling attachment, or by drilling overlapping holes and smoothing with a file. Cap square bolts (Figure 12) are made from $3/32''$ diameter steel rod, welded to the top of wood screws with the heads cut off.

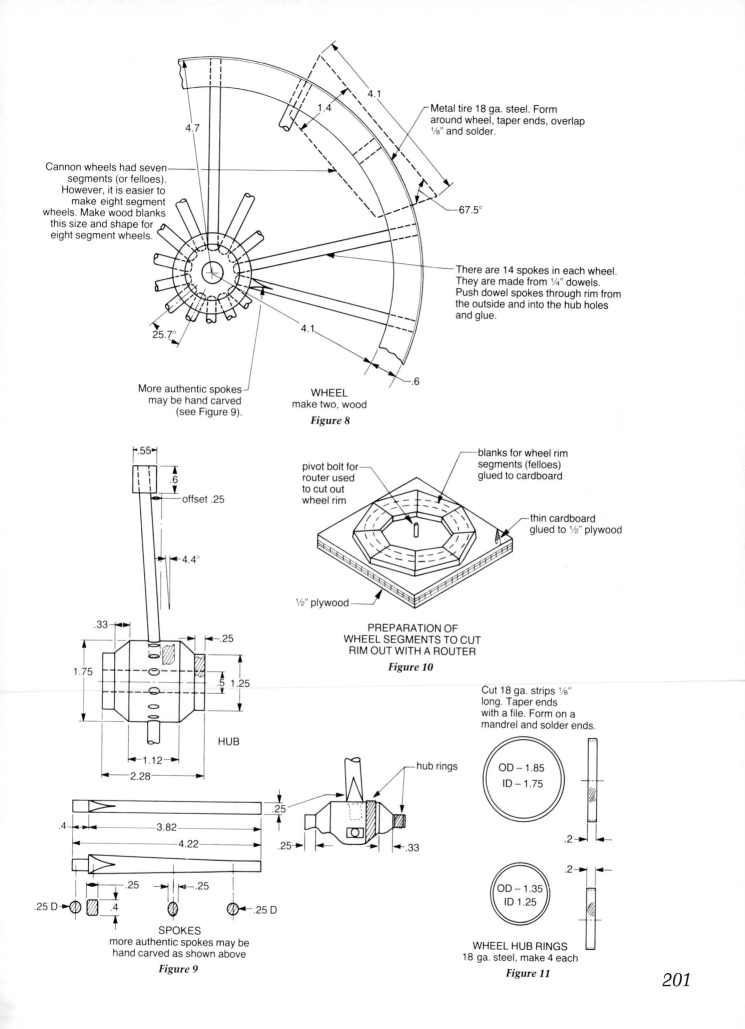

Metal tire 18 ga. steel. Form around wheel, taper ends, overlap ⅛″ and solder.

4.1

1.4

4.7

67.5°

Cannon wheels had seven segments (or felloes). However, it is easier to make eight segment wheels. Make wood blanks this size and shape for eight segment wheels.

There are 14 spokes in each wheel. They are made from ¼″ dowels. Push dowel spokes through rim from the outside and into the hub holes and glue.

25.7°

4.1

.6

More authentic spokes may be hand carved (see Figure 9).

WHEEL
make two, wood

Figure 8

.55

.6

offset .25

4.4°

.33

.25

1.75

.5 1.25

HUB

1.12

2.28

blanks for wheel rim segments (felloes) glued to cardboard

pivot bolt for router used to cut out wheel rim

thin cardboard glued to ½″ plywood

½″ plywood

PREPARATION OF WHEEL SEGMENTS TO CUT RIM OUT WITH A ROUTER

Figure 10

Cut 18 ga. strips ⅛″ long. Taper ends with a file. Form on a mandrel and solder ends.

OD – 1.85
ID – 1.75

.2

hub rings

.25

.25

.33

.25

.4

3.82

4.22

.25

.25

.25 D

.4

.25 D

SPOKES
more authentic spokes may be hand carved as shown above

Figure 9

OD – 1.35
ID 1.25

.2

WHEEL HUB RINGS
18 ga. steel, make 4 each

Figure 11

201

The jig (a block of wood) is clamped to the drill press for drilling the spoke holes in the rim.

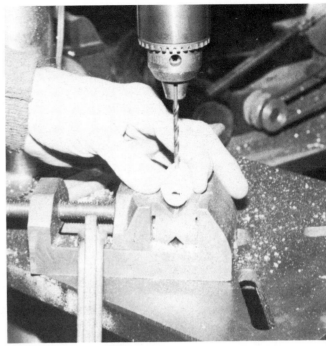

A "V" block is held in a drill press vise to use as a jig when drilling the spoke holes in the hub.

Each wheel is mounted to the assembly jig, used to put the rim, hub and spokes together. The rim is blocked to the proper height for the hubs and secured with C-clamps. The hub is bolted to the center. Spokes are glued in place.

The Napoleon 12-Pounder was a favorite of the artillery for both Union and Confederate forces.

Here is an alternate method for assembling the wheels, if your lathe is big enough.

Each wheel hub is fitted with hub rings and a drag hook (to be covered later).

Here in great detail is shown how the wheel hub should look once mounted to the end of the axle tree.

The top and part of the bottom of the cheeks are covered with a metal band (Figure 6). Metal banding, such as that used around crates and boxes for shipping, is ideal for this; if not available, cut banding from sheet metal. Solder the pointing rings to the lunett.

All metal parts, including the tube, are treated with a "cold blue" preparation, which gives them a dark blue gun finish. This is available at most gun shops and sporting goods stores.

Most of the hardware is attached to the wood parts with wood screws or brads. In either case, the heads of the brads or screws are filed square, to resemble the type of screws that were used in that period.

Locate the hardware, as shown in Figures 6 and 7. Part numbers 18, 24, and the metal bands over the cheeks are fastened with brads. Part numbers 16, 19, 25, 29, and 31 are attached with small square head wood screws. Part numbers 26 and 30 are attached over the threaded rods, which hold the cheeks and stock together. The two pivot pins on the "D" rings are pressed into holes in the cheeks and held with epoxy glue. Use .14" threaded rods through the three holes in the cheeks and stock to hold them together.

Rondelles (Figure 35) are used between the cheeks and the stock to space the cheeks far enough apart to fit the trunnions. Center the axle tree in position under the cheeks, and

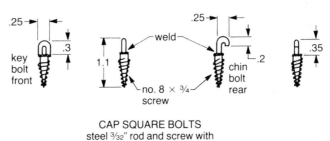

CAP SQUARE BOLTS
steel ³⁄₃₂" rod and screw with
head cut off, make two each

Figure 12

position the axle in the axle tree slot. Fasten the axle and axle tree to the stock assembly with a long wood screw, through the hole in the center of the axle. The axle and axle tree are further secured to the assembly by the metal cheek bands and the axle strap.

Form metal bands around each end of the axle tree (Figure 21). Drill pilot holes into the cheeks and screw the cap square bolts into position (see the detailed sketch in Figure 6). Slide the wheels onto the axle with a washer between them and the axle tree. Place a drag hook (Part No. 27) over each end of the axle and secure the wheels with a small tapered pin, forced into the holes at the ends of the axle.

203

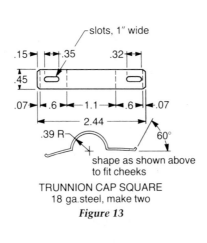

slots, 1" wide

.15 | .35 | .32

.45

.07 | .6 | 1.1 | .6 | .07

2.44

60°

.39 R

shape as shown above
to fit cheeks

TRUNNION CAP SQUARE
18 ga. steel, make two
Figure 13

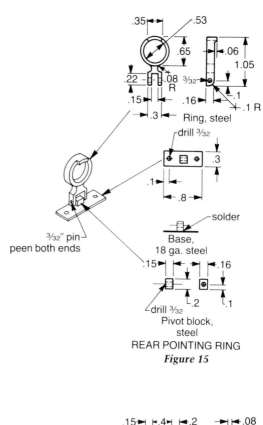

.35 | .53

.65

.22 | .08 R | ³/₃₂

.15

.3

.16

.06

1.05

.1

.1 R

Ring, steel

drill ³/₃₂

.3

.1

.8

solder

Base,
18 ga. steel

.15 | .16

.2 | .1

drill ³/₃₂

Pivot block,
steel

³/₃₂" pin
peen both ends

REAR POINTING RING
Figure 15

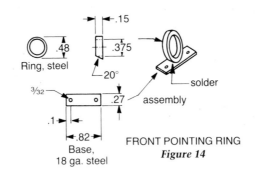

.15

.48

.375

20°

³/₃₂

.27

.1

.82

Ring, steel

solder

assembly

Base,
18 ga. steel

FRONT POINTING RING
Figure 14

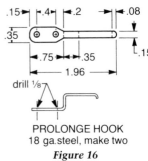

.15 | .4 | .2 | .08

.35

.75 | .35

1.96

.15

drill ¹/₈

PROLONGE HOOK
18 ga. steel, make two
Figure 16

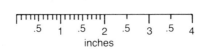

.5 | 1 | .5 | 2 | .5 | 3 | .5 | 4

inches

*A front view of the cheeks shows the implement hooks
and the "D" rings (to be covered later).*

*Note the chain used to hold the key in this view
of the trunnion cap squares, cap square bolts and cap
square key.*

204

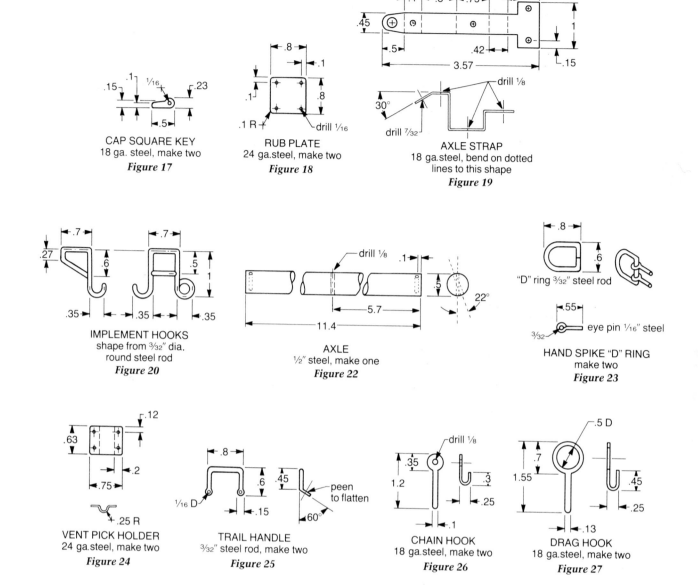

CAP SQUARE KEY
18 ga. steel, make two
Figure 17

RUB PLATE
24 ga. steel, make two
Figure 18

drill ⅛

30°

drill ⅞₃₂

AXLE STRAP
18 ga. steel, bend on dotted
lines to this shape
Figure 19

IMPLEMENT HOOKS
shape from ³⁄₃₂ dia.
round steel rod
Figure 20

drill ⅛

22°

AXLE
½″ steel, make one
Figure 22

"D" ring ³⁄₃₂″ steel rod

eye pin ¹⁄₁₆″ steel

HAND SPIKE "D" RING
make two
Figure 23

VENT PICK HOLDER
24 ga. steel, make two
Figure 24

peen
to flatten

60°

TRAIL HANDLE
³⁄₃₂″ steel rod, make two
Figure 25

drill ⅛

CHAIN HOOK
18 ga. steel, make two
Figure 26

.5 D

DRAG HOOK
18 ga. steel, make two
Figure 27

Here, the cap square keys are folded back. Note the holes and slots in the metal bands for the cap square bolts.

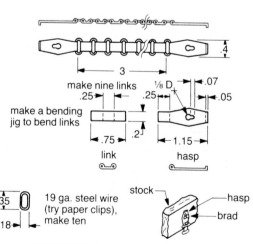

make nine links

make a bending
jig to bend links

link

⅛ D

hasp

19 ga. steel wire
(try paper clips),
make ten

stock

hasp

brad

SPONGE AND RAMMER CHAIN
24 ga. steel, make one
Figure 28

The lunett, front and rear pointing rings, trail handles, and prolonge hook are in place on the tongue.

The "D" ring, vent pick and trunnion cap squares are shown here. Note the method used to attach the implement hooks to the front of the cheeks. Metal strips that go around the top, front and part of the bottom of the cheek are illustrated here, also.

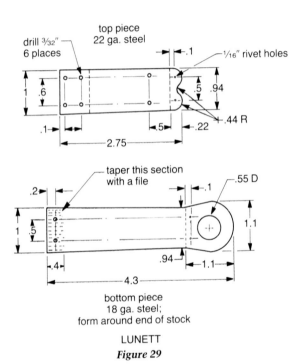

top piece
22 ga. steel

drill ³/₃₂"
6 places

¹/₁₆" rivet holes

1 ⎯ .6

.5 .94

.1

.5

.22

.44 R

2.75

taper this section with a file

.55 D

.2

1 .5

.1

1.1

.4

.94

1.1

4.3

bottom piece
18 ga. steel;
form around end of stock

LUNETT
Figure 29

Here we see the elevating screw, vent pick holder, and hand spike hook. Note the metal strips on the top surface of the cheeks.

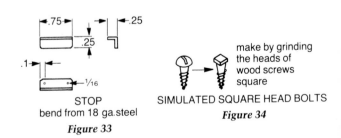

.75

.25

.25

.1

¹/₁₆

STOP
bend from 18 ga. steel
Figure 33

make by grinding
the heads of
wood screws
square

SIMULATED SQUARE HEAD BOLTS
Figure 34

This angle shows the details of the lift handle and bottom attachment of the lunett.

One of the prolonge hooks and the rub plate can be seen in this view of the sponge chain and chain plate.

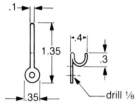

HAND SPIKE HOOK
18 ga. steel, make two
Figure 30

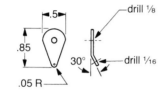

CHAIN PLATE
18 ga. steel, make two
Figure 31

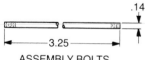

ASSEMBLY BOLTS
steel rod, make three
thread each end 6-32;
use square nuts
Figure 32

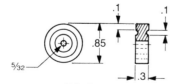

RONDELLE
turn from steel, used for
spacer between stock and cheeks,
make six
Figure 35

Glue the elevating screw assembly into the hole in the stock, and fasten part "C" onto position with two brads. Attach the cap square keys to the cheeks with a short section of chain, as shown in the detailed sketch of Figure 6. Fasten a length of chain between the chain plates and the chain hooks as indicated in Figure 7. Place the tube into position, and secure with the trunnion cap squares.

Build an Electric Gun

by Robert W. Metze

Photos by Author

Although it looks like a modern automatic, this pistol is really an old fashioned muzzle-loader with an up-dated ignition system. Building it is easy and straightforward.

The Barrel (Figure 4) is turned from a .22 caliber heavy-wall rifle, such as a Hornet. It could as easily be .30 caliber cut from a military barrel. Drill and tap the breach to receive a tempered bolt, which extends up to the Glow Plug (Figure 5). However, with black powder, it is not necessary to use a hardened bolt. The model engine glow plug that I used is a Fox, heavy-duty type rated at 1½ volts. Threads on it are 32 per inch, so you may drill and tap ¼-32

if you have such a tap available. I didn't, so I rethreaded the plug to ¼-28. I wired the plug to receive 3 volts from the two alkali penlight cells in the handle. Higher voltage lights the plug quicker than would be done with 1½ volts. This shortens ignition time, but do not hold the trigger down after firing as it might burn out the element in the plug. Two batteries, when fresh, will fire about one hundred times. However, after fifty shots, there is a noticeable delay in ignition. The wiring is routed through a safety switch shown in the schematic and photos. It is a miniature switch mounted low on the left side, as I didn't have room elsewhere. The two buttons adjacent to the switch are bright red and green plastic inlaid into the stock to indicate "fire and safe."

The Hand Grips are carved from walnut and are finished with Birchwood Casey *Tru-Oil*. Some carving-out of the inside of the grips is necessary to accommodate the penlight batteries and wiring (Figure 10).

Ⓐ Drill .125, on right side counterbore .312 by .070 deep on left side counterbore .187 by .110 deep.

Ⓑ Drill .187, on bottom counterbore .250 by .150 deep.

Ⓒ Drill and tap for 4-40   Ⓓ Tap 10-32

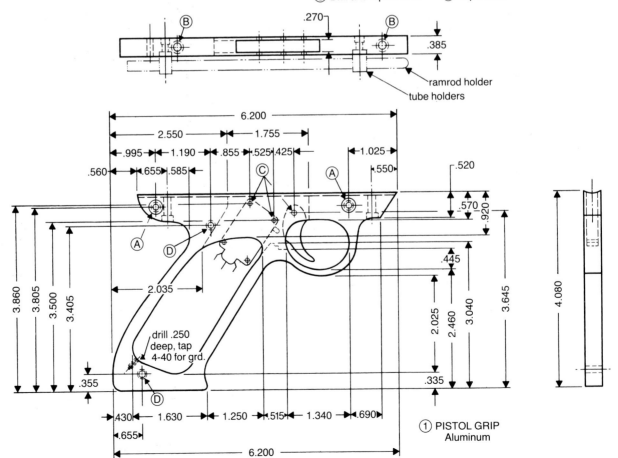

① PISTOL GRIP
Aluminum

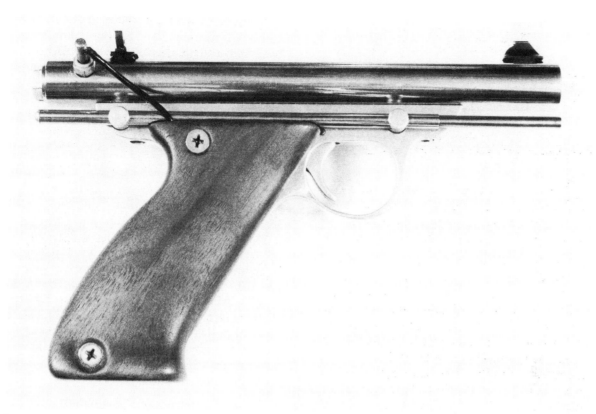

1

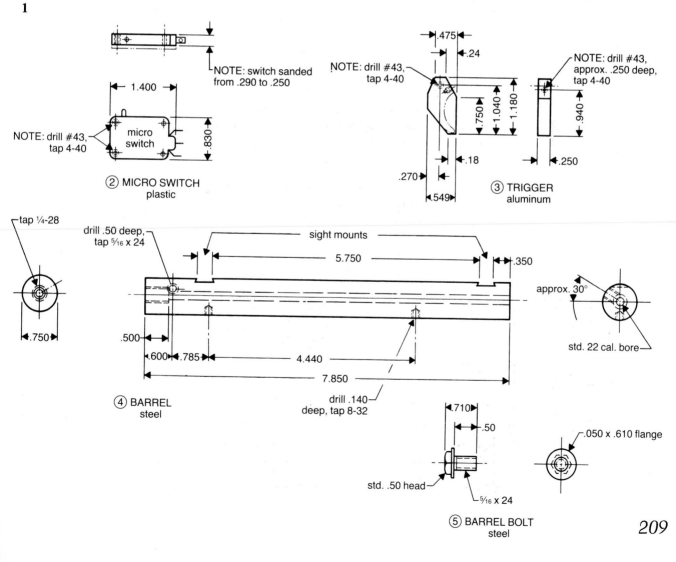

NOTE: switch sanded from .290 to .250

1.400

micro switch

.830

NOTE: drill #43, tap 4-40

② MICRO SWITCH
plastic

.475

.24

NOTE: drill #43, tap 4-40

.750 1.040 1.180

.270

.18

.549

NOTE: drill #43, approx. .250 deep, tap 4-40

.940

.250

③ TRIGGER
aluminum

tap ¼-28

.750

drill .50 deep, tap ⁵⁄₁₆ x 24

sight mounts

5.750

.350

.500

.600 .785

4.440

7.850

④ BARREL
steel

drill .140 deep, tap 8-32

approx. 30°

std. 22 cal. bore

.710

.50

std. .50 head

⁵⁄₁₆ x 24

.050 x .610 flange

⑤ BARREL BOLT
steel

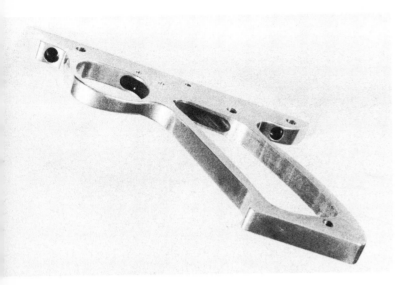

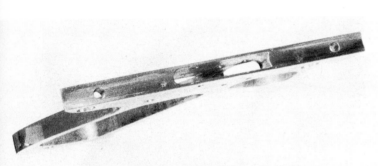

2

3

two smaller Allen head screws. It is a piece of thin-wall, chrome plated tubing. To finish the back end, a small aluminum plug is pressed or glued in with epoxy (Figure 6 and 9). The Ramrod is a piece of brazing rod which I nickle plated. It could also be made of polished steel. The tubing is held just tight enough to give the ramrod a snug sliding fit.

The Trigger (Photos 4 and 5) is aluminum and pivots on a headless machine screw. It presses the plunger on the micro-switch. This switch is a common one found in many surplus stores. It is marked with the name *Acro Switch*, Columbus, Ohio, 3 amp 250 v a-c. To press the actuating plunger on this switch requires only one ounce. Since the plunger is pressed at a mechanical advantage, the trigger pull is in the neighborhood of one-half ounce! This is a very light "target" type of trigger pull. And indeed it is, as the pull is so light that about half way along the squeeze the pistol fires without the shooter being aware of ignition...no time to flinch so the shot goes into the bullseye!

So, back to construction: The Switch is a little too wide for the quarter-inch milled slot, so I sanded the sides down a little to fit (Figure 2). This is a plastic housing with a thick enough wall to stand the thinning. It is held in place with two headless machine screws. The screw stub protruding from the front side of the trigger is a return adjustment to control its forward movement (Figure 3). In case it was not made clear, the only spring that returns the trigger is inside the micro-switch.

The Frame (Photos 2 and 3) is aluminum and carries the barrel in a groove. It is shaped to fit the contour of the barrel, which is secured to the frame by two Allen head machine screws tapped into the barrel (Figure 1). Just below and to the side of the barrel is the ram rod housing, held by

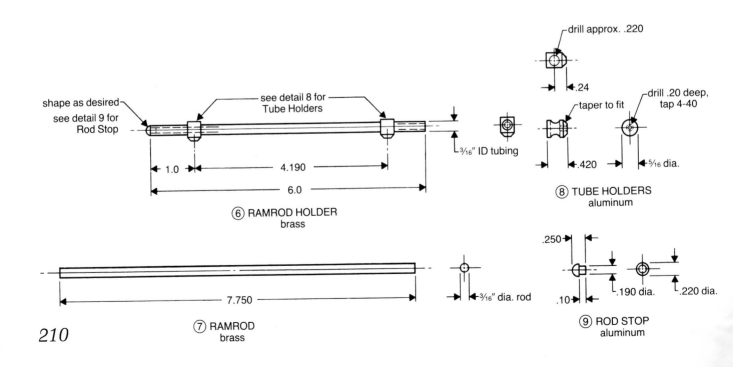

210

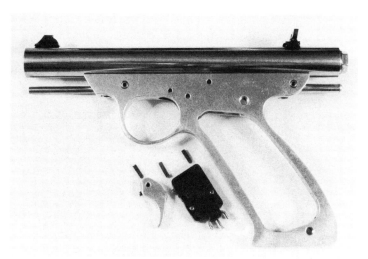

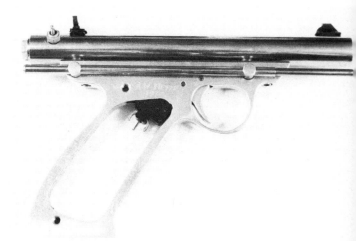

4   5

The entire pistol was finished "in the white," all metal parts polished to a high luster. The sights, which I purchased from a gunsmith, are Williams, and both are dovetailed into the barrel.

The location of the glow plug, as can be seen in Photo 6, is designed with safety in mind. In case of a blow-out, the plug should not hit the shooter (Figure 4). I have tested this pistol with a load of 3F black powder, enough to fill the barrel

halfway, topped by two tightly patched lead balls. The glow plug gave no sign of weakening and continued to operate perfectly. However, *do not use smokeless powders in this type gun* as the pressures are too great to be safe. As a powder measure, I use a cut down .22 short soldered to a piece of brazing rod. About half of a .22 short case of 3F black powder behind an air rifle pellet constitutes a mild load for the pistol. This

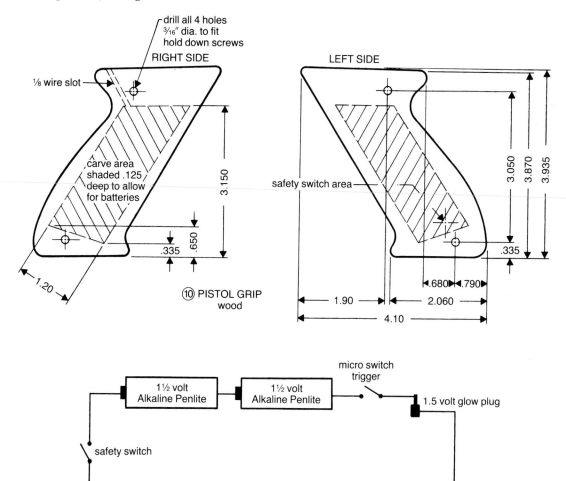

drill all 4 holes
³⁄₁₆" dia. to fit
hold down screws
RIGHT SIDE

⅛ wire slot

carve area
shaded .125
deep to allow
for batteries

3.150

.650

.335

1.20

⑩ PISTOL GRIP
wood

LEFT SIDE

safety switch area

3.050

3.870

3.935

.335

.680   .790

1.90

2.060

4.10

micro switch
trigger

1½ volt
Alkaline Penlite

1½ volt
Alkaline Penlite

1.5 volt glow plug

safety switch

ground to frame

ground to frame

211

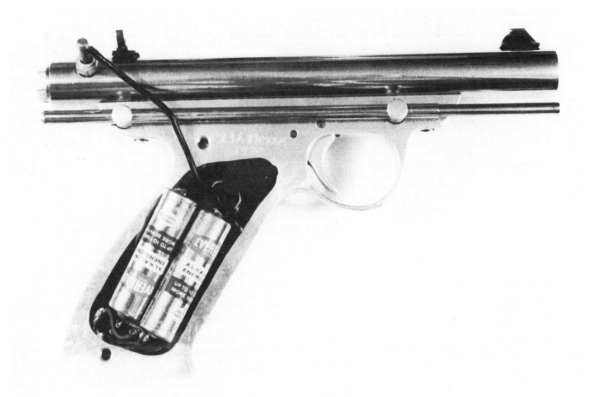

6

design permits easy cleaning. Remove the glow plug and rinse under warm water, then blow out with air, or shake it out. Then unscrew the breach plug and run a wet swab through the barrel, dry and oil lightly.

As a variation to this design, larger batteries could be carried in a pack attached to one's belt. A wire from this pack to a mini-plug would plug into the base of the handle. This would constitute a safety by unplugging during loading. The design might be simpler this way since it would eliminate the safety switch and batteries inside the handle.

There are many other variations, but I'll leave that to the imagination of the builders.

We hope that readers who undertake this or any other firearms project will approach both its fabrication and use with caution and an eye to safety. Ed.)

Build a Gimbaled Ship's Lamp

by William F. Green

Gimbaled oil lamps were used in the old sailing ships, so that the lamp remained upright when the ship was heeled over. This gimbaled lamp could be used in a boat. A pair will make an attractive accessory for the den or a family room.

CONSTRUCTION

Start by making the body of the lamp from solid brass stock 1½" in diameter by 6¾" long. Using the lathe, turn and bore the lamp body to the size and shape shown in Figure 2. Drill two ⅛" diameter holes in the top part of the body for the trunnions. Make sure these holes are exactly 180° apart, so that the lamp will balance properly.

Next, turn the top (Figure 1) as shown in the drawing. Make sure the top fits into the body properly (note: top will be soldered to the body). The threads shown fit most of the small acorn-size lamp burners; however, it will be wise to check the one you obtain for thread size and thread the top to fit the burner assembly. (Note: The burner assemblies I used were distributed by "Lamplight Products," Brookfield, WI. They are sold in some supermarkets and dime stores.)

Make the trunnions (two of each) from ¼" brass stock as shown in Figures 4 and 5. The trunnion in Figure 4 is soldered into the lamp body, and the ones shown in Figure 5 are soldered into the inter-gimbal ring. These positions are shown in Figures 6 and 8. Four gimbal pivot screws are turned and threaded from ¼" brass stock as shown in Figure 3.

The gimbal rings are made from ½" wide strips of brass ¹⁄₁₆" thick. The small ring is 2" in diameter and will require a strip 6⁹⁄₃₂" long. The large ring is 2²³⁄₃₂" in diameter and will require a strip 8½" long. Roll these strips into smooth circles and silver solder the butt ends. Lay out the positions for the four holes in the small ring so that they are 90° apart. Drill two of these holes opposite each other, with a ⅛" drill. The trunnions made from Figure 5 should be soldered into these holes. Drill the other two holes ³⁄₁₆" in diameter to fit the gimbal pivot screws. Now, lay out two holes in the large ring 180° apart and drill with a ³⁄₁₆" drill. Drill a ⅛" rivet hole halfway between these.

The back plate is cut from sheet brass stock ¹⁄₁₆" thick to the size and shape shown in Figures 9 and 11. Shape the "S" bracket from a strip of ½" wide by ¹⁄₁₆" thick brass in accordance with Figure 10. Drill ⅛" rivet and mounting holes in the back plate and the "S" bracket in the locations shown. This completes all of the parts for the lamp. These parts should be given a smooth finish with fine steel wool and buffed before assembly.

ASSEMBLY

Sweat solder the body trunnions and top to the lamp body. Rivet the large ring to the "S" bracket and the "S" bracket to the back plate with ⅛" × ³⁄₁₆" brass rivets. Attach the small ring to the lamp body trunnions with two of the pivot screws. Using the other two pivot screws, attach the large ring to the trunnions mounted on the small ring (Figures 6, 7, and 8). Finish by installing the burner assembly.

Your lamp (or lamps) is ready to mount on the wall or in your boat. Fill the lamp with lamp oil and you have an attractive source of emergency light.

BILL OF MATERIALS
Brass Round Stock – 1½" diameter × 7" long
Brass Round Stock – ¼" diameter × 6" long
Brass Sheet Stock – ¹⁄₁₆" × 3" × 9"
Brass Sheet Stock – ¹⁄₁₆" × ½" × 24"
Brass Rivets – ⅛" × ³⁄₁₆", 3 each
Lamp Burner Assembly – small to take 1¼"
    diameter chimney (Lamplight Products)

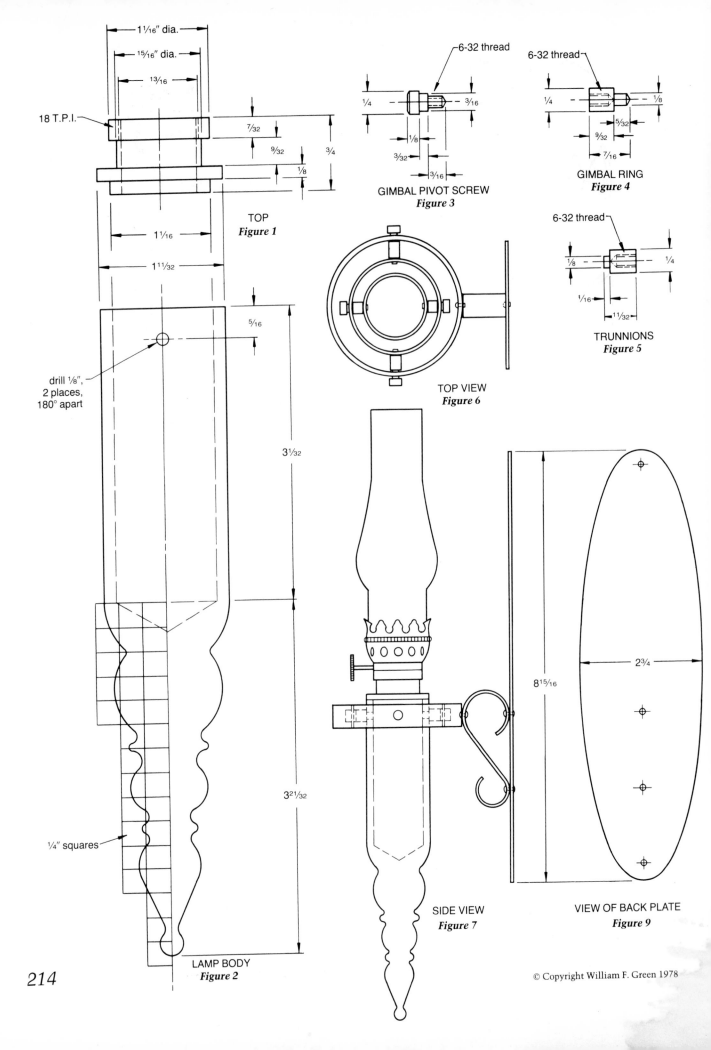

1 1/16" dia.

15/16" dia.

13/16

18 T.P.I.

7/32

9/32

3/4

1/8

1 1/16

1 11/32

TOP
Figure 1

6-32 thread

1/4

1/8

3/16

3/32

3/16

GIMBAL PIVOT SCREW
Figure 3

6-32 thread

1/4

1/8

5/32

9/32

7/16

GIMBAL RING
Figure 4

6-32 thread

1/8

1/4

1/16

11/32

TRUNNIONS
Figure 5

TOP VIEW
Figure 6

5/16

drill 1/8",
2 places,
180° apart

3 1/32

3 21/32

1/4" squares

8 15/16

2 3/4

LAMP BODY
Figure 2

SIDE VIEW
Figure 7

VIEW OF BACK PLATE
Figure 9

214

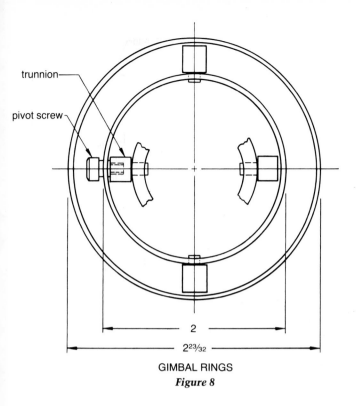

GIMBAL RINGS
Figure 8

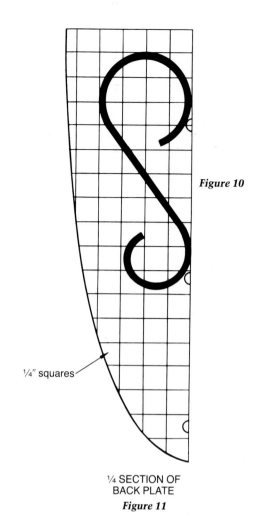

Figure 10

¼" squares

¼ SECTION OF
BACK PLATE
Figure 11